22

22

No Ordinary Man

The Life and Times of *Miguel de Cervantes*

Donald P. McCrory

Illustrated

Dover Publications, Inc., Mineola, New York

Bibliographical Note

This Dover edition, first published in 2006, is an unabridged republication
of the work originally published in 2002 by Peter Owen Publishers, London.

International Standard Book Number: 0-486-45361-8

Manufactured in the United States of America
Dover Publications, Inc., 31 East 2nd Street, Mineola, N.Y. 11501

ACKNOWLEDGEMENTS

It goes without saying that this present contribution to biographical studies of Cervantes owes much to others. Research into the Golden Age of Spain is of such a quality today that new material about life under Philip II and Philip III comes to light continually. The same may be said of the life and works of Cervantes. His ancestry, parents, birthplace, friendships and career, as well as his literary production, are constantly under scrutiny; so much so that my aim here is to bring to the general public an accurate account of what is known at present and to offer some account of his writing in relation to his life. In so doing I have had recourse to the remarkable works of others: urban and social historians, court chroniclers, geographers, envoys and ambassadors, travellers, as well as literary analysts.

I should like to express my sincerest thanks to Krzysztof Sliwa, who has unstintingly given his time to reading this text and offering invaluable advice throughout all its stages; to I.A.A. Thompson who advised me on historical matters; to Antonio Feros, whose groundbreaking work on the Duke of Lerma caused me to revise views no longer valid; to Paul Lewis-Smith and Eduardo Urbina, whose helpful comments have eradicated many an error; and to all those cervantistas and Hispanistas whose works have made this book possible. The notes to each chapter could easily have been trebled and signal my debt both to persons and sources. Many of those who helped me along the path are sadly no longer with us, but I remember their encouragement and enthusiasm. Lastly, I would like to express my deepest gratitude to the editorial team at Peter Owen and to my former employer, the American International University in London, in particular to Richard Resch, the Academic Provost, who kindly granted me study-leave to work on this text, and to Martin Winter, Head of Reprographics at the University, who patiently assisted in the assembly of the several drafts that led to the final copy.

Needless to say, any errors found in the text, historical or interpretative, are mine and mine alone.

Donald P. McCrory

CONTENTS

ILLUSTRATIONS
between pages 160 and 161

INTRODUCTION

In the study of Cervantes the dispersion of error is the first step in the discovery of truth. As regards biographies of Cervantes I have mainly used as sources those written after Astrana Marín's monumental study of 1947–58. For those interested in earlier biographies, the as yet unpublished doctoral thesis of Krzysztof Sliwa of Indiana University, *La Historia de las Biografías de Cervantes* (1997), is the best on the subject and highly recommended. In it Dr Sliwa examines nine major biographies – including those of Astrana Marín and Jean Canavaggio – and points equally to their contributions and failings. It is true to say that many of his findings lend support to the view that there has been too much of conjecture and fantasy and too little valid documentary evidence. His invaluable research also supports the method adopted in this work of mine.

Although Astrana Marín's text contains much that is not relevant to the needs and tastes of the modern reader, his discovery and use of 'one thousand hitherto unpublished documents' overshadows all previous works. A modern classic, with warts and all, his seven-volume study, which took twenty years of unceasing labour to complete, is a major contribution. No modern biography of note has been written without reference to it. But even his work is now over half a century old and relies on work carried out two decades before publication, and a great deal has been researched and published since then that needs to be considered. Scholarly work, in Europe but more significantly in America, has helped to clarify a number of the riddles surrounding the still enigmatic Miguel de Cervantes.

It may be surprising to learn that the first biography of Cervantes was commissioned not by a Spaniard but by an English aristocrat, Lord Carteret, who asked Mayáns y Siscar to write a full-length study worthy of the subject. And so it was that in 1738 the *princeps* biography appeared, that is, more than a century after Cervantes' death in 1616. Such a long delay proves that his contemporaries saw little reason to write about him, and he was never the target of biographers, unlike Philip II who refused to let his life be written while he was alive. Although superseded by later studies and rarely read nowadays, its publication marked the slow but sure beginning of a latent interest in the life of an exceptional man. But it was not until 1819, that is, over two hundred years after Cervantes' death, that Martín Fernández de Navarrete published a biography which included for the first time a documented account of Cervantes' military service and captivity derived from early research in the Archives of the Indies in Seville. As Dr Sliwa's thesis reveals, new documentation and details were unearthed by Spanish and British cervantistas in the nineteenth century and published piecemeal in literary journals or monographs. The search for additional documents regarding Cervantes and his family continued in the twentieth century, beginning with the memoir by James Fitzmaurice-Kelly (1913), followed by the seminal work of Rodríguez Marín in 1947 and of Luis Astrana Marín, whose avowed intention was to write the definitive work on his life and times. Research interest, mainly from outside Spain, has continued in fits and starts up until our own day. Most agree that the most important memorials to him are his written works, but our keen interest in the latter has awakened a renewed interest in the man behind the pen. Indeed, a first reason for reading and studying Cervantes is that his literary works are the medium in which a superlatively intelligent and unusually well-placed observer discerned and responded to numerous shifts in the bedrock of intellectual Spain and of a Europe 'on the move', in which Spain was a prime player.

Astrana Marín asserts that 'most of the early attempts at a biography of Cervantes were nothing more than a preamble to editions of the novel *Don Quixote*'. Editors and the reading public at large were seemingly far more interested in the life of the knight errant and of his squire than in the life of their enigmatic creator. And yet, arguably, the real-life experiences of Cervantes were as colourful, as richly diverse and, on occasion, as dramatic as those of his principal characters in his most famous work. It is probable that neglect of serious biographical studies on Cervantes may have been the price he had to pay for the almost overnight fame of his masterpiece.

As far as we know, Cervantes did not keep a diary or leave behind him volumes of official papers. He never wrote an autobiography and there is no evidence to suggest that he was the author of countless letters. Unlike Johann Wolfgang von Goethe, for example, whose conversations run to some four thousand printed pages and of whom contemporary gossip – extracted from the correspondence and diaries of third parties – fills three volumes, Cervantes was rarely in the public eye. In fact he became increasingly marginalized and aloof. In this regard his social standing could not be more different to that of his rival and literary opponent, Lope de Vega, who was extremely successful and adulated beyond measure.

Enough time has elapsed since Astrana Marín's contribution was made half a century ago for modern readers to demand a new appraisal of an extraordinary individual. Elusive as Cervantes was, it is the intention of this biography to remove the conscious aura of mystery that he wove around his extensive output. The distinct but varied voices heard in *Don Quixote, Persiles and Sigismunda* or in the *Exemplary Novels* belong to no ordinary man; on the contrary, they belong to a self-effacing genius who has come to enshrine all that is meaningful in Spanish consciousness. And that recognition is both at home and abroad, for it is true to say that his works have achieved, especially outside the Iberian Peninsula, much more than any of his famous contemporaries. Although Spain has produced brilliant writers, artists and poets, few are known – and even less are studied – outside her borders. Even those men of power and influence, such as Cardinal

Acquaviva, Hasan Pasha, the Count of Lemos, Juan de Urbina and Avellaneda, are remembered primarily because of their contact with Cervantes; it is his name that helps to keep alive the memory of others who otherwise would have sunk into oblivion long ago.

Any genuine attempt at a biography of Cervantes inevitably faces inherent problems. It is well known that we have lost a considerable number of his works and that there are doubts as to the authenticity of some attributed to him. With regard to the best of his prose works, we often do not know their genesis, and, to cap it all, of the several por-traits of Cervantes, not one, it is alleged, is genuine – and that includes the portrait that embellishes the cover of several biographies, this one included. Of course, where gaps and uncertainty exist, conjecture and speculation thrive, giving rise to legends and myth that are even more difficult to dislodge. It is not for nothing, therefore, that Cervantes has been labelled 'the man behind the mask'. This is doubly so, for when we visit his writing to discover the authentic Cervantes, what do we find? A series of first-person narrators whom Cervantes, when and wherever possible, disowns at the first opportunity. Moreover, so much is said in his creative works that it would be impossible to limit the man to any one set of ideas or beliefs.

In this biography, which aims to be comprehensive, I have neces-sarily touched on his known and not so well known texts and tried, where relevant and possible, to key them to his living experience. It has to be said, however, that a number of his works have accrued histories of their own and will continue to do so. Our knowledge of the man is refined in new editions of his diverse works – and in adap-tations of the same, as the musicals and ballets prove – as well as in discoveries of documents that have lain hidden for centuries. We still await the discovery of a first edition of *Don Quixote* from the several batches sent to Mexico and Peru in the New World. What is interest-ing to see is how critical appreciations of his works based upon the most recent literary theorists – Derrida, Bakhtin, Deleuze, Kristeva, Calvino – provide new and often hitherto unsuspected insights. We also now know much more about his living and working conditions under the Habsburgs: recent excellent studies of both Philip II and of Philip III add much to sharpen our picture of Cervantes and his family. The remarkable work of Anton van den Wyngaerde, who drew detailed drawings of many major and now not so major cities in Golden Age Spain and throughout Europe, further help us to visualize the cityscapes that Cervantes would have seen on a daily basis. Wyngaerde's drawing of Alcalá de Henares in about 1560 is by far the best illustration we have of the birthplace of Cervantes.

This attempt of mine differs from those previous biographies which imagine a Cervantes embroiled in political intrigues, a victim of impotency, a homosexual, a writer who supported the viewpoint of the minority *converso* population (Rosa Rossi, *Sulle Tracce de Cervantes*, 1997), those which employ imaginative reconstructions and elaborate psychological theories about him (Fernando Arrabal, *Un Esclavo Llamado Cervantes*, 1996) and from those who fictionalize their accounts, no matter how amusingly or skilfully (Stephen Marlowe, *The Death and Life of Miguel de Cervantes: A Novel*, 1996), to name the three most recent full-scale biographical studies. Nevertheless, the issues raised by such researchers have to be faced, for, as data accumulates, so do myths. What emerges is that the factual truth, in so far as we are able to piece it together, is often more exciting and suggestive than the fictions dreamed up about him. This being so, I have tried to incorporate as much relevant material from a variety of authentic sources as space would allow in order to furnish a picture of a man who has proved notoriously elusive. However, much of that elusiveness has stemmed from the rather blinkered approach adopted by those biographers who have looked to Cervantes' literary works to explain – often to explain away – any gaps or uncertainties we have about his 'real-life' experience. But even when we have evidence of the experiences and can put a date to them, questions will always remain: if we agree, for example, that not all his work is of the highest quality, how did he come to create *Don Quixote* and the *Exemplary*

Novels? Does the answer lie in the reality of his social and historical contexts?

To answer this fundamental question we have to make use of historical documents but in conjunction with other facts relevant to the time. To establish little or no historical context for Cervantes' five years in Algiers, his time as a court petitioner, his marriage or his spell as a purveyor for the Armada, to name but a few turning-points, would do a disservice to biography. Fictionalized accounts or purely literary approaches to the subject of biography poorly accommodate the much-needed bona fide documentation offered by other research areas.

What would be ideal is a continuous factual account of the life of Cervantes from birth to death. From today's perspective that must remain an ideal, for, despite renewed interest and serious research into his life and times, considerable gaps still remain. Why did he leave his family home after three years of marriage? Why did Hasan the Venetian treat him so leniently when in Algiers? What was the true nature of his relationship with his mother-in-law, his wife, his sisters and his bastard daughter Isabel? Differences of interpretation will always exist – and that is healthy – but if we can base our interpretative differences on established historical-social contexts our discussions will bear greater fruit and lead to a clearer picture of Cervantes the man as well as Cervantes the writer.

I have used the English rendering of place names where possible (Corunna for La Coruña, Saragossa for Zaragoza, Lisbon for Lisbôa, Naples for Napoli, Peru for Perú) but have given the original, with due accentuation, in all other cases: Alcalá de Henares, Cádiz, Córdoba and so on. Although Spanish family names are relatively long, I have endeavoured to provide the full name in order to avoid confusion. To illustrate my meaning, the name Rodrigo was the Christian name of Miguel's father, his younger brother and a first cousin. A casual glance at the family trees of Miguel's parents further proves the necessity for full nomenclature, even if repetitious on occasion. When referring to Miguel de Cervantes I have used throughout the surname Cervantes rather than Miguel, but on those occasions where two or more of the family are mentioned in the same context I have reverted to first-name usage without losing, I hope, clarity of meaning.

1

HUMBLE ORIGINS: THE MAKINGS OF A HERO
(1547–69)

Verifiable documented references to the family of Cervantes go back four generations before the birth of Miguel de Cervantes Saavedra and begin with the mention in Córdoba of Ruy Díaz de Cervantes, who, in March 1463, 'took possession of a vineyard'. Ruy Díaz, a cloth merchant, was the paternal great-grandfather of the Cervantes who rose to become Spain's most celebrated writer. The son of Ruy Díaz was a Juan de Cervantes, and he first appears in a summons to the court to explain 'certain transactions and claims related to cloths' that is dated 17 June 1500. It was also in Córdoba in October 1483 that we find the first mention of Juan Díaz de Torreblanca who was the father of Cervantes' paternal grandmother and is recorded as 'leasing out an orchard for two years to the gardener Andrés Martínez for an annual rent of 2,500 maravedís'. Such entries suggest that, in the century before Cervantes' birth, his father's family was affluent and well established in Andalusia. This is in line with an early reference to the origins of the name of Cervantes that is found in the work of a famous poet of Córdoba, Juan de Mena (1411–1456), who served as the chronicler to King Juan II.[1] In a curious and incomplete work on genealogy, Juan de Mena makes the undocumented claim that the ancestors of what was destined to become the family name of Cervantes originated in Galicia, in the remote north-west of the Iberian Peninsula. He writes:

Those from the lineage of Cervatos and Cervantes are of noble blood and stem from the Munios and Aldefonsos, rich families in León and Castile who are buried in Sahagún and Celanova; they were Galicians and sprang from the loins of Gothic kings and were related by marriage to the kings of León. From Celanova the Aldefonsos went to Castile and took part in the capture of Toledo and having settled in the village of Cervatos took that as their new family name.

Mena goes on to say that one of these men, named Gonzalo, 'so as to distinguish himself from the rest of the Cervatos clan took the name of Cervantes'. When the same source later tells us that the family name of Cervantes is mentioned in connection with the capture of Seville it is clear that new roots in the south of Spain had been established. From this branch we find a Don Juan de Cervantes, who became the Archbishop of Seville as well as a cardinal of the Church of Rome and was buried in Seville Cathedral in 1453. But that was not all. For, arising from that same branch, there is record of 'the grand prior of the Order of St John, named Rodrigo de Cervantes the Deaf'. It is this ecclesiastical offshoot of the ancestry based in Andalusia that will prove significant in the biography of Miguel de Cervantes. Indeed it was the grandson of Rodrigo the Deaf who was to become the Knight Commander of the Order of Santiago and who married into the Saavedra family. Although Cervantes' father, Rodrigo, was to use the surname of Saavedra, it was left to Cervantes himself to make greater use of it, but for causes and in circumstances neither man would have envisaged.

It is clear from the account of Juan de Mena that the campaigns in which the Cervantes family took part helped to shape the political, religious and social conditions that later members of the family were to encounter. A little-studied aspect of the life of Miguel de Cervantes Saavedra is the role played by his ancestors, although there is no denying the rivalry among Spanish towns and cities to claim the family as theirs. This has resulted in the creation of a number of false documents that, in turn, have spawned spurious claims. And it is not only in relation to his birthplace that such inauthentic documents occur.[2] Their existence has hindered progress in the discovery of the truth about the man the Spanish affectionately call the 'prince of geniuses'.[3]

There is nothing inauthentic, however, about the documentation relating to Cervantes' paternal grandfather, Juan de Cervantes, an eminent lawyer who was born c. 1470 in Córdoba, a city that from 711 until 1236 was under Moorish rule and which, because of its culture and learning, had earned the title 'the Athens of the West'. The earliest reference to Cervantes' great-grandparents on his mother's side is to a Juan de Cortinas, who, in Arganda, Castile, in 1485 donated a chalice to the parish church. Indeed, of the few surviving records from Arganda most concern family donations to the Church, whereas those of Córdoba relate mainly to the buying, selling or renting of lands and of houses. The ability to either give or buy possessions indicates success and suggests that both families enjoyed comfortable lifestyles. The fact that Juan Díaz de Torreblanca, the father of Cervantes' grandmother on his father's side, was a physician and surgeon is a further indication. Active in Córdoba, his success is seen, *inter alia*, in the ability to purchase houses (with their winepresses) in 1490, in the joint company he set up in 1495 for the 'leasing of the sales-tax on cloths' and in the 55,000 maravedís he paid for 'the purchase of houses' in June of that same year. From the few records that relate directly to the great-grandparents of Cervantes in Andalusia and in Castile, it is clear that they were prosperous and respectable citizens of their communities. Fortunately, documentation for the families of both of Cervantes' grandparents is extant, especially so with reference to Juan de Cervantes, and it is with the help of bona fide records relating to his life and activities that we are able to place the family in a clearer social and historical context.

Despite early attempts at collecting material for the purposes of writing a biography of Juan de Cervantes that were made known in 1887 by Julio de Sigüenza, no biographical study has yet appeared – there are as many as 288 extant documents relating to his life most of which refer to accusations against him: accusations of abuse of office (theft or appropriation of goods) or of serious breaches in common courtesy.[4, 5] Although the context in which these accusations and alleged breaches of etiquette has been lost, the picture that emerges from a study of the documentary evidence is that Juan was ambitious, restless, short-tempered and enjoyed the good life. He was also resilient and always made a point of responding to charges levelled against him, and whenever he lost a case he almost always appealed against the decision.

Recent research proves that Juan was also a man of prominence who, despite setbacks in his long and active career, was highly regarded in the circles that mattered. Proof of this is seen in the substantial sum of 10,000 maravedís he received from the king in 1508 for his services over several years as a scholar and lawyer 'in lawsuits and disputes relating to the revenue for the city of Córdoba'. It is no surprise therefore to find Juan as the mayor of that city in 1516 and, after one year in office – the post was temporary – as its chief magistrate. After various similar offices in both Toledo and in Cuenca, the Duke of Alzadas appointed him as his deputy in Cuenca (where Juan apprehended a Miguel Ruiz, who had stabbed to death 'as many as twelve or thirteen constables') and one year later as his judge in Guadalajara. Juan went from strength to strength, and, when appointed Judge in Residence for the city of Plasencia (1538–41), to be followed by the post of mayor for the Duke of Sessa's estates in Baena (which included Cabra, a city many believe to be important in the early life of Cervantes), his success had turned full circle. When, in 1551, he returned to Córdoba he was welcomed as 'one of the city's most esteemed scholars'.[6] The professional career of Cervantes' grandfather is also significant in that those who posit the notion that Jewish blood ran through his veins point to the grandfather's university education and career as a lawyer, a profession that Juan's own father and his father-in-law both practised, and one in which Jews flourished. Although the bulk of documentary evidence argues against such and similar claims, the 'converso' issue – were the Cervantes family converts from Judaism? – remains a bone of contention. It is clear that Juan enjoyed high social standing in Córdoba and valued his status among the nobility. When he finally retired to Córdoba to work for the Inquisition, he could look back upon a varied and successful career.

Successful as he was, there was one major blemish on the family record which was possibly to have bearing on his grandson's career.[7] The origin of this lay in a dispute concerning payments to do with illegitimacy, and it is well documented. Juan de Cervantes had a very desirable daughter named María who caught the eye of the archdeacon of Guadalajara. As luck would have it, the archdeacon Don Martín de Mendoza – nicknamed El Gitano (The Gypsy) – was himself the illicit fruit of the union between his father, the duke Diego de Hurtado Mendoza, and a gypsy woman, who had been pensioned off and long forgotten. The liaison between María de Cervantes and the archdeacon led to an illegitimate daughter, named Martina de Mendoza. When Juan de Cervantes discovered what had happened he compelled the archdeacon to sign an obligation to the tune of 600,000 maravedís, in order to pay for the upkeep and maintenance of both mother and child. Marriage was out of the question, and the child was sent to Madrid to be brought up. This private arrangement held up well until the duke died and was replaced by his successor, who immediately set about clearing all the family debts. Discovering the obligation imposed on the archdeacon, he immediately sacked Juan de Cervantes who, although he tried to exact just retribution, soon realized that he was fighting a losing battle, so he decided to go to Alcalá de Henares and from there continued his lawsuit. When we learn that one year before the old duke died that he had secretly married a commoner and had left her some 2 million maravedís we can better understand the fury of his successor, who believed that his father's friend and confidante Juan de Cervantes – whom he believed had conspired with his father against him – was to blame for his dramatic loss of revenue. The 'dowry' to the commoner amounted to one fifth of the total value of the successor's inheritance.

In 1532 the tribunal in Valladolid finally decided in Juan's favour, but the decision was hotly disputed and the rancour continued. The affair very soon became public knowledge, and the scandal – that was what it became in the kingdom of Toledo – was reputedly the most talked-about matter during the early years of Charles V's reign.[8] With so much money at stake, a whole series of accusations and counter accusations inevitably ensued in which attacks on Juan's sexual morality loomed high. Unhappily for Juan such acrimony brought the family name of Cervantes into the spotlight. Even two years after the tribunal's verdict in Valladolid we find a reference to a 'letter sent by the graduate Mejía to Dr Vaquer, the inquisitor for Toledo, about the charge brought against Juan de Cervantes of acting as a pimp'.[9] Records prove, however, that litigation was very common in Spanish public life. Juan's determination to defend his corner explains his family's return to Alcalá de Henares, for he had worked in the city from 1509 to 1512. His second child, Rodrigo, the future father of Miguel de Cervantes, had been born there. During his second stay in Alcalá de Henares, Juan de Cervantes worked for the constabulary as a magistrate in the local courts. Together with his wife, Leonor Fernández de Torreblanca, he set up house in what was becoming a fashionable and prosperous city. It was quite the place to be in early sixteenth-century Spain.

The generally agreed year of Rodrigo's birth is 1509, although the absence of a birth certificate has inevitably led to controversy as to the place of birth. The date is significant in the history of the city because it was the year that Cardinal Cisneros founded the university there. Thanks to the foresight and energy of Cisneros, Alcalá de Henares was soon to become the focal point of Renaissance Spain. Known in Roman times as Complutum and later occupied by the Muslims – the prefix 'al' tells us of its Arabic past – the city had been recaptured by Alfonso VI in 1085 and its site was given to the archbishops of Toledo in 1126. It is well known that the church played an active role in resettling the lands won back from the Arabs, and the archbishops did everything in their power to attract colonists and to make Alcalá de Henares a thriving metropolis. As a result it became an important medieval communication axis, capitalizing on its location on the road from Madrid to Saragossa. Alcalá de Henares also attained early prominence for its fairs and markets and as an agricultural centre. It was for these reasons that the city received the special support of the Catholic Monarchs in the 1490s. By the time Cervantes was born, no less than eight city gates gave access to rising numbers of university students who attended the city's twenty-four colleges. By 1565, with a population of some 13,000, Alcalá de Henares had matriculated over 3,000 students, a figure exceeded only by the universities of Salamanca and Valladolid.[10] Clearly, with this sudden influx of students, the town was transformed. Most of the students lived on their own, in private houses or in special student houses, the *pupilerías*. With its colleges renowned for theology, classical languages, philosophy and architecture, the city also offered its visitors more than twenty convents, two major seminaries, five monasteries, three parish churches and two hospitals. In a detailed drawing of Alcalá de Henares by Anton van den Wyngaerde in 1565, mounted travellers are seen using the wide approach to the city, while in the foreground there is an inn with a spacious courtyard. 'By minimizing his references to secular life', states Richard Kagan, 'Wyngaerde seems to be suggesting that the city of Alcalá de Henares was dedicated to the study of theology and to the service of the Catholic Church, two of the university's avowed goals.'[11] Had the concept of the cultural city of Europe been in vogue at that time Alcalá de Henares would certainly have been a strong candidate. Not only was the city in its prime, it was a prosperous period for the Cervantes family, too.

Not only was Juan's son Rodrigo born in Alcalá de Henares but also Rodrigo's son, Miguel de Cervantes. Endorsed by a notorial statement made by Juan Sánchez de Lugo in Valladolid in July 1552, it is clear that excluding the year 1532 (when the litigious dispute with Diego de Hurtado was at its height) the years in Alcalá de Henares from 1533 to 1538 number among the happiest for the Cervantes family, especially for Rodrigo. But things were to change when Juan agreed to accept the post of magistrate in Plasencia.

Despite the acknowledged 'high life' enjoyed by the family not all, so it seems, had been harmonious at home, and the offer to leave Alcalá de Henares provided Juan with the excuse he had been seeking to part from his wife. From the beginning of 1536 until late in 1537 he had been working in Ocaña, Castile, where he had fallen in love with a María de Córdoba, a girl described as between 'seventeen or nineteen years of age'.[12] Although this secret love affair did not progress it caused Juan to desert. When we learn that in 1551 (five years before his death) he left 50,000 maravedís to María Díaz, his housekeeper-cum-mistress, 'for the services rendered to him over twelve years' – that is to say, shortly after his acceptance of a post in Plasencia – it is plain that involvement with his housekeeper followed hard on the heels with that of Maria de Córdoba. We have no record of any matrimonial problems between Juan and his wife, but the family well knew that its situation had not been at all helped by the demands of the fourth duke, Diego de Hurtado Mendoza, for the return of the gifts – gold jewellery, pearls, silks and rich clothes – and monies made to María, Juan's pretty daughter.[13] By 1538 most or even all of the money may have been spent. The outcome of such liaisons and litigation was a desertion that was as sudden as it was harsh, especially for Leonor. It clearly brought with it a dramatic end to the family's halcyon days in Alcalá de Henares. Taking his older son, Andrés, Juan left behind a distraught wife, daughter and two other sons, Juan, who died in his youth, and Rodrigo.

It is known that Juan went on to spend successful years in Plasencia before taking up the offer by the Duke of Sessa to supervise his estates in Baena and in Cabra, although no actual documentation of the time Juan spent in Plasencia has come to light. This suggests that his stay there may have been free of the acrimony that was intrinsic to his work and that had followed him from his first summons in 1500. Whereas Juan went on to further success and ended up living a comfortable life with a mistress, slaves and servants in Córdoba, the fortunes of the family he left behind went from bad to worse. This is especially true in the career of Rodrigo, who, at the age of twenty-nine, suddenly found himself facing an uncertain future.

Rodrigo clearly enjoyed the prosperity of his parents' home up to the time of their sudden separation. The out-of-court settlement paid to his sister ensured that, and so, as records prove, he spent his days jousting, horse-riding and in tournaments. He also attended the highest civil and social functions in the city. Thanks to the resilience of his hard-working father, Rodrigo took part in the good life of the leisured classes. In a society based on display and spectacle nothing less was deemed appropriate for those who had wealth. Rodrigo had entered a world of power and privilege in which pageantry had set its seal and he lived according to its code. In such a setting one's social position was sustained by a network of friendships, affinities and social obligations. As a result, contacts were established which were to prove helpful, initially for Rodrigo and later on for his second eldest son, the author of *Don Quixote*.

Juan de Cervantes' desertion forced Rodrigo to reconsider his lifestyle. Frustratingly nothing is known of him until his marriage four years later in 1542. Did he exploit the hospitality of his jousting friends or was he dependent on what may have remained of María's 'dowry'? After all, 600,000 maravedís, if spent wisely, could have comfortably supported the Cervantes family for several years. But already six years of opulent living had eaten into the money, and the likelihood of a tidy sum remaining by this time is therefore not great. The fact that nothing has been found to prove that Rodrigo began working immediately suggests that the family was not yet on the breadline. However, four years later, after his marriage, Rodrigo was compelled to find employment – but he did not turn to law. One of the reasons given for this is that he apparently suffered from deafness. Despite the lack of documentary proof to date of such a disability, it is generally believed that Rodrigo was deaf – although to what degree is unknown – and had been so since his early years.[14] If the general consensus is correct, has his deafness any connection with that of his ancestor, Rodrigo the Deaf?

Compelled to make his own way in the world, Rodrigo became a *médico cirujano*, a surgeon, although at the time this meant little more than a barber. Surgery at that time was a branch of medicine very much in its infancy. Aged thirty-three, he had no time to go to university, so he undertook something that could be learned relatively quickly. Underlying his choice of profession was perhaps an expectation that he could profit from his former contacts and friendships. This was doubly important, because those who practised surgery were generally regarded as quacks. His choice of occupation, therefore, may be found wanting, but he really did have very little option. The fact his mother had been the daughter of a doctor may have influenced his choice. Besides we have no record of any advice about careers given to him by Juan, his father.[15] Had his father stayed in the family home it is probable that Rodrigo would have married into a family rich enough to offset his lack of a university education and his possible deafness. He was rudely thrown into life's realities and forced to face the severe tensions of a society undergoing rapid changes without the cushion of his father's support – changes that were to continue throughout the rest of the century.

As with Rodrigo's education, no diploma or any similar documentation relating to his profession has yet been found.[16] The main task of such 'surgeons' was to set bones, let blood and attend to wounds; anything else was left to the superior hands of the physician. Nevertheless, he would have studied the major medical text of the time, *Libro de las Cuatro Enfermedades Cortesanas* by Luis de Ávila Lobera, which dealt specifically with the quaintly termed 'four courtly ailments', gout, catarrh and complaints to do with the kidneys and liver.[17]

Although no official marriage certificate is extant, it is believed that Rodrigo married Leonor de Cortinas in 1542. Her parents were rural landowners whose origins were in Old Castile but who had settled in Arganda, close to Madrid. Little is known of the circumstances in which the courtship and marriage took place, but, given that Leonor's parents did not attend the baptisms of any of their grandchildren, it is probable that they disapproved of the union. Furthermore, the fact that none of the three boys born during these years was named Juan suggests that attitudes towards Rodrigo's father since his desertion continued to be hostile. Both Rodrigo's mother, who had brought to her marriage a dowry of 50,000 maravedís – no small sum in 1504 – and Rodrigo, who had been left behind without the support of either his father or his brother, had good reason to feel hostile. No reason is given as to why Juan chose to take Andrés, but Rodrigo would have resented the fact that he was left to fend for himself and, in effect, for the rest of the family. With their families' blessing or not, other more pressing problems were to burden the newly-weds. Rodrigo's mother had to face increasing financial strain after her husband's desertion, and in her struggle to survive she was in no position to help Rodrigo and his wife financially. The break with her husband had been total, and, as far as we know, he did not send one maravedí to alleviate her situation.

Unfortunately for the new breadwinner, competition for work in Alcalá de Henares was intense. It had become a major centre for medical studies and there were too many doctors seeking too few patients. Having to support his mother and a family circle that grew to six by 1550, Rodrigo's adversities were to begin in earnest and never truly left him. Their first child, born in 1543, was a son named Andrés, who died in infancy. In 1544 Andrea, their first daughter, was born, followed by Luisa in 1546. The next year Miguel arrived and three years later another son was born, named Rodrigo after his father. All the children were born in Alcalá de Henares, except for Magdalena, who was born in Valladolid in 1552, whence, prior to her birth, Rodrigo had decided to move in order to find better-paid work. One of a number of factors leading to his decision to leave his birthplace was, it seems, the refusal of a notable client to pay his bill, claiming that Rodrigo had not cured his son. Whether true or not, it was a painful slur on his professionalism, the bill was never paid and Rodrigo, in no position to pursue costly disputes, decided to leave.

With 35,000 inhabitants, Valladolid was at the time the capital of Spain and one of the most prosperous cities in the land. It was also very proud of its religious orthodoxy, and proof of this was to be seen in the public burnings of heretics in its main square which the Inquisition sanctioned during the reign of Philip II. Whether Rodrigo approved of such punishments or not is not mentioned or discussed. His mind was on more immediate matters. To a father seeking gainful employment, the city would have seemed to offer prospects he could not ignore. The move there marked one of several attempts to find regular work and, thus, a degree of security. However, despite the opulence in the halls of the chancery and in the antechambers of the councils, Rodrigo met only with continued hardship in Valladolid, which included time in a debtor's prison around 1552–3 and the threat of total confiscation of his goods. This arose because, on his arrival, he took out, together with his sister María, a loan to be repaid within the year to Pedro García (who had also co-signed the agreement) and Gregorio Romano. In return he pledged a good part of the family's silverware. Unable to meet his pledge, an acrimonious dispute then arose between Rodrigo and the two guarantors, and the upshot was a nasty spell in gaol. According to Canavaggio, Rodrigo's wife gave birth in July 1552 to Magdalena before his release.[18] If Canavaggio's dating is correct – for there is no surviving birth certificate – it must have been humiliating for her to discover that at the time she was born her father was behind bars.

Noblemen were exempted from imprisonment in a debtor's gaol, and so Rodrigo immediately invoked immunity. It is unlikely that he had read Juan de Mena's treatise on genealogy, but he would have learned from his father and grandfather of his high-born forebears in Andalusia. By definition noblemen were orthodox Christians and were 'pure of blood', a concept which became increasingly important in the Spain of Philip II and Philip III. By laying claim to nobility,

Rodrigo was therefore claiming to be a thoroughbred orthodox Christian. His embittered creditors, however, were having none of it and contested his claims. Luckily the high court of Valladolid, together with that of Granada, had as a primary function the resolution of cases of disputed nobility.[19] Seemingly, therefore, Rodrigo could not have been better placed, but, despite this, a protracted dispute followed and he was not released until seven ignominious months had passed. To offset the portrayal of him as a down-at-heel barber-surgeon was his claim made in the court in Valladolid that he owned properties in other places and even outside Spain and, if he were set free, would be able to pay for everything.[20] True or wishful thinking, nothing has emerged to prove such claims. Fortunately, his goods, which his creditors had temporarily confiscated, remained with him because Leonor enlisted the help of a solicitor named Francisco de Pedroso, who persuaded the judge that the goods belonged to Leonor and not to María, Rodrigo's sister. Records show that Pedroso worked tirelessly to have Rodrigo freed, and, when unable to bring proof of Rodrigo's nobility, it was he who asked the presiding judge if statements of witnesses would suffice. Interestingly, in April 1553 there is record of the Emperor Charles V demanding the authorities of the realm 'to require that witnesses specified by Rodrigo be brought before the courts for questioning'. [21] The fact that the office of the highest authority intervened points to the gravity of the dispute and reminds us of the litigation between Rodrigo's father and the Duke of Hurtado Mendoza that had scandalized the realm. Not for the best of reasons the family name of Cervantes was brought a second time to officialdom's notice. Seven witnesses testified on Rodrigo's behalf and, because his creditors could not disprove such evidence, Rodrigo eventually won his hard-fought freedom. The question arises, however, as to whether Rodrigo entered into his debts knowing that he could have recourse to the law of exemption. The documentation clearly shows that his creditors acted justly and were rightly annoyed at the use of what was, effectively, a legal loophole. They stood to lose 44,472 maravedís, and nowhere in the dispute is it mentioned that the debt was ever paid. After his release another move was inevitable.

Arguably, Rodrigo had been naive to try his luck in the capital, which was already full of the top doctors and physicians. It was not only in Valladolid that his judgement, in terms of residence and employment, would be found wanting. Indeed from 1551 to 1566 the Cervantes family spent fifteen years in what is best described as vagabondage. It is because of his wanderings around Spain that relatively little is recorded of Cervantes' early years. The number of times Rodrigo moved house in search of work or to shun creditors indicates the measure of financial hardship he faced as a matter of routine. Yet his situation was by no means uncommon, as village censuses of the early 1600s often list people who fled home to avoid imprisonment for debt. In 1586, for example, the Rioja hamlet of Neguerela was fast in the process of disappearing because its men were leaving to escape unmanageable debts.[22] Rodrigo and his family were left to struggle on despite the fact that his father was in a position to offer assistance. Evidently the bitterness that arose on account of the desertion still rankled. There is no record of any correspondence whatsoever between Juan and his family, so it is doubtful whether Rodrigo knew at this point that his father in 1551 had given over all his wealth to María Díaz. But changes were in the air.

In 1553, after twenty-five years, Rodrigo, undeniably *in extremis*, decided to visit his father in Córdoba, a journey that took eight days by horse and cart. In his earlier years Juan de Cervantes had made that same and similar journeys when *in* employment, whereas the journeys undertaken by Rodrigo were prompted by the need *for* employment. The journey was long and arduous, but it must not be thought that Rodrigo would have been a solitary wayfarer leading his hungry family to the safest haven. As the exploits of Don Quixote demonstrate, the roads of Spain witnessed a great variety of activities and travellers, especially itinerant doctors, for it was common practice for Castilian villages to share the services of a qualified doctor. The contract of a certain Juan de Salas, drawn up in 1555, clearly indicates the type of career that a country doctor could expect. Working in the province of Burgos, de Salas agreed to work for a three-year period and 'to go to those places and see the sick as many times as he was called, and to examine the urine of all of them without charging a fee'.[23] In return, his annual salary was to be 30,000 maravedís, the free use of a house, exemption from local taxes, guaranteed salary even in the event of a disability and the right to offer his services to the monasteries within a three-league radius. The figure of 30,000 shows how generous María's compensation of 600,000 maravedís had been. Clearly, poorer villages could not offer such generous terms, but it shows how things could have been different if Rodrigo had been properly qualified and prepared to work in rural communities that housed most of Spain's estimated population of some 7 million. What is interesting is that the most famous surgeons of the time also led highly migratory careers. Anastasio Rojo Vega claims that constant mobility was the norm in the sixteenth century for surgeons.[24] After all, Spain had a long tradition of population movements. The eight-centuries-long Reconquest of Muslim territories produced a rural population accustomed to moving when conditions so dictated. The career of Rodrigo's own father attests to that also.

On arrival in Córdoba, the first thing Rodrigo did – as before in Valladolid – was to borrow money. It was clear that he did not wish to face his father as a pauper. The fact that he had to borrow only proved the point, however, and Juan was not deceived; with his legal contacts he would have been one of the first to hear of his son's spell in prison, and bad news travels fast. Besides, he knew that his long-absent son was in dire straits otherwise he would not have come to see him. What may have sweetened the pill somewhat for Rodrigo was the knowledge that Juan in his early days had over twenty-one lawsuits brought against him and would not have forgotten the short spells inside Valladolid gaol in 1532.[25]

Juan clearly had enemies and had certainly been involved in what can be confidently described as shady deals, yet his reputation, at least in Andalusia, remained unblemished. Had Rodrigo been able to follow his father's profession he would have had all the prerequisites to make a successful career. After all, his brother Andrés, who became the mayor of Cabra, had presumably followed his father's advice and recommendations and did indeed lead a relatively successful and secure existence.

In keeping with his father's good standing in the town – still an eminent lawyer and now working for the Holy Office – Rodrigo probably found employment in hospital administration. The issue of reputation – in the sense of one's good name – has always loomed large in Spanish society. It is to be remembered that when brought to trial in Valladolid Rodrigo never mentioned his profession. But now in Córdoba, in the relative safety of a town in which he was unknown and where his father was a valued citizen, Rodrigo could start afresh. It must have seemed to him that his family had landed on its feet in a city that was in the midst of a minor building boom. Indeed, since its reconquest in 1236, it had been growing steadily – its population in 1553 was some 25,000 – while still retaining its courtly air of having once been the capital of Moorish Spain. The difference in architecture and lifestyle when compared to the barren contours of Castile would have been clear not only to Rodrigo but also to the young Cervantes. The geography of the region, together with its cultural, religious and historical past, would have shown him aspects of life he had not yet encountered. And here he was to make his first contact with the Moriscos, the Moors who had supposedly converted to the Church of Rome, a contact that would reappear in circumstances unimagined by any of the Cervantes family as it rumbled its way down through central Spain.

In 1555, two years after his enforced return, another son was born. It is no surprise to learn that the latest addition was called Juan, suggesting that a degree of reconciliation had occurred between Rodrigo and his father. However, next to nothing is known of Rodrigo's youngest child – not even a baptismal certificate has ever been found. Recent research into the genealogy of the family shows that Juan was certainly alive in 1585 because he is clearly mentioned as one of the heirs in his father's will. The wealth referred to in that will, although not specified, must refer to saleable items, for they 'are to be sold in a public auction or privately' and what is left of his goods was 'to be shared equally among his offspring, that is, his three sons 'Miguel, Rodrigo and Juan and his two daughters, Andrea and Magdalena'.[26] No mention is made in his will of Luisa, probably because of the renunciation of 'earthly goods' entailed in her vow of poverty taken when she entered a convent in 1565.

Accompanying Rodrigo throughout his travels and tribulations was his wife, Leonor. The fact that Rodrigo took her as his wife may have had more to do with her dowry – although precious little it turned out to be – than of Rodrigo's undying love, as in those days the resources of the bride or the bride's family were very often the most important aspect of any marriage. From what has been said so far of Rodrigo's adult life, it is clear that her life was never destined to be an easy one. Cervantes says very little of her, and, apart from a number of documented desperate measures which she undertook to protect her sons, it was inevitable that her situation would compel her to suffer the hardships unleashed by her husband's unenviable fate, dogged as he was by debts, impatient creditors and sheer bad luck. Her lifestyle lends support to the notion of that 'separate spheres' model of society, in which women lived in sealed communities, without autonomy or direction. According to such a view, women were little more than passive victims of the whims of men who dominated social and institutional life. Despite the constraints of a patriarchal society, Leonor did indeed have her moments of self-assertion, however. Constantly faced with the adversities occasioned by Rodrigo's repeated failures, she proved to be his main and often sole support throughout his frustrating efforts to find regular employment.

In an attempt to portray Leonor, successive biographers point to what they consider to be the characteristics of certain Castilian

33

women: piety, faith, resourcefulness and good housekeeping; they also employ the same tactic when they come to envisage Cervantes' future wife.[27] Unfortunately, not one print or drawing exists of either woman, nor do we have one physical description of them. What can be known of Cervantes' mother, however, is the sort of existence she would have led up until her marriage. For a woman in Castile the ritual of the mass would have been central to her existence. In a nation that was the right hand of the Pope nothing less could be warranted. The occasional burning of heretics served as a forceful reminder to citizens of their allegiance to king, country and to the Divinity. No Spaniard in Habsburg Spain was unaware of the forceful tentacles of the Inquisition, which reached as far into rural life as it did into urban.[28]

The pageantry that surrounds the feasts of Corpus Christi, the Nativity and of local patron saints were the highlights that gave life and the locality a meaning and measure. In general terms everything in sixteenth-century Spain revolved around the power and pomp of the Church and its authority; its festivals matched the changing seasons on which landowners and workers depended for their livelihoods. Leonor would have imbibed the virtues of propriety and good housekeeping in a culture where ceremonial order was intrinsic. From this relatively harmonious and stable existence in one locality, Leonor, soon after her marriage, was wrenched away to travel the unpaved roads of Imperial Spain searching for security. Her duties were to change dramatically when she was burdened with the obligations of a mother always on the move. She could not have foreseen a life on wheels, more akin to that of the gypsy than of a landed gentlewoman, but that is what her fate decreed. The change must have both bewildered and disorientated her. In response to her changing circumstances she was to rise to become her family's saviour.

Our knowledge of Leonor stems from some thirty-two documents about her, although 'not one of these sheds any light on her childhood, youth, education, ambitions, properties in Arganda or how she learned to write'. [29] We know that she could read and write because her signature is found on her letters and legal documents. Although no marriage certificate has been found we know that she bore seven children, a not exceptionally large family at that time but big enough when the breadwinner was rarely in permanent employment. When, because of debts, Rodrigo spent from October 1553 to April 1554 in Valladolid prison all the furniture in her home had been removed and, although she was pregnant with Magdalena, 'there was nothing to sleep on or anything to serve her person'. We can only imagine the misery she suffered in this period and even though, as we have seen, her goods were eventually returned, it was clearly at this time that Leonor came into her own. Six months without support had awakened within her that spirit of independence that the family needed to survive. She turned her hand to business; she sold and bought goods and entered into contracts and public loans with merchants and received rental from houses. She was clearly a woman of energy and initiative with an eye for business. It was her resourcefulness that had kept the family afloat through this time.

The generally accepted date of Miguel's birth is St Michael's day, 29 September 1547, the year in which both Henry VIII and Francis I of France died. It was also the year in which Ivan the Terrible of Muscovy assumed the title of Tsar, an event that went unnoticed by most Spaniards at the time. On the wider canvas, it was the year that saw Charles V defeat the Lutherans at Mühlberg (Luther had died the previous year) and, on a more local note, it was the year when Philip II spent Christmas in Alcalá de Henares. [30]

It is commonly accepted that Miguel's early schooling took place in Córdoba, a city that in 1553 saw the opening of its first Jesuit school. It is likely that Miguel attended the college from the age of seven, but from six to seven he would have gone to the school run by Alonso de Vieras, a friend of a cousin of the Cervantes family. Jesuit teaching manuals of the period reveal that in their colleges their youngest pupils were introduced to the rudiments of grammar and rhetoric.

What is often forgotten is that pupils listened rather than read. In other words, learning was by ear and the use of memory. From the praise lavished on the Jesuits as teachers in Cervantes' story 'The Colloquy of the Two Dogs', some argue that he must have studied under them, but nothing is known for certain. Fortunately, records do exist of what teaching materials were used and which subjects were taught throughout the Jesuit school system. Whatever school he attended in Córdoba, it is agreed by his biographers that Cervantes was to make three important discoveries there: the love of learning, the magic of theatre and the presence of the picaresque.

Two sudden deaths in the family – that of Juan de Cervantes in March 1556, followed one year later by his estranged wife – brought new vicissitudes for the household. For the next seven years documentary evidence of both Rodrigo's and his family's whereabouts is practically non-existent. Lack of documentation over such a considerable time-span in the early life of Cervantes has led a number of biographers, especially those who wrote before the findings of Astrana Marín, to make wild speculations.

With the death of his father Rodrigo was made to reconsider his family's future. Luck would have it that in Cabra, some sixty-five kilometres (forty miles) away from Córdoba, his brother Andrés was mayor. As a result, the backwater town of Cabra seemed to offer Rodrigo distinct possibilities and, given his brother's presence and influence there, became the obvious, perhaps the only choice. After all, Rodrigo could not return to Valladolid, Madrid was not yet the capital and Alcalá de Henares, after his mother's death, held nothing for him. Without evidence of the contrary it has been generally assumed that Rodrigo went to Cabra with his family in 1558. If indeed he did go there Miguel's early education in Córdoba would have come to an abrupt end.

The year 1558 was a bad one in absolutist Spain. The first real signs of famine were visible and a plague was sweeping the country. Fortunately for the Cervantes family, however, the jurisdiction of

Cabra fell to the Duke of Sessa, a remarkable Spaniard, who in 1541 had named Juan de Cervantes lawyer of his estates. Andrés was a leading member of the council in Cabra; he made all appointments and it is reasoned that a job for Rodrigo in one of the local hospitals was arranged. Without documentation to show otherwise, it is commonly believed that Rodrigo and his family – not Luisa who had returned to Alcalá de Henares – stayed in Cabra until 1564.

Recaptured from the Moors in 1240, Cabra was a walled fortress town with a palace, gardens and fountains surrounded by a moat. It was where El Cid had won a notable victory against the king of Granada. Mentioned by Cervantes in *Don Quixote, Part Two*, the town was famous for its ravine. At the time that Andrés was mayor its population totalled 3,000 and was served by four churches, three hermitages, two convents and two hospitals. If we follow the reasoning that Rodrigo did go to Cabra, the town, in comparison to the towns and cities in which they had previously lived, would have struck the family as a quiet, pleasant, even idyllic backwater. It offered the type of environment Cervantes praises, both in the prologue to *Don Quixote* and in his pastoral novel *La Galatea*, as ideal for the muse of poetry. As such, Cabra would have offered the young Cervantes an unruffled prelude to the storms and stresses of later life, but that does not mean that his parents, irrespective of any support proffered by Andrés, found life there any easier.

If we go by extant documentary evidence, the next time Rodrigo appears is in October 1564 in Seville. The document claims that 'for several months Rodrigo had been a resident of Seville and was subletting property'.[31] In that same year a lawsuit was issued against a Juan de Ureña who owed Rodrigo three months' rent. Atypically, Rodrigo won the case.[32] Interestingly, the document recording the amount awarded to Rodrigo was signed in the presence of his brother Andrés, now a junior magistrate of the city. What prompted the move, whether from Cabra or elsewhere, to what arguably was the most colourful and vibrant city on the Iberian Peninsula, the major port to the amazing wealth of the Americas? And, what of Cervantes' education which had been so abruptly interrupted?

Andrés had a son, also named Rodrigo, only six months younger than his cousin Miguel. A man in Andrés' position would have had private tutors for his children. Both fathers knew the importance of education and would have seen to it that the two boys continued their schooling. The assertion by a number of biographers and critics that Cervantes, because of his love of reading, was self-taught is probably expecting too much of a young mind. Even if, like the celebrated protagonist of his novella *The Glass Graduate*, he studied intensely and devoured books or, like his engaging knight, he 'so buried himself in books that he read all night from sundown to dawn', a boy of eleven needs tuition. In all probability Cervantes resumed schooling in Cabra or wherever the family settled. Even if we assume that his education continued, whether in Cabra or not, we cannot say that it proceeded along the lines first introduced in Córdoba.

The move to Seville was to be deeply significant. At the time Spaniards referred to the capital of Andalusia as the 'gateway to the Indies', that is, the New World. Cervantes regularly saw galleons leaving the port bound for Mexico or Peru and returning laden with precious metals, especially silver from Potosí in Bolivia. Contemporary records show that some fifteen gates gave access to what was a walled cathedral city surrounded by some of the most idyllic and fertile lands in Spain. Reclaimed by King Ferdinand III in 1248, after the discovery of America and its colonization throughout the sixteenth century it rapidly grew to prominence as a centre of trade with the New World. With a population of 85,000 in 1565, Seville was famed for its oils, hams, fish, olives and wines. Indeed, a proverb of the day talks of the eight rivers that flowed into its bustling port: water, wine, oil, milk, honey, sugar, gold and silver. The Inquisition had its headquarters there, too, probably because the city was the main focus of Lutheranism in Spain and Portugal. In 1562, the year before Rodrigo's arrival, there had been public burnings of heretics. To any dispassionate witness it was clear that religious intolerance was widespread and not just the prerogative of the Barbary States, Reformation England or Constantinople.

Rodrigo's job in Seville was as the manager of rented accommodation; the owner of the properties was Andrés. Apart from the educational needs of his children – although mention is of Cervantes alone – it is not difficult to understand why Rodrigo should have tried his luck in Seville. The city, after all, was in the midst of an even greater building boom than Córdoba had been. For once it seemed Rodrigo could profit from circumstances rather than suffer from them. However, despite what seemed very favourable conditions – the support of his elder brother, his father's contacts, the numerous hospitals – Rodrigo's stay would not even last two years. It is not at all clear why Rodrigo abandoned his new life as a managing agent, although it has been suggested, somewhat unkindly, that he may have been showing proof of his incompetence.[33]

To those who doubt whether Cervantes joined his father in the Andalusian capital, what other option did he have? The Jesuit school in Seville had expanded within four years to embrace five hundred pupils. Biographers and commentators tend to agree that Cervantes probably did attend the Jesuit school in Seville, and, if so, he would have met Father Acevedo, who in 1561 had moved from the Jesuit school in Córdoba to the one in Seville. Acevedo would most probably have taught him Rhetoric. Twenty-five of Acevedo's plays have survived for the period 1556–72, and it was he who fixed the norms of what may be called school drama, an important step in the evolution of the theatre in Spain.[34] Although in Jesuit schools drama was initially employed as a teaching aid for moral and rhetorical instruction, the emphasis on entertainment grew, which meant greater use of the vernacular. If we accept that young Cervantes was in Seville, he would have noted public interest in an art form that was to undergo enormous changes in his lifetime.

In the Jesuit method of education great emphasis was given to performance. Pupils mounted public shows to celebrate the opening and closing of the school year, national holidays and the great festivals of Nativity, Easter and Corpus Christi. This attracted local patronage and helped to integrate school drama and, by extension, the schools themselves into community life. Pupils of all ages were actively encouraged to produce their own work that they could recite, sing, act or accompany with an instrument. From his later work it is clear that Cervantes had a passion for the theatre and it is likely that it was innate; any exposure to drama during his schooldays therefore helped to develop an interest that became lifelong and that was to be nourished by the arrival in Seville in 1564 of Lope de Rueda, one of the founders of Spanish theatre.

Curiously enough, at the time when Rodrigo was working for his brother we learn that he had Rueda as a neighbour.[35] In later life Cervantes recalls having seen the great Lope de Rueda and praises his use of pastoral poetry, although his most vivid memories were of the interludes performed between the acts of plays. It is entirely possible, therefore, that Cervantes saw Lope de Rueda in Seville at this time. Other influences, however, were also at work on Cervantes.

Some have found it difficult to believe that an impoverished Rodrigo would have sufficient funds to send Cervantes to the best college in Seville. Records show that the locals considered the Jesuit-run college in Seville to be the best in Andalusia and, thus, one of the best in Spain. There is no record whatsoever of Rodrigo having studied to any worthwhile level – unlike his father and grandfather – and so it is likely that he would have wanted the very best education for his children, especially after suffering the shock of his father's desertion, an action that had brought home to him the real need of a well-rounded, formal education. His life had not been a success and the hardships he had to suffer resulted in part from the lack of appropriate qualifications. And as for financial support, the money earned from his latest career in real estate could have provided the wherewithal for Cervantes to attend the college. Militating against this notion is the fact that Rodrigo finds himself involved once more in a lawsuit over debts. While in Alcalá de Henares in 1565 attending the vow-taking of his daughter Luisa – who entered its Carmelite convent as Sister Luisa de Belén y Cervantes – a creditor in Seville named Rodrigo de Chaves demanded seizure of Rodrigo's goods.[36] Although saved by his daughter Andrea – she claimed that the goods were *her* personal property – Rodrigo once again felt obliged to leave Andalusia and decided to settle in Madrid.

Luisa is a very shadowy figure in biographies of Cervantes. She was to spend over half a century as a nun and became the prioress of the convent in which she took her first vows. In contrast to the calamitous events that constitute the life of her brother, she remained fixed to a life of contemplation and prayer. Towards the close of the sixteenth century, after discipline in the order had become relaxed, efforts to reform the order were introduced by St John of the Cross and St Teresa of Ávila (Ávila at the time was a walled city two days' journey from Alcalá de Henares). The reforming zeal of these two great Spanish mystics – who were also poets – had reached Luisa's convent, and so her daily existence was highly disciplined and, if judged by today's standards, harsh. The convent became the centre of great spiritual devotion and similar in its practices to the contemplative order of the Carthusians, an order founded by St Bruno in France in 1084. A description of the life of the monks in Charterhouse in London in the early sixteenth century bears comparison to the austerities of that of Sister Luisa's and is not for the faint-hearted. It was a life of dedication and simplicity in which the hours of the day were measured by the 'perpetual chant of psalms, canticles, antiphons, responsoria, prayers and hymns'.[37] And yet, in Spain at least, such austerities led to the inexpressible heights of mysticism. We know that from November 1567 to February 1568 St Teresa visited Alcalá de Henares, and it is highly likely that such a visitation would have aroused widespread interest, both inside and outside the Carmelite convent.

Perhaps another good reason for Rodrigo to settle in Madrid was the death of his wife's mother, Doña Elvira de Cortinas, who lived in Arganda, not far from the city. When we learn that Elvira had left property to her daughter we can see an added incentive. Curiously enough, there is no record of Elvira's husband. Rodrigo received twenty ducados (ducats) for the sale of part of the land inherited by his wife. Although not a great sum it was thought sufficient to meet the needs of the moment; such needs almost always dictated Rodrigo's life.

When in 1561 Philip II chose Madrid to be the new capital of Spain he was merely following the express wishes of his father who, once *his* wars in Europe were over, intended the capital to lie at the geographical centre of the Iberian Peninsula. After all, up until that point the court of Charles V had been itinerant. Yet, in mid sixteenth-century Spain, the new capital-to-be could not compete with Seville, Toledo or Barcelona. Modern Madrid owes its origins to Muhammad I who, as the emir of Córdoba, built a fortress called Maýrit in c. 875.[38] The town was captured from the Moors by Alphonsus VI at the end of the eleventh century but only came into relative prominence during the reign of the Catholic Monarchs in the late fifteenth century. Their achievements – political unity, the creation of an effective administration, the capture of Granada, solid defence at home, the discovery of the Americas – created the world into which Cervantes would make his entrance.[39] And when in 1544 Charles V, the grandson of Ferdinand and Isabella, awarded to Madrid the right to carry the emblem of the crown on its coat of arms, its future seemed assured. Not even Seville, the thriving gateway to the Indies, could boast the emblem of the crown.

No more than 14,000 people lived in Madrid at the outset of Philip II's reign, but with the arrival of the court another building boom was imminent. Between 1550 and 1600 the city expanded from around 20,000 to 65,000 inhabitants. Thanks to the work of Wyngaerde, we have excellent perspectives of the city as it was in the 1560s, the Madrid Cervantes would have seen grow around him in his late teens.

From such illustrations it is clear that it had remained 'a late medieval city, surrounded by walls that marked off the city's western edge and its substantial eastern suburbs. The town extended from the banks of the river Manzanares which was crossed by three bridges from north to south.'[40] The modern suburb of the Casa de Campo, clearly visible in the drawing as a green mass of woodland on the west bank of the river, was purchased by Philip II to be used as a hunting ground. Nowadays it functions mainly as a park for the capital's inhabitants, known as *madrileños*.

During the reign of Philip II, which spans most of Cervantes' life, Madrid remained primarily a political centre, while Toledo and Seville continued to dominate the country's economic, social and cultural life. What the choice of capital meant for the economy and infrastructure of Spain has been well studied, and it is clear from such studies that the government of the day tended to treat the rest of the peninsula as merely another part of its colonial empire, to be exploited as necessary for its own well-being. Geographical factors forced Madrid to 'regulate the economy of the rest of the country, to guarantee itself a dependable supply of foodstuffs, fuel, and other necessities'.[41] Like most larger towns Madrid possessed seigniorial rights over the villages in its jurisdiction, which included the right to compel its subject villages to provide bread for the city at regulated prices. Research has shown that at the time Cervantes was in Esquivias in the 1580s (his future wife's native town in Castile) the radius of control of Madrid was some seventy-two kilometres (forty-five miles).

A strong flavour of the Madrid he and his family members would have known towards the end of the century is captured in the plan of the city drawn by the Dutchman Frederik de Wit in the early seventeenth century. With its fountains, trees and fences, de Wit plotted the city, clearly labelling each street, church and house. Juxtaposing the perspectives of Madrid drawn by Wyngaerde with the detailed plan of de Wit there emerges a clear image of the city at the time. Amid the streets and churches depicted by de Wit the young Cervantes, aged

nineteen, would have walked, having his first real taste of a royal city –
and one only five years old. Using as a guide the self-portrait given in
the prologue to his *Exemplary Novels* of 1613, it is not too difficult to
imagine Cervantes as a bright-eyed, fair-haired, lean-framed teenager
having his first experience of Imperial Spain, the capital of which was
to witness his frustrations and disappointments; his triumphs, too. The
Prudent Monarch, the term given to Philip II by Spanish historians,
ruled over an expanding empire, and, to a talented and ambitious individual like Cervantes, it offered possibilities that his father could
hardly have envisaged. As young Cervantes roamed the streets of the
capital he must have felt part of that empire and believed he had a
future in it. And so he had until the element of chance, so intrinsic
an ingredient in his writing, was about to play a cruel card, the consequences of which were to change his life for ever.

The Cervantes family arrived in Madrid in the autumn of 1566.
Madrid may also have appealed to Rodrigo because civil unrest with
the Moriscos in Andalusia was growing in momentum. When in 1566
Cardinal Espinosa, in an attempt to accelerate social integration,
'invited' the Moriscos of the kingdom of Granada to abandon their
language, customs and rites they stubbornly refused. Unsurprisingly,
the collapse of their economy (the silk industry), accusations of aiding
and abetting Barbary pirates and the dispossession of their lands and
properties without receiving any compensation brought about civil
disturbances that finally erupted in the rebellion on Christmas Eve
of 1568. It was to last three years and led to some of the most savage
conflicts ever seen on Spanish soil. Inevitably, brutal massacres were
the outcome.

It was in Madrid that Cervantes was to meet his next teacher, Juan
López de Hoyos, curate of the parish of San Andrés and a known
humanist. He was also the royal chronicler and was the author of the
voluminous work on the illness and death of Elizabeth of Valois,
Queen of Spain and King Philip II's third wife. This became the standard manual and was known in every official circle in the land, and it

was in this book that Cervantes saw his first work published, four poems to commemorate the sudden death of the queen, who died at the age of twenty-three while bringing a stillborn child into the world.[42] Although today Elizabeth is no more than a name in history books, the news of her death was as shattering to her contemporaries, especially throughout the courts of Europe, as that of Princess Diana in our own time. Given that López de Hoyos was commissioned to draft the official account of the funeral it is clear that Cervantes was moving in high circles. His education was apparently bearing early fruit, and he was being talked of as an 'extraordinary and precocious poet'.[43]

Three months after the publication of the four poems, Cervantes was living in Rome. His hasty departure from Spain in December 1569 signals the beginning of a welter of life's adventures that for the most part led to misfortune and frustrating poverty. The flight from Madrid clearly marks the first climacteric in Cervantes' early life.

2

EXILE AND THE FORTUNES OF WAR
(1569–75)

In a document discovered in the archives at Simancas during the nineteenth century by an early biographer of Cervantes, Jerónimo Morán, we learn that a royal warrant, dated 15 September 1569, commanded the bailiff, Juan de Medina, to arrest a Miguel de Cervantes, accused of having wounded Antonio de Sigura in a duel that occurred within the precincts of the Royal Court. The summons authorized the police, who were to have all expenses paid, 'to seek out, arrest and bring back the said Cervantes and his possessions to the royal prison in Madrid for trial'.[1] Clearly the offence was deemed serious, and he did well to flee. Antonio de Sigura came from a reputable family of builders and had worked in the royal palace in Aranjuez. Commentators tend to believe that the dispute between them involved the concept of honour and that possibly Sigura had cast aspersions on one of Miguel's sisters. Whatever the cause, the punishment, to have 'his right hand cut off and exile for ten years from these kingdoms as well as other punishments contained in the said warrant', seems excessive and must have horrified the young man. One of the other punishments was the public shame to which all culprits of such crimes were exposed. Disgrace in the eyes of men was one thing, but the fact that Cervantes had fled the rule of law had clearly angered the authorities and must explain the harshness of the summons. How could a young upstart – so at least runs the sentiment of its subtext – imagine that he could escape the clutches of Imperial Castile? From being a man on the make in Madrid, he now became a fugitive from justice. He went first to Andalusia, a dangerous move, because at the time the region was in open conflict with the authorities. The War of Granada (1568–71), a

47

war against the Moriscos, has been described as the most brutal of all wars in sixteenth-century Europe.[2] That said, there were advantages in his choice of city, Seville. At the time it was the third largest city in Europe – only Paris and Rome were bigger – and was enjoying an economic boom. For a man on the run there was safety in numbers. Besides, in Seville, a city he already knew, and elsewhere in Andalusia, Cervantes had family connections.

Impulsively or not, the twenty-two-year-old saw no option but to flee first to Seville and eventually the country. He was not safe in Spain, but even outside her borders he was not free because the summons clearly authorized the police to seek everywhere in the 'kingdoms and domains' where Spanish law ruled. What is rarely discussed is why he did not surrender to the authorities. Had he gleaned enough from his father's – and his grandfather's – skirmishes with the law to infer that any punishment meted out through the courts would be far worse than that decreed in his absence? He would have known about Hurtado de Mendoza, former ambassador in Venice and Rome, the chosen representative of Charles V at the Council of Trent and ex-governor of Siena, who had been banished from the palace grounds for 'fighting in the court precincts', and this only five months before the affray with Sigura.[3] No doubt he later sympathized with Luis Cabrera de Córdoba, the court chronicler, who was exiled in 1601 for putting his hand to his sword in the king's presence. Cervantes' punishment is much harsher than that of either of his two countrymen.

What should be mentioned is that, when Jerónimo Morán first published details about the summons and sentence in 1863, he was attacked by those who saw in Cervantes an impeccable being who could not possibly have been the person referred to in the Simancas indictment.[4] And yet three other major writers of Golden Age literature, namely, Lope de Vega, Calderón de la Barca and Francisco de Quevedo, all fell foul of the law. Had Cervantes been blameless, would he have left Madrid so abruptly? Although an aura of mystery surrounds the episode, the very existence of the summons serves to elucidate his subsequent behaviour. Having fled to Seville in December 1569 – the warrant claims that he had been 'seen in Seville and in other parts' – Cervantes then showed up in Rome the following February, in the household of the prelate Giulio Acquaviva, the son of the Duke of Atri, who, in May of 1570, became a cardinal. Cervantes worked for the cleric until April 1570 as a chamberlain, while, at the same time, Acquaviva acted in that same capacity to the Pope. Thus the prelate and his new employee would have known of the excommunication of Queen Elizabeth I, declared in February 1570, an event that infuriated Philip II and which would have been a talking-point for Acquaviva and his new employee. We know that the prelate had been sent to Madrid in 1568 to offer the condolences of Pope Pius V to Philip II on the death of Don Carlos. There is no record of any meeting between the future cardinal and Cervantes, but that does not exclude the possibility that Cervantes met Acquaviva during the latter's visit to the Spanish capital. Besides, whom else did he know in Rome, a city where the Pope and not Philip II held jurisdiction?

To work in the prelate's household Cervantes needed proof of his orthodox Christian ancestry, known under the statute of 'purity of blood'. Nobility, honour and purity of blood (by which was meant that the holder of the certificate was not a bastard and that there were no Moors, Jews, converts or persons reconciled by the Holy Office among his ancestors) constituted the sacred triad of criteria by which the nation most openly expressed its cultural and social values.[5] Proof of the purity of one's blood was a usual requirement of those who sought employment in the houses of the powerful and influential, and so Cervantes asked his father to produce such a document, which he did. We already know that to seek immunity from imprisonment Rodrigo had earlier laid claim to his nobility and purity of blood, which seemingly had been accepted (although no document actually proves his assertion), so all that he required was a witness. This done, Rodrigo applied for and was granted on the same day, 22 December 1569, the necessary certificate for his son. The document is important, for it proves that Miguel was in Rome, in the employ of the prelate and, arguably, an orthodox Christian. Arguably, because, the method adopted by Rodrigo to prove so says nothing about the family's genealogy. This is because the proof of purity submitted by him relied totally on accepted notions of social reputation and belief and these were based on the opinions of chosen witnesses. It worked, however, because his son found both home and employment in Italy. But nothing is added to our knowledge of the Cervantes' pedigree. All that can be said about the document is that it proves that Cervantes was facing difficulties in Italy. All those working so close to the papacy clearly needed proof of their Christian orthodoxy. As argued by the critic and cervantista Ellen Lokos, this document that explicitly addresses Cervantes' ancestry, possesses a purely notarial content and that from a judicial viewpoint must be considered as 'entirely invalid and inconsequential'.[6]

Social historians tell us that notions of nobility and purity of blood were not necessarily associated until the middle of the sixteenth century, when statutes requiring purity of blood spread throughout many of the most important institutions of Spanish society.[7] Rodrigo's appeal to his nobility as grounds for immunity from the debtor's prison in 1552–3 clearly involves both concepts. His appeal makes evident the fact that purity of blood became an increasingly necessary prerequisite for nobility. Nevertheless, the document he sent to his son, although it met the needs of the moment, was by no means a patent of nobility and in fact leaves us with more questions than answers. The document sent by Rodrigo was hastily concocted solely to help his son survive in an alien environment.

The Rome Cervantes entered can be seen best in the map drawn by Pyrrho Ligurio in 1570, which shows the eternal city to be surrounded by a wall enclosing its seven famous hills. Crossed by the Tiber, the city's major landmarks, squares, public buildings and wide avenues are clearly indicated. To walk freely through a truly Renaissance city and capital of the Papal States would have been a welcome relief after his enforced flight, but, beneath its façade of splendour and elegance, he may have seen that 'den of iniquity', which is how Luis Gálvez de Montalvo described the city in a letter dated July 1587 to the Duke of Francavila. Montalvo claims that in Rome 'the prisons are full of Spaniards, the streets full of prostitutes and the city full of priests'.[8] Three months after Cervantes' arrival Acquaviva was made a cardinal, and it was around this time that his chamberlain left his service to go south.

Successive biographers quickly pass over this period, mainly because it was brief and seems to have been no more than a stepping-stone. Cervantes' stay in Rome was certainly brief but significant in that employment in the home of a prelate on the verge of becoming a cardinal introduced him not only to the etiquette of courtly and social life but also to the world of privilege and authority and to the customs of a ceremonial and hierarchical society. In Toledo, the spiritual centre of Spain, Cardinal Tavera's entourage – one which had a comparable status to that of Acquaviva – numbered over four hundred.

Not yet twenty-three, Cervantes' time in an ambitious prelate's household in Rome, the centre of the universal Church, would have shown him the power of a culture where ceremony ruled supreme; a world of patronage, faction and worship. It was also his entry into the world of a Christian prince being educated for high office. This granted, his sojourn in Rome would have been much more valuable than generally credited. He would have seen aspects of courtly and ecclesiastical life as well as the functioning of the diplomatic process; no prince of the Church was free from the machinery of statecraft and political intrigue. The history of alliances, truces, secret affinities and clandestine negotiations which involved the Papal States and other states at the time prove this.[9] Aware of these or not, while working for Acquaviva he was soon to hear rumours of the growing conflict between Venice and Turkey; it was the talk of the town.

Ever since the fall of Belgrade in 1521 and the siege of Vienna in 1529, the Ottomans had been building an empire that was to rival that of Catholic Spain. In particular, the Turkish rule in the Barbary States posed a constant threat to the Iberian Peninsula, giving rise to several conflicts. Spain had been routed at Djerba off the coast of Tunisia in 1560, although Malta had been saved in 1565. The astonishing expansion of the Ottomans served to stiffen resistance to Philip II's rule in areas where the Moriscos dominated, such as Granada. The revolt in the Low Countries (that is, Flanders) also took place in 1565. Scores of Catholic churches had been sacked and in August 1566 Calvinists had seized control of municipal governments in Utrecht, Delft, Leyden, all supposedly Catholic towns. Philip II was desperate and summoned the Duke of Alba to resolve what one commentator has called the work of 'creeping Protestantism'.[10] While the Duke of Alba was busy quashing rebellion in Flanders, the Moriscos at home chose their moment to rebel, an event that saw the emergence of Don John of Austria, Philip's younger brother and the man destined to be the soldier of the age.[11]

The outcome of such events meant that Spain needed soldiers, and in Spanish-ruled Naples Philip II had one of his most important garrisons. Given that accounts and testimonies differ, it is not known for certain when Cervantes went to Naples to enlist. Nor is it known whether his decision to join Diego de Urbina's company was premeditated or the result of necessity. His flight to Rome had not been planned, but once caught in the web of events he had to act. Offering his services to king and country was one way to protect himself from a life on the run, and good service offered a desperate fugitive a means of restoring the family's honour. What is curious is that he first served under the Papal banners and not the Spanish. He probably still harboured fears about Spanish justice in the military, for it seems likely that the summons for his arrest followed him also to Italy.[12] As he made his way south he may have remembered the plight of the king he was to serve, Philip II, who, at a similar age had been left a widower, a father and an apprentice head of state.[13]

A popular saying of the time used by Cervantes in 'The Captive's

Tale', an interpolated novella in Don Quixote, Part One, claimed that 'to thrive one went to sea, joined the church or served the king'.[14] The last is what the story's protagonist did and it is also what Cervantes did. Interestingly enough, years later, in Don Quixote, Part Two, the chastened knight meets a page on his way to the wars, driven by necessity and deeply worried about his future. Although the meeting is brief, he is the only character in Part Two who neither ridicules nor admires the ageing knight. Described as having a 'cheerful face' and being 'nimble', is he not possibly the young Miguel de Cervantes, who, having decided to leave the prelate's service, had no other recourse but join the garrison in Naples? It is well known that Cervantes often smuggled a self-portrait into his works and this could be one. Useful as these are, perhaps the most accurate portrait of the type of man Cervantes was may be drawn from the several critical decisions he was to make. In this light the decision to turn soldier would prove central to any such portrait.

In Naples Cervantes met Álvaro de Sande, an old family friend and colonel of the Neapolitan regiments. With his support the new recruit was to serve under Álvaro de Bazán, the Marquis of Santa Cruz, a man for whom Cervantes would hold the highest esteem. Although dates are imprecise, we know that Rodrigo, Miguel's younger brother, joined him in Italy and went to sea with him as a soldier. This fact allows for the possibility that it was Rodrigo who presented Cardinal Acquaviva with the documents verifying Miguel's purity of blood. In those days Spain did not have a separate army and navy; soldiers served on both land and sea.

In 1570 the Turks had to decide whether to go to the aid of the Moriscos in Spain or to attack Cyprus. After thirty-four years of what had always seemed a fragile peace accord with Venice, the Turks decided to take Cyprus, and, with a fleet of over three hundred vessels and some fifty thousand men, they attacked the island.[15] Nicosia fell in September and, so it is claimed, twenty thousand of its inhabitants were put to the sword. Events led Venice into a frantic diplomatic offensive because it lacked men and material for a war with Turkey and had no wish to lose what was left of the Eastern trade in silks and spices on which its declining wealth was based. And so the Holy League was reformed in May 1571, by which Venice, Spain and the Holy See determined to defeat the Turks. It was the best moment to become a soldier and serve the nation.

As a soldier Cervantes was to travel the length and breadth of Italy and so, indirectly, was to experience the benefits of the Grand Tour that writers, poets and artists undertook in later centuries as an integral part of their education. Equally as significant were the numbers of scholars who had preceded his footsteps in Italy. Influential English scholars such as William Grocyn, John Colet, Thomas Linacre and the famous Dutch reformer and humanist Erasmus had all studied in Italy. Seven decades on, the fruits of their scholarship and of what became known as Christian humanism would greatly influence Cervantes' own outlook and writing. It is impossible to quantify the impact on him of the works of writers and thinkers such as Erasmus, Tasso, Castiglione, Hebreo, Ariosto, to name but a select few, but it is significant that he was able to combine a comprehensive understanding of what might be called 'European' humanistic culture with a specific instinct for the life and times of Madrid in Counter-Reformation Spain. Furthermore, by virtue of Spanish possessions in the peninsula of Italy he was able to maintain an interest in all things Italian throughout his life.

Cervantes' flight to freedom in Italy proved to be of immense benefit as well as a major turning point in his life. The comparison with the Grand Tour is doubly important because one of the greatest errors ever made by Philip II, although one easily overlooked in the welter of political and economic events yet to occur in his reign, was to forbid Spaniards from leaving his dominions to study, a ban brought about in November 1559. Having witnessed what happens when religious disputes divide communities, Philip II had no desire to see sedition and heresy enter Spain, and, after the discovery of Protestant circles in

Seville and Valladolid, his adherence to the decrees of the Roman Church intensified. Censorship by means of the Index Librorum Prohibitorum (an official list of books which Roman Catholics were forbidden to read) was introduced in 1577 and *autos-da-fé* (the public burnings of heretics) became common. Reasons for the ban on students studying abroad were valid and persuasive to a king who had been brought up by his father to 'keep God always in mind' and to 'accept good advice at all times'.[16] Prudent or not, Philip II found it necessary to instigate the ban and to recall all those students who were abroad. And yet he knew the benefit derived from his extensive educational journeys to the seventeen provinces that began when he was fourteen. As a soldier Cervantes was not to suffer from such a ban, and, with his extraordinary love of learning, where better to continue his education than in Italy? A soldier's life meant travel and exposure to different cultures, attitudes and lifestyles. It also promised a regular income – even if it was a promise more often breached than kept.[17] Although there is nothing in his background to suggest that he wanted to be a soldier, we have to admire his willingness to adapt to circumstances. It is in his reaction to events where perhaps the true measure of the man lies.

An overriding factor in his decision to follow the course he did may have been an innate desire to seek in military service that seal of distinction that alone could restore his family name. It was clearly honourable to serve his country, especially if it led to recognition by his commanders and his king. Not one of the 1,661 documents relating to the life of Cervantes explains why he joined Diego de Urbina's company in Naples, the same company in which the two Cervantes brothers would fight at Lepanto.[18]

But why, if not to carry the purity of blood documents for his elder brother Miguel, had Rodrigo left Madrid? There is no evidence to suggest that he was being pursued by the authorities for Miguel's misdemeanours. Rodrigo's situation was clearly quite different to that of Miguel who, in the light of literary success, however limited, would have far preferred to remain in the capital and continue his close friendship with López de Hoyos. At twenty Rodrigo wanted to experience the world. His older brother's flight into exile offered him such an opportunity. Besides, his life in Spain – a life on wheels – had never been easy, yet it was one that had indirectly prepared him for the restless life of a soldier.

Cervantes almost always depicts soldiers as quarrelsome, boastful or beggarly, although the discourse Don Quixote delivers on 'arms and letters' is a rallying call to all of us to sympathize with the hardships and vicissitudes that soldiers everywhere suffer. With the Battle of Lepanto only five months away, there was but little time to learn about armed conflict before active participation in what Cervantes later described as the most glorious naval battle ever. According to John Guilmartin, the one who has done most to trace the ever-changing face of naval warfare in the Mediterranean in the sixteenth century, new recruits could learn the use of the harquebus in a few days, whereas years were needed to train an archer.[19] Nothing is said of Rodrigo's participation in the battle, but he, as well as his brother, may have joined the ranks of the harquebusiers. What Spanish commanders could not have forgotten was their crippling defeat at Djerba. The loss of shipping had been severe, but a deeper blow was the loss of trained manpower; it was the latter fact that explains the disasters of the years following the battle. It is no surprise then that a thorough evaluation of Spain's strategic situation was carried out and was submitted to the Council of Galleys in 1564 by the Captain-General of the Sea, Don García de Toledo. His report examined the options open to the Ottoman fleet and ranked them according to the danger each one posed to Spain, concluding that Malta would be the most likely target. And indeed, in 1565 Malta was attacked but survived. So, with a recent defeat on their minds, the Turks had no desire to wage war and lose a second time. In the light of events that led up to Lepanto, it is clear that its outcome would prove decisive. Don García's assessment of his country's defences and those of the likely enemy proved that to triumph strategically it was necessary to survive tactically; it was tactics that carried the day at Lepanto. But within the objectives of the strategists there was ample room for individual bravery and daring.

Prints of the period show the extravagant dress of Spanish troopers. Because many such were Catalan whose language was incomprehensible to other Iberians, they were given the nickname '*papagayos*' (parrots).[20] Cervantes would have been equally flamboyant as he carried his harquebus, a gun weighing some 5.4 kilograms (twelve pounds) and measuring 1.52 metres (nearly five feet) in length.[21] In the sixteenth century, naval battles were ordinarily fought near land; naval warfare in the Mediterranean had always been amphibious, and this explains why soldiers fought in both arenas and why the war galley was born. By the end of the century, however, the appearance of the broadside sailing ship was to usurp what had been the realm of the war galley. Nevertheless, it was the latter that played such an important role in the victory at Lepanto and in the life of Cervantes the soldier. He lived to see the significant changes to shipping brought about by advancing technology that affected the size and make of artillery and of individual firearms such vessels could carry.

The history of shipping has changed beyond recognition since the mid sixteenth century, but prints, paintings and navigational records exist that show us various types of sea-craft, from galley-ships to frigates, as well as the conditions under which sea-soldiers served. There were three types of *galera* (warship), with the *galeaza* (battleship) by far the biggest with its cumbersome sails; such impressive craft were manned by galley-slaves (*forzados*). Lines from the unforgettable ballad written by Luis de Góngora in 1583 illustrate the gruesome plight of galley-slaves:

Chained to the hard bench of a Turkish galley, with both hands on his oar and both eyes fixed on the land, one of Dragut's prisoners off the coast of Marbella groaned to the harsh noise of the oar and chain. Oh, sacred seas of Spain . . . bring me news of my wife, and tell

me if the tears and sighs she expresses in her letters have been
sincere . . . since I've lived ten years without freedom and without
her . . . At this six ships of our navy were sighted and the commander
of the slaves ordered the prisoner to pull harder.[22]

Described as 'a land battle at sea', the campaign against the Turks
was one of the most carefully planned and best-fought battles in
the annals of warfare.[23] Both sides engaged in the conflict knew that
the war galley, for logistical reasons, could not stand out to sea for
extended periods of time. Therefore the configuration of the nearest
shoreline, which army occupied it and in what strength, were critical
factors in determining the eventual victor. The Venetians had already
fought against the Turks in the Gulf of Lepanto in 1499, in what
historians call the battle of Zonchio, although not much has been
written about it.[24]

Before the invention of gunpowder, the only decisive way to conclude a naval engagement was by boarding a vessel. And even with
cannon the need to board the enemy vessel continued. The naval
historian Guilmartin explains how the introduction of cannon influenced only the way hand-to-hand encounters took place. It was here
where Cervantes was to show his valour. Despite suffering from
malarial fever and being urged by his captain, Urbina, to remain below
deck, he insisted on fighting, even if it meant death. His insistence
paid off and he was put in charge of twelve soldiers in a skiff. Given
that skiffs were intended for grappling and were used for attack but
lacked the assault rams which some galley-ships carried on their
prows, soldiers in skiffs faced the greatest danger.[25] Cervantes lodged
himself at the head of the skiff, a particularly exposed combat position.
Although documentation about Lepanto abounds, observers disagree
on numbers of casualties but not about the sea, that all agree was
tinged red with blood. The king's chief minister, Cardinal Diego de
Espinosa, compared Lepanto with the drowning of Pharaoh's army in
the Red Sea.[26] One satisfying outcome of the conflict was the freeing of

some 15,000 Christian galley-slaves; this is the same number given by Cervantes in his story 'The Captive's Tale'.

During the onslaught Cervantes received three shots from an harquebus resulting in deep bullet wounds to his chest and to the permanent loss of the use of his left arm. His skiff belonged to a galley ship called *La Marquesa*, which suffered the loss of forty men including the captain and 120 wounded. Such was young Cervantes' valour that it brought him to the attention of Don John of Austria, who came to visit the wounded in hospital and was moved to write recommendatory letters on Cervantes' behalf. This recognition would have severe repercussions for Cervantes, and nothing like those envisaged as he convalesced for six months in the military hospital in Messina. As he slowly recovered – his chest wounds took over two years to heal completely – his brightest moments perhaps were the two visits made by Don John of Austria and the award of no less than four pay increases authorized by Don John himself.[27] Six months to heal a wound can prove frustratingly overlong to a man eager to make his mark and remove the blemish of exile. Although documentation of treatment and conditions in Messina has not come to light, Cervantes clearly had time to reflect on one inescapable fact: he could no longer use his left arm. Unable to take part in the nine days of festivities to celebrate Lepanto's triumph, he would have heard the cannon of victory. Coins and medals were struck and songs composed to mark what was a turning point in European naval warfare. A fleet considered invincible had fallen to the navigational and strategic superiority of the allied Christian forces. Lepanto was more than a Spanish victory, however. Mercenaries from several European countries commonly fought under the Spanish flag. Indeed, the campaigns of Djerba, Malta, Lepanto and of Tunis in 1573 were all equipped in Italy and 'predominantly Italian in conception and composition'.[28]

For a nation constantly at war and harbouring imperialistic dreams, a permanent standing army was a prime necessity. Moreover, the need for permanent military establishments, such as the garrisons in Naples and Orán and the fortresses in North Africa – Bugía, Larache and La Goletta – led to the creation of a permanent military administration and to the growth of bureaucracy. Lepanto had made Cervantes into a hero but also an invalid, and it was this that focused his thoughts on a career in military administration. While doing so, and amid the jubilation of the Holy League, the news in Constantinople of defeat was received with numbed disbelief. Ali Pasha, the leader of the Turkish fleet had been decapitated while his ship was attacking that of Don John; Uluch-Ali, however, had escaped and fled back to Istanbul with the sombre news of the rout and of Pasha's gruesome death. The response of Selim II was to commission Uluch-Ali to rebuild the Turkish fleet and thus restore Islamic pride. The order for the reconstruction of Turkish sea power meant little to weary Christian troops, who, together with freed galley-slaves, had their minds set on the spoils of war. With typical foresight Don John wrote to his brother, the king, who was now hailed as the defender of the faith – a mantle once worn by Henry VIII of England – advising him that the Turks had been defeated but not conquered and that he planned a follow-up. Pope Pius V likewise wrote to Philip II urging him to make haste and prepare a new offensive. With the onset of winter, however, the members of the Holy League went their separate ways without having reached an agreement on any future campaign. When Pius V died in May, his successor, Gregory XIII, also urged Philip II to act, but nothing happened. And then the world saw why. Philip had got wind of a possible revolt in the Low Countries and would need his troops for that emergency. Cervantes, meanwhile, remained in Messina hospital. Fortunately, although he had lost the use of his left arm, it was not amputated – despite a number of paintings and drawings which depict him as one-armed – so he did not have to join that vast band of war-wounded found in Spain begging for a living. In July 1572 Cervantes rejoined his regiment and went to Corfu from where he was to make a number of journeys in the Mediterranean. The next documented record of his whereabouts is given as February 1573 in Naples; his wounds had still not healed.

What Lepanto meant for Spain and for Cervantes as a Spaniard may have been revealed in his drama based on the conflict entitled *The Naval Battle*, but it has been lost. Its theme, so relevant to his contemporaries, would have made it very popular with theatre-goers. The loss of 127 Turkish galleys and galiots was 'an event unprecedented in Mediterranean history', suggesting a massive loss of trained Muslim manpower.[29] But, because of the revolt in the Netherlands and the routing of the Portuguese in Morocco in 1578, the extent of the defeat on the Ottomans was not fully apparent. After Lepanto Cervantes joined the regiment led by Lope de Figueroa and took part in a series of campaigns described in 'The Captive's Tale'. But no matter how willing he may have been, with his left arm incapacitated, he could no longer serve as an harquebusier and so his services to the regiment must have been limited. And yet there is no mention of this at all in any of the documents relating to him. In fact he was to serve another four years in significant campaigns. In Corfu, Navarino, Tunis and La Goletta he witnessed the vicissitudes of war and saw how Spanish troops failed to exploit their advantage after Lepanto; had they done so, Modón and Navarino would both have been captured. Cervantes was to learn the life of a sea-soldier, whose fortunes so often depended on the weather, that master of navigation and of all naval conflict, and explains why Cervantes and his comrades-at-arms were holed up for long periods in ports waiting for storms to pass or for spring to arrive.

An ambitious but perfectly feasible plan to break the Turkish fleet once and for all had been agreed on by Philip II and the Venetians. A fleet of 300 vessels was to be launched against Uluch-Ali's forces, and Spain's shipyards worked at fever pitch to construct their quota of 150 ships. However, when near completion, Philip II was told of a bilateral peace pact signed on 4 April 1573 by Venice and Constantinople. Pope Gregory XIII was dumbstruck and threatened to excommunicate the whole republic. This was the second time within a generation that Venice had betrayed its allies, as in 1536 Venice and the Ottomans had signed a bilateral peace accord *vis-à-vis* Cyprus. The upshot was that Venice was guaranteed its trade and Selim II promised to defend Venice against any attack by its former allies. The sole positive note for Philip II was that he could now focus on Flanders.

Although he saw his way clear to quash insurrection in Flanders he could not crush the pirates operating from North African ports, especially Tunis and Algiers. Only the coastline and shipping of France were safe from their attacks. France was spared because she had a bilateral agreement with the Turks, a source of deep resentment for Philip II. Most of the revenue that poured into Algiers stemmed from the work of pirates; it has been estimated that in the period 1520–1650 over six hundred thousand captives passed through the slave markets in Algiers.[30] So irksome was the action of Barbary pirates that Philip II resolved to launch an all-out attack against them. But lack of funds deterred him and so he devised a very cunning ruse. If he could restore to the throne of Tunis Muley Hamid, a faithful ally of Spain, who had been deposed three years before by Uluch-Ali, loyal to the Sultan, not only would he strengthen his friendship but he would have a fortress free of charge. The Spanish duly recaptured Tunis and its fortress La Goletta. There had been no combat: the Turks had fled, leaving all behind so Cervantes and his regiment returned to winter in Sardinia in 1573. It was here that he probably cultivated his passion for card-playing, and one or two earlier biographers posit the notion that the island also offered his fertile imagination the ideal location for his first major work in prose La Galatea, a pastoral novel published in 1585.[31]

The fall of Tunis provoked an immediate reaction in Constantinople. The captured fortress of La Goletta had been rebuilt by Don John and held 8,000 men but was no match for the newly launched Turkish fleet of 300 ships with a force of 40,000 men led by Uluch-Ali, which left Constantinople in high hopes of revenge. The Turks planned to attack Tunis and the fort simultaneously. Don John had to move fast to galvanize his troops. With his forces marshalled from Naples and Palermo, storms twice prevented their departure and, while waiting for better weather, he learned of the fall of La Goletta in late August and of Tunis in early September, one of the worst defeats for Spain in the sixteenth century. And so, in 1574, just three years after Lepanto, Cervantes was to witness the disaster of Tunis. It is clear from 'The Captive's Tale' that he did not agree with the criticism levelled at Don John, who, brilliant though he was, could not dictate the weather nor read the minds of his so-called allies. Leaving Tunis with the fleet led by Don John, a disillusioned Cervantes returned to Palermo, where he was given, in November of that same year, twenty-five escudos signed by no less a figure than the Duke of Sessa. This is the last recorded payment made to Cervantes for his services as a soldier. Interestingly, he is described in the document as 'an outstanding soldier', and from what the Duke of Sessa claimed in a written statement three years later it seems likely that Cervantes used the last meeting with Don John, who ordered the payment, to request letters of recommendation for his return to Spain.[32] If this is the case, Cervantes knew that his career as a soldier was over. He also knew that he had left Spain in disgrace, but with Don John's assistance he would return as a distinguished bearer of recommendatory letters that he hoped would bring recognition and a royal post at home. Cervantes then left for Naples where in December he met up with his brother Rodrigo.

The next document relating to Cervantes is dated 7 September 1575, and it states that he left Naples bound for Spain. Some ten months were to pass before the departure and what Cervantes did in the interim is related to us, decades later, in what many regard as a semi-autobiographical poem, *Voyage to Parnassus*, in which he claims to have spent more than a year in Naples. He clearly holds dear memories of his time there. Indeed, he was to make serious efforts to return to the city when aged seventy-three. Although views differ, a major reason for his affection for Naples is found in his love affair, possibly his first, and outlined in the poem just mentioned, with a local beauty called Silena. Conjecture has it that she bore him a son, Promontorio. Opinions diverge because her existence is based solely on clues left in his writings. Those who believe the affair occurred point to Book 4 of *Voyage to Parnassus* in which the writer describes an imagined re-encounter between himself and his son, fruit of a passionate love that ended in bitterness. Powerfully evocative and convincing, the cause of its ending – bitter jealousy – became a recurrent theme in his work, suggesting strongly that it did indeed occur and that his experience of jealousy had left a deep mark. Most probably more than a 'literary game', which is how Canavaggio views the episode, the relationship with Silena, if it happened, closed in the summer of 1575. We know this because his best friends, including Pedro Laínez, a fellow poet and soldier, had left the city, the Duke of Sessa had returned to Palermo and Don John's future was in the balance.[33] And, to cap it all, Cervantes must have known that, with his disability, promotion was very unlikely. There was no better time to return home. Although he had enjoyed Naples, a city so Spanish that even bullfights took place there every Sunday, home was calling, where Magdalena, the younger of his two sisters, was deeply embroiled in a love affair with Pedro de Portocarrero that had gone wrong. The latter's brother, Alonso de Portocarrero, had already badly deceived Cervantes' other sister, Andrea, whose demands for compensation for breach of promise proved unsuccessful.

Obtaining leave of absence, Cervantes and his younger brother Rodrigo left the port of Naples in the Spanish galley, *El Sol*, escorted by three other ships. In an age when piracy ruled the waves, no vessel ever sailed the seas alone. Favoured with good weather, the Spanish convoy set out for Barcelona in September 1575 with high hopes of a speedy return. Their journey was a straightforward one and the two brothers were looking forward to a welcome rest from the vicissitudes of life as professional soldiers.

The unexpected – such a central feature of his writings later – intervened, in that violent storms, not uncommon in the Gulf of Lions, drove their ship near to Corsica, making it lose contact with the others.[34] While struggling to rejoin the convoy, and when not far out from Cadaqués on the Costa Brava and therefore tantalizingly close to Spanish soil, it was sighted by enemy vessels who gave chase. With Barcelona within shouting distance, a worse moment could not have been chosen. Records show that a flotilla bearing the green banner spangled with stars – the ensign of pirates from Algiers, Spain's sworn enemies – with their lighter and faster vessels accustomed to daring raids, repeatedly attacked *El Sol*. Obvious to all, the passenger ship in which the two brothers were travelling, having lost its escort, was decidedly ill-equipped for confrontation.[35] Reluctantly, they could do nothing but wait; their destiny, and all those with them, lay at the mercy of the elements. Despite stout resistance, Cervantes and his fellow passengers succumbed to the pirate vessels. Their surrender, however, was not without serious injuries and fatalities. Along with several eminent soldiers, the captain of the ship, a Pedro Gaspar de Villena, met a violent death.

It was not until most of the able-bodied survivors were taken as captives (records show that Cervantes was captured some hours after his brother) that the ships escorting *El Sol* appeared on the horizon and, although posing a threat to the captors, they could not match their vessels for speed.[36] Before reaching the wounded and dying left on board, they had to witness the abduction of their comrades-at-arms. The knowledge that the majority of oarsmen hauling their fellow countrymen away to captivity were also captives longing for freedom only deepened their grief. As they watched powerless and in disbelief, it would fall to them to report the event to those relatives and friends – if they could be located – back home in Spain, never an enviable task.

But their sense of disbelief could not have equalled that of those captured. Not only had they been taken, but they had also fallen into the cruellest hands operating in the waters of the Mediterranean. Even to their hapless crew on whom their lives depended, pirates at the best of times showed little mercy. Of all the fates that befell captives on the high seas, that of the galley-slave was by far the worst. It is not difficult for today's reader to imagine the pain, both physical and psychological, such slaves must have felt on having to row away from the very ships that could have rescued them.

Victims of man's inhumanity, their predicament perhaps finds a modern counterpart in the slave-camps described so poignantly in the works of Alexander Solzhenitsyn.[37] For prisoners in both regimes, life, being cheap, was often unimaginably cruel. Times then were different, and Christian captors in Spain could be, and frequently were, equally harsh, particularly to heretics and renegades, those who converted to Islam.[38]

Within a few days Cervantes found himself in the cosmopolitan port of Algiers, which at that time was under the control of the Turkish Sultan. It therefore functioned as a frontier zone, that dangerous meeting point between the two superpowers. Irreconcilable religious differences between the two cultures help to explain the cruel treatment of captives, but other factors, social and economic, played their part, too. In the lifestyles and attitudes of the rulers of Algiers it is possible to see the principles of conduct expounded in 1513 by Niccolò Machiavelli in *The Prince*. Indeed, the beys, or governors, of Algiers, especially during and after the rule of Aruch Barbarossa, behaved as if born with the text in their hearts, as they matched Machiavelli's descriptions of the autocrat, the new man: ruthless, efficient and defiant. As a consequence, ambition, espionage, intrigue and double-dealing were the order of the day and permeated all levels of society.

Modern historians claim that the Barbary States – known today as the Maghreb – were nothing less than emergent societies, showing all the birth-pangs of the absolutist nation state. The waves of lawlessness that accompanied early settlers in the USA and the attitudes that prevailed in the gold-rush towns of the nineteenth and twentieth centuries were but faint reflections of patterns of behaviour documented in Algiers and elsewhere in the region. The severe culture shock also helps to explain the numbers of captives who converted to

Islam, some of whom rose to heights of power undreamed of in so-called civilized nations. If Spanish authorities had been given one boon, it would most probably have been for abiding peace with Barbary. But wishes and boons, when most needed, are rarely granted, and, despite clandestine efforts by the Spanish secret service, no such luck fell King Philip II's way. Of all the thorns in His Majesty's flesh, Algiers and Flanders were the sharpest, and Algiers was much closer to home.

Although stretching from Tripoli in the east to the Atlantic coast in the west, the term Barbary, at least for Spaniards in Cervantes' day, came to mean the 'kingdom of Algiers', a political entity created and sustained by the two ill-famed Barbarossa brothers, Aruch and Jeredín.[39] Ever since the conquest of Granada in 1492 by Castilian forces, the region of North Africa had experienced political collapse and fragmentation, made worse by the threat from Christian Spain. But a dramatic change occurred in 1516 when Aruch Barbarossa took control of the city of Algiers. Within twelve years of his arrival in 1504 he had not only created the first Barbary State he had also founded the nucleus of a new political order in North Africa. With the succession to power of his brother Jeredín, who set about consolidating his brother's work and wisely decided to fortify the city, Spain reluctantly realized it was facing an incipient nation-state and a serious enemy to its interests in the western Mediterranean. After Lepanto, despite the defeat of the Ottomans, the whole of the southern coast of the Mediterranean was, except for the Monarchy of Morocco and the city of Orán, under Turkish control. Algiers saw itself as a proud city-state. Its maritime situation had helped to create its wealth and cosmopolitanism, but unquestionably the rapid emergence of Algiers owed much to its piracy in Sicilian and southern Italian waters, which at the time were zones controlled by Spanish forces. The chief instigators of such attacks were exiles from Spain, especially from Andalusia, many of whom were classed by Spain as renegades. Throughout the sixteenth century, Spanish coastal areas and shipping would prove prime pickings for pirates and corsairs, most of whom operated from Algiers. It is a compelling subject and far too vast to be done justice to here; suffice to say that when the two Cervantes brothers fell foul of Barbary pirates they had entered a world of Machiavellian intrigue and subterfuge, of espionage, greed and violence.

Illustrations of the period reveal a society on the make; a thick labyrinth of roads and houses led to and from the several souks or markets that catered for the needs of its 120,000 inhabitants; several palaces, a series of public gardens and baths, fountains and mosques, a theological school, a mint and, inevitably, the prisons. This thriving city-port, which half a century later would reach its zenith, was bigger than Palermo and Rome and housed a fascinating array of languages, customs and traditions.[40] It was also the haven to an underworld that matched those of Naples and Seville.

One can only speculate about the psychological blow to the Cervantes brothers as they stared captivity in the face, but, as later events were to prove, Miguel de Cervantes' defiance, despite repeated setbacks and betrayal, was remarkable. Nevertheless, both he and Rodrigo must have stood aghast at the colourless dust into which, in three short days, their dreams of a happy reunion had crumbled.

Although undocumented, it seems probable that Cervantes spent his twenty-eighth birthday aboard the pirate vessel. If so, instead of a celebration, he had to suffer the consciousness of an impending doom. Instead of a hero's welcome, he had to endure the insults thrown by the guttersnipes and greedy ship and slave-owners as he walked off the boat.[41] In a letter in verse allegedly written by Cervantes, delivered some two years later by a ransomed captive to the king's secretary, Mateo Vázquez, the writer confesses that he entered Algiers with 'tears streaming down his haggard face'.[42] Although some dispute the authenticity of the letter, Cervantes had good reason to cry. To be captured by Spain's sworn enemies after exile was bad enough, but then to see those royal letters of recommendation snatched and used against him as proof of his great worth added insult to injury. To his jubilant captors Cervantes was a licence to rob; to himself he was a maimed but defiant hostage.

He was to spend five years in one of the several prisons known as the 'bagnio' in the Lingua Franca, the language spoken by the captive community, a shifting population made up of men and women from every walk of life. The social structure in Algiers was dominated by Turks and Berbers, who controlled administration and the military, aided and abetted by corsairs. At the bottom of the hierarchy were the 25,000 Christian slaves imprisoned in the city and in between were the Moors – mostly artisans – and the renegade Christians; in addition there was a sizeable Jewish community. In other words, the triad of cultures and religions which had characterized southern Spain for centuries obtained in Algiers as well.[43]

The walk from the port to the slave market is described in detail by Antonio de Sosa, a fellow captive of Cervantes and the author of what is one of the most remarkable histories of Algiers ever to be written.[44] It includes conversations, entitled 'Dialogues with Martyrs', held with Cervantes and several others while in prison. His account of Cervantes' life there provides biographers with fascinating material. In general, however, de Sosa's study makes for harrowing reading. Slaves were manacled and fettered and auctioned to the highest bidder. Heavy irons were a reminder to them of their status and ensured that escape remained only a remote possibility. Indeed, any attempt to escape was considered an act of sabotage and exacted the strictest penalties.[45]

A map of 1571 depicts seven bagnios, four of which formed a line behind the main square and market, well within the walled city, which was surrounded on three sides by its protective moat.[46] Nevertheless, the two Cervantes brothers would not have been spared the taunts of the children who would have sung to them that Don John would not save them and that they would die behind bars. Lines taken from Cervantes' play about the prisons in Algiers illustrate this: 'Thieving

Christian / No ransom, no escape / Don John no come here. / Here die dog, die here!' It was true that Don John, who had publicly acknowledged Cervantes' valour and was the one man the Turks feared most, would never set foot in Algiers. Despite the children's reproaches, however, Cervantes proved to be no ordinary captive. Records show that prisoners with a ransom enjoyed much greater freedom – in terms of movement as well as from irons and chains – than those without. This distinction should not be overlooked, because it is clear that Cervantes was not chained and fettered all the time he was in captivity. There were times when he could freely walk, not only inside the compound but outside in the city, too. This relative liberty explains how he was able to do the things that he did – and repeated – while in the royal prison. If there was one thing that animated him throughout his imprisonment, it was the thought of freedom. It became the aspiration that was to steer him from one plan of escape to another, culminating in an outcome even more unexpected than his capture.

In the bagnio where, as a ransomed slave Cervantes was confined, life was less harsh than in the so-called *almacén* or public prisons occupied by slaves who were unransomed and had no one to bargain for them. Apart from the distinction that Cervantes in 'The Captive's Tale' and de Sosa in his *Topographia* of Algiers draw between both categories of prisoners, little is said of them. Misery and deprivation faced both categories of prisoner, however. Ransomed slaves, if deprived of material comforts, so ran the logic of greedy captors, would seek the quickest means to raise the money with which to buy their freedom. And yet, undoubtedly, it was the unransomed prisoners who made up the vast majority of unfortunates mentioned by historians and envoys of the period. The staggering number of those sold in the slave markets of Algiers in the sixteenth century shows how relatively common capture and captivity were.[47] In other words, the plight of the Cervantes brothers was by no means exceptional. What distinguishes Cervantes' situation from that of his brother Rodrigo and from countless others stems from two principal facts: first, that he carried the seal of Don John of Austria; second, that he defied the Turkish authorities so persistently. The former determined his ransom, the latter defined his attitude and conduct in the bagnio.

Cervantes' covetous captor, Dalí Mamí, a Greek renegade, set the figure of 500 escudos in gold for a ransom, a sum beyond the pocket of Cervantes' family and friends. The amount asked probably strengthened the resolve of an already defiant Cervantes to plot his escape. Despite his protestations that he was merely a soldier – a maimed one at that – without connections or savings, he was housed with some 2,000 other ransomed prisoners. His brother Rodrigo was not with him for he had been bought by Ramadan Pasha and valued at a ransom of 300 escudos. It is clear that the financial burden put on the Cervantes family was intolerable. While the newly arrived captives were awakening to the reality of captivity, their jubilant captors mounted a boisterous fiesta involving wine, women and song. But not just women, for it is well documented that corsair owners of pirate vessels took enormous pride in their capture and possession of young men whom they would dress lavishly on festive occasions and parade before their peers and superiors. Given that homosexuality was officially encouraged – government food and housing was denied to all janissaries (the crack Turkish forces) who married, and their sons were barred from the military and all public office – the reis, owners of ships used by the corsairs and pirates, spent large sums of slave-generated income to adorn their 'bearded wives', the term given to their young men, many in their teens.[48]

Although the ransom fixed for Cervantes was high, the fact that he was redeemable was no small blessing, for not all prisoners could be or would be sold. Any prisoner who could be used in the shipyards was equally as precious and sometimes even too valuable to lose through ransom. The same was true of some officers who might be persuaded to become renegades. From all accounts Cervantes never succumbed to such offers. Indeed, we know from reliable sources that he moved heaven and earth to help renegades renounce their adopted religion and return to the Church of Rome.[49] It should be remembered that several rulers of Algiers had been renegades from Christianity, including Hasan Pasha, the most ruthless of rulers that Cervantes was to encounter while in captivity.

3

CAPTIVITY IN ALGIERS
(1575–80)

On his arrival in Algiers, Cervantes could not have been expected to know the full historical evolution or the political developments of a society that was founded in the so-called heroic era of the Muslim corsairs that persisted even beyond the French invasion of 1830. More relevant to him was the process of adaptation by European Christian powers to the problems presented by the existence of a corsair community committed to a holy war against Christendom. This process was complicated by the fact that the regency in Algiers was technically part of the Ottoman Empire and yet it often acted independently of the Sultan and ignored his edicts, so the government in Spain had to contend with policy-makers in Algiers as well as decision-makers in Constantinople. Delicate and ongoing negotiations between the courts of Madrid and Constantinople, conducted by agents of the secret services of both nations, came to a head after Lepanto. Precisely at the time the two Cervantes brothers were captured, such talks, which had a truce and eventual long-term peace as their theme, were the main concern of both governments. Such dealings, highly clandestine and the cause of huge expenses to the Spanish treasury, were further complicated by the subterfuges of the French and Venetians, who in turn had their secret agents and spy rings in both camps.[1]

Cervantes would not have known of the painstaking and ultimately futile attempts of Spanish agents to woo Uluch-Ali to the side of King Philip II in 1569. But, amid much of the feverish activity behind the scenes, the name of Don John of Austria was a constant. It is possibly for this reason that Hasan Pasha tended to treat the daring exploits of Cervantes when in Algiers with unwonted respect. A world of double agents, intrigue and underhand diplomacy operated in Barbary – as it did also in the courts of Madrid, Constantinople, Venice, Paris and London – a world into which the brothers had unwillingly been forced to enter. Without a trial or any due process of law they were viewed, when captured, as pieces of merchandise to be sold to the highest bidder. In order to exit from such a world the two brothers would have to adapt to a social code they considered barbaric. These Machiavellian rulers of the Barbary States, who were the forerunners of the new monarchs in sixteenth-century Europe, held absolute sway over the world in which Cervantes was now imprisoned. The events that befell him in Algiers proved that little had changed in political circles since the beginning of the century when Machiavelli's *The Prince* was published.

In those early months in captivity we know that he met other captives, men of eminence, dignitaries of church and state, all condemned to await the arrival of missionary priests, mainly from the Trinitarian and Mercedarian orders, who periodically were sent from Spain and Portugal to ransom as many captives as their funds allowed. It was a waiting game, but how long could one wait if one knew that one's family lacked the required funds? Cervantes, unlike Don Quixote, had no magicians or wizards in his pockets. Having already eluded Spanish justice, he was determined to test his mettle against Muslim law as well. It was to be a fraught-ridden campaign. Years later, when he claims he learned patience in adversity, he was referring, at least in part, to his captivity in Algiers.

But in Algiers he learned much more. His experience of the lawlessness that ruled there served only to strengthen his vision of a Golden Age of mankind in which, according to his famous discourse in *Don Quixote, Part One*, 'the words "me" and "mine" do not exist, for everything is shared for the benefit of all', a philosophy that has its practical application in the mournful knight's sound advice to his elated squire Sancho when a governor.[2] Based on his humanistic education, the views Cervantes held on kingship, government and the conduct of society were severely tested when exposed to the cruel practices and punishments of the rulers – with the exception, perhaps, of Ramadan Pasha – in Algiers.

Faced with irreconcilable attitudinal differences and made aware of the politico-historical relationship between Spain and Constantinople – no Spanish monarch ever signed a peace accord with the rulers of Algiers, although short-term peace accords wrought in the utmost secrecy were signed with Constantinople – Cervantes attempted to escape not once but four times. These attempts distinguished his service as a hostage and contributed to his legend in the city. Given that few attempts were made, and of those even fewer succeeded, what was it that drove Cervantes onwards in the face of betrayal? As we study these escape attempts, it will be interesting to note the role of the unexpected and how it relates to the will of divine providence, aspects of major concern in Cervantine writings.[3]

The first escape attempt was ambitious: the sea route, suicidal in mid-winter, left no option but to flee over land. Yet a land-route was arguably no less hazardous. An oddity, however, is the timing of the undertaking, because the moment to escape would have been when most of the slave-owners were away on acts of piracy, and that was a month or so later. He must have been informed of the seasonal activities of life in the bagnio, and that March to October constituted the raiding season for buccaneers, privateers and pirates. Possibly the change in temperature that occurred between January and March came into the equation. The distance to be covered on foot was no trifle, but innate impatience and youthful defiance clearly got the upper hand. But there was something else. The attempt to walk across semi-desert terrain peopled by hostile nomad tribes suggests a man *in extremis*. Hostages in our own time tell us that the early days in captivity unleash so many diverse thoughts and emotions that individuals can easily crumble.[4] For countless captives in Algiers the transition from Christian Europe to Barbary was deeply traumatic.

One obvious option did remain open to all captives, including

Cervantes, and that was conversion. Judging by the numbers of rene-gades that fill the chronicles of envoys, soldiers, travellers, captives and priests sent to ransom captives the temptation to turn coat must have been very strong. But Cervantes' desire to escape proved stronger and much more hazardous, for it was common knowledge that the coastal road swarmed with Algerian patrols eagerly hunting fugitives for bounty.[5] Cervantes therefore chose the inland road intending to foot the 320-kilometre (200-mile) stretch to Orán, a Spanish possession. He enlisted the aid of a Moor who was bribed to guide the party of eight to freedom. In this band were two of Cervantes' close friends, Gabriel de Castañeda and Antonio Marco. It is not known whether Rodrigo was included, although biographers tend to believe he was. Ahead of them lay fourteen days of hard walking across rugged enemy terrain. They left at nightfall some time in January or February 1576, and how far they reached remains unclear. In a signed statement relating to his time in captivity in Algiers, Cervantes claims that they had been gone for several days before the guide abandoned them. Deserted, the small band of hopefuls returned to their covetous owners, who were, not unreasonably, furious at the break-out. The owner of Cervantes was particularly incensed for he got to know that it had been Cervantes who had led and masterminded the escape plan. But it had failed and so the captives rightly expected the worst, but in the event no one lost a nose or an ear or was flogged. Mercifully for Cervantes his life was spared, although he was treated 'much worse than before with clubs and chains'.[6]

His life was spared because Ramadan Pasha was a more compas-sionate ruler than his predecessors and successor, the notorious Hasan the Venetian. But even Ramadan could act out of character. His sanc-tion of the public burning of Father Aranda in May 1577, in retaliation for the same fate meted out to a Morisco corsair named Alicax in Valencia in November 1576, proves the point. Moreover, other cap-tives who engineered escape attempts while Cervantes was in prison were unceremoniously put to death. And when we learn that at the time Cervantes chose to flee prison Ramadan Pasha was involved in frantic preparations to go to either Fez or Orán in order to support Abdel Malik's claim to the throne of Morocco, such leniency is remarkable. Indeed, even before the capture of the two Cervantes brothers, such military preparations had been the major preoccupation of both Uluch-Ali, operating from Istanbul, and of Ramadan Pasha, whose rule in Algiers lasted from May 1574 until June 1577.

One month later, both Castañeda and Marco were ransomed, and when in Spain told the anxious Cervantes household of the brothers' imprisonment. But not immediately, it seems, because the date of Antonio Marco's official statement in Madrid about the captivity of the Cervantes brothers was 9 November 1576. Given that Rodrigo, their father, made strenuous but unsuccessful efforts to recover 800 ducats owed to him by Pedro Sánchez de Córdoba in October 1576, it is likely that the Cervantes family already knew of their sons' plight. Easily overlooked, a significant aspect of the brothers' captivity is the anguish and suffering endured by the Cervantes household in Madrid. News clearly did not pass that quickly between Algiers and Spain, but even from his disadvantaged position as a captive Cervantes was all too aware of his family's financial situation. He knew that the sum demanded by his captors was beyond his family's means and so he had no choice but seek his freedom the best way he could without their help. The situation faced by his brother was no different.

His family's frustrations were exacerbated by their seemingly futile attempts to collect debts or to secure funds allocated by the authorities to help pay ransoms for Spaniards held in captivity. Bona fide documents prove that the Cervantes family was living on its nerves, frantically trying to collect money from every source. Indeed, nineteen days after Antonio Marco's statement, Leonor applied to the Crusade Council, to whom, in her despair, she claimed she was a widow.[7] Her ruse worked, but she received no more than the paltry sum of 60 ducats, a fraction of the sum required. Besides, there were conditions attached to the offer. The money would have to be refunded unless a signed receipt was submitted by the two brothers within one year. It was assumed that both brothers would be ransomed simultaneously; the fact that this did not happen only added to the family's plight. The day following Leonor's petition (although in the records two alternative dates in November are given) Rodrigo compiled a petition providing information about the capture and captivity of his sons. An important document, it was intended to support the claim for financial aid made by his wife. Aware of events at home or not, Cervantes began plotting a second escape. Given that he knew the consequences of such actions his seemingly cavalier disregard of the prison's cruel code of practice appears foolhardy.

It also strongly suggests, however, that the fear of punishment, even of death itself, did not pose the kind of deterrent the authorities intended. The heroic fearlessness Cervantes displayed at Lepanto was still his guiding star; he valued freedom more than a life without it. In this he differed from his captors, who could view a prisoner's situation only in terms of money. The maimed Spaniard that Dalí Mamí had captured was not just another redeemable commodity but a man who had been an exceptional soldier – his several pay awards proved that – and one who held for the profession the highest regard. Cervantes intuitively knew that if he stood by what he firmly believed that he could face anything. As at Lepanto, he would fight on regardless.[8]

Through his exploits in captivity he became acquainted with other eminent captives, one of whom was Antonio de Sosa. It was he who later testified that Cervantes often worked at his poetry, especially on poems that had as their theme praise for Christ and the Virgin Mary. De Sosa was also to provide the most reliable account of Cervantes' second attempt at escape and of the circumstances surrounding what proved to the most hair-raising and protracted of all.[9] It was also the most daring and later gave rise to the Cervantes legend in the city.[10]

In April 1577 Mercedarian missionary priests arrived in Algiers armed with money supplied from both private and official sources to ransom as many captives as possible. They had arrived at the time the captives call the 'cherry season', although it is doubtful whether many of them enjoyed such delicacies. Ramadan Pasha was at the end of his three-year term of office and therefore anxious to convert his 'properties' – one of whom was Rodrigo – into cash. Bearing in mind that Dalí Mamí, who at that time was in Constantinople, had left strict instructions that Cervantes' tariff was to be held at 500 escudos in gold, a choice had to be made between the two brothers, and therefore Cervantes, realizing that the sum asked for his own ransom was too high, urged his brother to go instead. Rodrigo accepted on the understanding that he was to return with an armed frigate with which to assist in the escape of Cervantes and other chosen captives. And so Rodrigo, unexpectedly a free man, set sail from Algiers on 24 August 1577, along with 105 others.[11]

Although he was ransomed in April, no one could have foreseen the five months' delay that elapsed before he left for Spain. For it was also in April, as soon as Rodrigo had been ransomed, that Cervantes persuaded fourteen eminent captives to hide in a cave located in a garden outside the city. They were to stay there until Rodrigo returned with a ship of some eight to ten oars manned by skilled mariners who knew the Barbary Coast. In disguise, the rescuers would land their craft at a prearranged location; those who spoke the local language best would go ashore at dusk and seek out the waiting captives. It was altogether a most precarious business, fatal to any captive or slave caught in what the Turks considered a blatant act of sabotage. Clearly, both Cervantes and his fellow captives assumed that Rodrigo would be released in April and would return within a month.

The timing of the planned escape seemed propitious, for at that moment Ramadan Pasha was busy preparing to leave for Constantinople, and both Dalí Mamí and Arnaut Mamí – Dalí Mamí's deputy – were out of town. De Sosa claims that some captives remained as long as seven months cooped up in their hideout, not daring to emerge until nightfall. The cave in which they hid was at the bottom of the garden of Alcaide Pasha, the mayor, some five kilometres (three miles) east of the city. Their concealment for such a length of time was made possible by the connivance of a Spanish slave-gardener from Navarre, called Juan. What is curious is that the Turks do not seem to have noticed the disappearance of so many valuable captives. Although it is hard to believe, no search seems to have been made for them. Even if their absence had been noticed, would the guards ever have searched the mayor's country residence?

Ramadan Pasha could not leave for Constantinople until his replacement, Hasan Pasha, the Venetian, arrived, which was to be in June 1577. Official records show that Hasan Pasha was not Spain's preferred choice of replacement. Indeed, agents working for the Spanish secret service had supported, with no small amounts of money, the candidature of Mahamet Pasha, the son of Salah Pasha. This manoeuvre of the Spaniards was discovered by Uluch-Ali and his retinue of renegades and may have worked in Hasan Pasha's favour.[12] The formalities associated with a change of personnel explains why Rodrigo had to wait until 24 August before being allowed to return home and why therefore the anxious captives had to spend months in a cave. Hasan Pasha took immediate charge of captives under ransom – this was against the corsair code – and proves the allegation that his sole concern as ruler was to amass a personal fortune. Fortunately he did nothing to interfere with ransoms of prisoners already settled. Rodrigo sailed for Spain a free man indebted to Jorge de Olivar, one of the Mercedarian priests, compelled to stay behind in Algiers as guarantor, but more as a voluntary hostage in exchange for some captives whose ransom was still unpaid. But there were other reasons, too. Hasan Pasha came to suspect that the friar had been involved in Cervantes' second plot to escape and so wanted to exact revenge. It took a petition sent by Cervantes and forty-two other captives to the Pope, Gregory XIII and to Philip II to negotiate the friar's release several months later and at no small cost to the Mercedarian Order.

While Rodrigo was unavoidably delayed, the fourteen captives in the cave had to be cared for and their morale sustained. How a penniless

Cervantes managed to achieve both is remarkable because several contemporaries claim that Dalí Mamí provided him with neither food nor clothing. In fact, according to Juan de Valcázar, one of the signatories to the affidavit drawn up by Cervantes when in Algiers, Cervantes was sometimes heard bemoaning the fact that he had to borrow to keep himself alive. Undoubtedly then he had to borrow for others, too, and to do so he would have used his good name. But that would not have been enough to repay his creditors. Perhaps he was hoping that, once freed and on home soil, the sunshine of liberty would melt all debts incurred in captivity. Whatever the truth may be, we have to admire the courage, ingenuity and patient organization needed to carry out the operation.

No sooner had Rodrigo arrived in Spain than he set into motion the plan devised by his brother. Within four weeks he had hired an armed frigate and returned to Algiers; the long-suffering runaways were joined by Cervantes one week before the expected arrival of the frigate on 28 September, but things went badly wrong. Antonio de Sosa claims that he personally spoke later to a number of seamen from the hired frigate, who described how they had approached the shore twice and on the second occasion, two nights after the first, some sailors had landed only to be captured. They were not to know of the treachery of one of the conspirators, another renegade, nicknamed El Dorador (The Gilder). Fearful of discovery or hopeful of a reward he had revealed all to Hasan Pasha who immediately had the gardens surrounded and the captives rounded up and brought under guard to his dungeons. Whichever version of events we prefer, nothing can alter the depressing outcome: Cervantes' second escape bid had failed.[13]

He immediately accepted responsibility, declaring to Hasan Pasha that the others had done no more than follow his instructions. This being so, he argued, not one of them was guilty of any crime. This was extraordinary behaviour when we realize how natural to Hasan Pasha acts of cruelty were. The very least Cervantes could have expected as punishment was to have his ears and nose cut off. And yet he and the others were all spared. Such leniency was unprecedented and borders on the incredible. In the 'collective' pardon we ought not to forget Jorge de Olivar, the priest acting as guarantor, whose life throughout this affair had been hanging on a thread.

Unfortunately, there was to be one victim. Three days after the rescue attempt failed all the conspirators were led out from the royal prison and escorted to the mayor's gardens that had been their home for so long, where they were compelled to watch the torture and death of Juan the gardener. Strung up to a tree by one foot he died choking on his own blood. It was a death demanded by the Alcaide who raged at what he saw as his gardener's act of betrayal. No doubt the barbaric death was meant to deter Cervantes and others from further attempts at escape. The matter of Juan's death is generally passed over without comment by biographers, but to a man of Cervantes' integrity, aware of his enormous debt to the gardener over several months of constant vigilance and support, the spectacle of wanton murder served only to steel Cervantes' resolve to escape. He was to defy Hasan Pasha on two more occasions in what became a personal feud: an engrossing but often overlooked aspect of Cervantes' captivity is the relationship between master and slave – of which, more later – culminating in his dramatic ransom.

Following his recapture, Cervantes was not allowed to leave the royal compound. Burdened with fetters and chains for the next five months, he was to undergo the harshest of prison conditions. Hasan Pasha was not a man to cross, and he no doubt felt determined to teach the ex-hero a few home truths. By this time Cervantes knew that Christian slaves were very often stoned, tied to a horse's tail and dragged over cobbled streets, impaled, buried alive and commonly had their ears and noses lopped off gratuitously. And yet Cervantes soldiered on, seemingly regardless. Events prove that Cervantes ignored Hasan Pasha's threats, but no doubt the death of the gardener made him re-examine his life in captivity. After all, he had now been inside some three years, culminating in five harsh months of incarceration.

One consolation was the knowledge that Rodrigo was free, although at times he may well have questioned his generosity towards his younger brother. No doubt the latter also deeply regretted the failure of the second escape. Nothing is recorded of his feelings as he returned empty-handed to Spain, knowing that the attempt had failed but not knowing what would befall his brother and the others. Instead of a welcome return the joy at his own release must have been tempered by the bad news he carried to his anxious parents, victims more than ever of uncertainty and foreboding.

Amid these daring events the attempts of the Cervantes household to gain their sons' freedom went on unabated. Five months before Rodrigo's eventual release his father had drawn up what is now known as the first *Información* (a sort of affidavit signed by witnesses before lawyers) and formed a petition designed to help the cause for Miguel de Cervantes' ransom. In this crucial document, Rodrigo senior claims that he is a 'nobleman and very poor and on account of having ransomed his other son . . . has no wealth whatsoever'.[14] Rodrigo enlisted the support of four witnesses who corroborate the information supplied in the petition that is then further endorsed by the acknowledgement of the Duke of Sessa, dated 25 July 1578. It is also recorded how Cervantes' parents and sister Magdalena on 29 June 1578 stood as guarantors to pay the 200 ducats that his other sister Andrea had already pledged as well as anything over and above that amount needed to finalize the ransom. The pledge was made to Hernando de Torres, a merchant from Valencia. The family was pledging everything they had; it was a desperate measure but one that bore fruit over two years later, a long time to wait when everything was at stake.[15]

The third escape attempt in March 1578 was a feeble affair compared with the second and the fourth that, eighteen months later, would prove to be his final bid for freedom. Only five months after the failure of the second attempt, when conditions for him in prison were being relaxed, we find him writing a letter to Don Martín de Córdoba, the general in charge of Spanish forces in Orán. It contained nothing less than a direct appeal to the general, beseeching him to send help so that Cervantes and three other eminent captives could be rescued. Don Martín would have sympathized with this request, for he himself had been a captive twenty years earlier and had tried to organize an uprising of the Christians in Algiers. Unfortunately, his plan was betrayed, resulting in the death of many captives. Not long afterwards, however, Don Martín was ransomed for the considerable sum of 23,000 escudos.[16]

Confiding in a Moor, who was to be his messenger, Cervantes' plan was thwarted at the entrance to the city of Orán. No reason is given why the Moorish messenger should arouse suspicion in the gatemen, but he was stopped and searched and the letter was discovered. What seems likely is that the messenger may have been stopped at the gates leaving Turkish-ruled territory before crossing the 'border' into the Spanish outpost. Recent historical studies clearly demonstrate how such frontier towns were a natural gathering point for spies and informants and that it was the common policy of both the Spanish and Turkish governments to employ secret agents. This practice assumed greater importance after Lepanto: the Spanish wanted to maintain their dominance, and the Turks had no desire to repeat their losses in any subsequent conflict, whether military or political.[17] Despite this, the discovery of the letter, given the mistrust that seems to have existed in all sections of the community at that time, may well have been no more than a quirk of fate. Whatever the motive, the outcome for Cervantes was bitter failure.[18]

Frontier towns housed every type of exile, turncoat, double agent and spy. As a consequence, Spanish outposts in North Africa were particularly vulnerable because Spain had made enemies of Moriscos from within its own kingdoms, especially from Aragón, Valencia and Granada. Moriscos who had suffered persecution at the hands of the Spanish authorities and had fled to North Africa were readily employed as informants by the Turks and actively worked against

Spanish interests everywhere. Spain's acclaimed anti-Islam policy, however well intentioned in terms of national unity, had united Turk, Berber and Morisco against them. Algiers also housed a sizeable number of *conversos*, who had fled Spain as early as 1473 after riots against them in Cádiz. With the establishment of the Inquisition in Córdoba in 1482, their situation had become increasingly precarious.[19] Hence, although unfortunate for Cervantes, the capture of the Moorish messenger was a possibility both men must have considered. Given the network of informants and spies operating in Barbary, failure was more likely than success. The gatemen brought back the messenger to Hasan, who had the messenger impaled. He died without giving anything else away. Cervantes was sentenced to 2,000 strokes of the rod – in other words, to certain death. Yet not one stroke was ever laid on him. Commentators speak of 'kindly mediators' working on Cervantes' behalf and leave the episode shrouded in mystery.

One reason for Hasan Pasha's leniency is found in the secret truce agreed upon between Spain and Turkey, signed in Constantinople, and engineered by one of the most important figures in the employ of the Spanish secret service, one Giovanni Margliani.[20] The truce, a 'suspension of arms', although unheeded by the corsairs and pirates operating from Algiers, was signed on 7 February 1578, only weeks before Cervantes' third escape attempt. The truce, known to Hasan Pasha but not to his unruly prisoner, was the result of frantic, long-drawn-out clandestine negotiations between the two superpowers. A major condition of the agreement called for the leader of the Turkish Armada, Uluch-Ali, a self-made man who was vehemently against having any dealings with Spain, not to leave Constantinople with his fleet, thus securing for Spain and its territories immunity from attack by Turkish forces. The intentions of the Spanish were clear: to negotiate a permanent peace settlement with the Ottomans. It was an opportune moment for talks, because Turkey was facing war with Persia, and Spain with Protestant Europe, especially in the Netherlands. Furthermore, the death of King Sebastian of Portugal in Alcazarquivir,

Morocco, that same year had repercussions on Philip II's government and was to have direct bearing on Cervantes' later activities when a petitioner at court.

King Sebastian's death, known to Hasan the Venetian, certainly influenced his dealings with Cervantes in the latter's second and third escape attempts. Indeed, no high-ranking official in Spain or Turkey would have been unaware of events in North Africa. The frenzied diplomatic negotiations around the battle of Alcazarquivir, which historians familiarly name the 'Battle of the Three Kings', prove yet again the importance of timing and the complex interconnectedness of events in the life of Cervantes. It was to such events, clearly outside the control of both Cervantes and his overlords in Algiers, that we must look to begin to appreciate the somewhat bizarre relationship between master and slave. In fact their mysterious rapport – long an enigma to biographers – lies mainly in the work and influence of the Spanish secret services, so active for years in Barbary and in Turkey. As already discussed, their clandestine activities took on renewed vigour after Lepanto. And it so happened that much of the control of their activities lay in the hands of both Don John of Austria and the Duke of Sessa, the two signatories to letters carried by Cervantes. Those in high places in Barbary and in Turkey, therefore, would have read a far deeper significance into the signatures, although they erred in thinking that Cervantes was a prize catch or that he may have been a spy. To Hasan Pasha, recently returned from the court in Constantinople, prior knowledge of the negotiations carried out by Spain's secret services was a clear advantage in his dealings with his captive. In short, he had every reason to treat Cervantes with the greatest of leniency; he was too valuable a hostage to treat any other way. Both men would have known of the death by stoning and burning in public of Father Aranda in May 1577 and of the execution of a Castilian named Cuéllar who tried to escape with others in April 1578. In context, therefore, the treatment of Cervantes was remarkably mild, explained largely by the fact that Hasan Pasha exploited every situation to exact the greatest profit and prestige. Even one year later, in December 1579, Juan Vizcaíno was executed for attempting to escape to Orán. Those who read into Hasan Pasha's inexplicable leniency evidence of homosexuality in Cervantes are probably mistaken. But such conjectures are not uncommon, and that is why in the study of Cervantes the dispersion of error is still the first step towards the discovery of truth; the weight of evidence of Cervantes' conduct in captivity points to a man who would not bargain with his captors.[21]

It is not known whether at this or any other point in his captivity Cervantes knew of the machinations off-stage to secure an accord with Turkey. But his wily ruler, acutely aware of the intense efforts of Spain's secret services to woo him to their cause, shrewdly kept his options open. Towards the end of his notorious reign he continued to view his captive, even after the death of Don John, as a prize commodity. The career of Hasan Pasha, born in 1544, some three years before Cervantes, is a model of how to thrive in a society based on piracy and booty. Hasan himself had experienced captivity under Dragut and been taken to Tripoli where he converted to Islam. When Dragut died he became, at the age of twenty, the property of Uchali Ali. It was when with the latter that Hasan, described variously as 'astute, meddlesome, brazen, and forward', rose in favour and became renowned for his 'sexual diversity'.[22] He eventually rose to become head of the Turkish fleet.

While riding the disappointment of three failed escapes Cervantes learned, in October 1578, that his most powerful referee, Don John of Austria, had died from typhoid. He was only thirty-one. If anyone could have rescued him and the other captives it would have been Don John, the one Christian soldier the Turks feared the most. The striking portrait of him by Titian shows a man who embodied the virtues of his age. A true prince of his times, his passing was a serious blow to Cervantes who could ill afford to lose such a powerful ally. Although overjoyed at the premature death of Don John, Cervantes' captors saw no reason to reduce his ransom. They believed that with

Rodrigo safely at home Cervantes would leave no stone unturned to join him. They failed to see that his efforts to escape arose in part from his parents' inability to pay. With one notable exception, Cervantes won universal approval and respect in Algiers. Even his overlord, whom he describes as 'the murderer of the entire human race', was compelled to recognize his outstanding virtues while in captivity.[23]

Tragically, just two months after the sudden death of Don John, his other staunch ally, the Duke of Sessa, died in December 1578. These must have been bitter blows to Cervantes' morale, undermining even further his self-confidence, which was already weakened after successive failures to escape. Unsurprisingly, a period of quiet ensued in which Cervantes took stock of his situation and resumed writing, seen in the poems he sent to Antonio Veneziano who was captured by the Turks in spring 1579. We also know from Antonio de Sosa that while in prison Cervantes cultivated friendship with the elite. That this is so is borne out by the events of September 1579.

In the interim, efforts in Madrid gained momentum. Despite progressive economic decline it is clear that with the return of Rodrigo, the whole Cervantes family worked towards collecting debts owed to them. But, with sickening monotony, their debtors wriggled out of payment after payment; the 800 ducats owed to Rodrigo senior by Pedro Sánchez de Córdoba and the 300 owed to Magdalena by Fernando de Lodeña were never paid but not through lack of trying.[24] And yet we know that if the sums promised to Magdalena and Andrea, who was owed 500 by Alonso de Portocarrero, the full ransom would have been met with money to spare.[25] However, because of breaches of contract, they were never paid. But without a dowry and bona fide proof of their Christian ancestry what hope had they of a financially viable marriage? Sheer economic hardship probably explains their apparent moral laxity and their several dubious liaisons.

After the return of her son Rodrigo, Leonor asked for an extension to her loan of sixty escudos (thirty had gone towards Rodrigo's ransom and the Trinitarians had the rest), an audacious request because the expiry date of one year after the ransom had been paid had already passed. She was in dire straits. She applied in November 1578 for 'a licence to be granted to her son Miguel de Cervantes to transport from Valencia goods to the value of 8,000 ducats'. No more is heard of this until King Philip II granted in August 1579 an extension to the licence of six months but for goods to the value of 2,000 ducats only. Five months later there is record of a licence to 'carry merchandise from Valencia to Algiers so as to help the ransom of her son Miguel de Cervantes Saavedra' that was granted in January 1580. Nothing ever came of the scheme; she had no goods to sell. Her plan was to sell the licence for a fee that she could then put towards the ransom. These were desperate measures and made public the iron determination of an impoverished mother to regain a lost child.

Having survived 1578, the following year was no less frantic for the family, especially for Leonor. She was helped somewhat by her two daughters, who had spent most of their lives in the shadow of poverty. The family were doubly on edge because they knew that another ransom mission was being planned. In their desperation they promised the Trinitarian priests – rivals to the Mercedarian order with regard to ransom successes – to make up any shortfall in their son's ransom. It was a do-or-die gesture and recognized as such by Juan Gil, the attorney general of the Trinitarian Order and its senior negotiator in ransoms, who, together with Antón de la Bella, received on 31 July 1579 some 300 ducats from the family (250 from Leonor and fifty from Andrea) for the ransom payment. Years later Cervantes was to claim that his two sisters sacrificed their dowries to help pay for his and Rodrigo's ransoms. Whether true or not it was a miracle that the family had scrambled together as much as 300 ducats. On 4 September 1579 the priests left Madrid to tour Spain to raise funds. They also carried with them the family's fortune and desperate hopes.

Whether Cervantes knew of the impending visit of the Trinitarian priests is not certain. He had been 'quiet' for eighteen months, a long time for a restless spirit. But behind the scenes he had been busy, as in

September 1579, precisely four years after his capture, he was to make another bid for freedom. His aim was to escape with sixty captives, 'the flower of Christian prisoners in Algiers', using a twelve-benched frigate. The two key figures in this enterprise were a businessman from Valencia named Onofre Exarque – a shadowy figure who operated between Spain and Algiers and who paid 1,300 doblones to buy the boat – and the purchaser, a renegade called Girón from Granada, who now desired to return to the Church of Rome. Envy, so the proverb tells us, is seldom idle, and when all was in place for the escape a renegade named Caiban betrayed their plot to Hasan the Venetian. Caiban's account was immediately verified by Juan Blanco de Paz, the real culprit behind the betrayal. The enterprise, on which so much had depended for so many desperate captives, resulted in yet another depressing failure. The cause of the failure, betrayal at the very last moment by a fellow Spaniard, must have driven Cervantes to despair. Moreover, sixty other eminent captives were left helplessly in the lurch.

When Onofre learned of the treachery he offered to pay Cervantes' ransom in full and to send him to Spain on the very next ship to leave Algiers. Cervantes stoically declined the offer, accepting total blame for the affair. He refused to put his own well-being before the plight of sixty individuals who had given him their total trust. He went into hiding; but in vain, for after learning that Hasan threatened to torture anyone found sheltering him he surrendered to the authorities. In so doing he knew that another confrontation with Hasan Pasha, who stood to lose very substantial sums of money from the loss of so many valuable captives, was inevitable. When brought before Hasan, Cervantes had a rope around his neck and his hands tied behind his back. The portents were clear, but he remained undaunted: not only did he confess his guilt but his explanations differed considerably from the evidence proffered by the renegade Juan Blanco de Paz. It may well be that Hasan believed Cervantes' version – since he knew him to be a man of integrity and one who had won the highest regard from other captives – rather than trust the splenetic views of Blanco de Paz, an overtly disgruntled ex-monk who clearly envied Cervantes and who had been ostracized by the majority of captives.

Unlike many of the Christian slaves and renegades whose names crop up in official documents associated with the captivity, considerable information about Blanco de Paz exists. Expelled by the Dominican order, he was captured when travelling from Rome in 1577. For reasons unknown, his jealousy of Cervantes was obsessive. Whereas Blanco de Paz was shunned, ignored or actively despised, Cervantes was respected, liked and his leadership applauded. The defrocked cleric had not been included in the plot to escape, but he knew of it and it must have rankled. Sour grapes or not, he saw in the plan an opportunity to wreak revenge, not only on Cervantes but on the others, too. His reward was one gold escudo and a jar of lard. Inevitably, commentators liken him to Judas Iscariot. Although Cervantes was spared, there were those who wanted to use cold steel on the defrocked friar. If ever Cervantes felt tempted to panic it must have fallen now. Five long years had passed and yet his prospects of freedom had not improved; in fact they had deteriorated. He had to endure strict confinement and was not freed until Easter 1580. When he emerged he had a new owner: Hasan had bought him from Dalí Mamí. It is claimed by Antonio de Sosa that Hasan was once heard to say that 'with Cervantes under lock and key his ships and the city itself would be safe'. The legend of Cervantes in Algiers had already taken shape.

Meanwhile hunger stalked the streets of Algiers, causing some forty deaths a day, according to Antonio de Sosa. Things were so bad that an attempt at mass escape took place in December 1579. More than a hundred Christian slaves fled to Mallorca, abetted by the Genoese renegade Borrasquilla. Six months later another twenty-five Christians fled to Spain in a boat aided and abetted by a Turk. Cervantes would have known of such attempts, which were similar in scope and design to his last effort. Such attempts point to the severity of the situation in Algiers. There is, curiously, nothing to indicate that Cervantes was involved in either bid for freedom. Had he learned his lesson or did he consider their plans too precarious?

So grim was the situation in Algiers that a delegation had been sent to the Sultan begging for the reinstatement of Ramadan Pasha, the ex-owner of Rodrigo. Hasan's days were numbered, but before the change of office – Yaffer Pasha was to be his successor – Hasan Pasha saw the recapture of fifty of those who had fled, including one of the leaders of the mass outbreak, a Juan Genovés who had escaped along with Borrasquilla. On the last day of August Hasan Pasha had Juan Genovés executed. The execution would have made Cervantes realize how much he owed his very survival to the unfathomable workings of fate. Others were executed for doing only once what he had done four times. And fate was yet to play one more card, coming without warning.[26]

On 19 September 1580 Cervantes was taken in irons on board one of Hasan Pasha's four ships. He was fastened to a bench with two chains and several shackles.[27] Other captives accompanying Cervantes included a young aristocrat named Jerónimo Palafox. When Hasan Pasha came on board, he was accompanied by the Trinitarian Juan Gil. The men with Cervantes held high ransoms and Hasan wanted 500 escudos for each prisoner except for Palafox. For him he demanded 1,000 escudos. The sum the priest had for Palafox was much less, but by adding to it the 300 ducats given by Cervantes' family the priest was able to ransom Cervantes instead. Although Hasan Pasha agreed to release Cervantes for 500 escudos he demanded that the payment be in gold. This was a cruel request because the priest had to return to shore, bargain with the money-lenders and return before the ships set sail. Despite the inevitable wrangling the priest returned with the money, paid the ex-governor and escorted Cervantes, a free man at last, back to the shore.

It is all too tempting to try to imagine what was going through Cervantes' mind as he waited for Juan Gil to return, and thereafter as he walked with the priest back to the city where he had been such an unwilling captive. There may have been one thought uppermost in his mind at this time: the fate of young Palafox. Two years after Rodrigo, it was Cervantes' turn to walk a free man.

Before he left for Spain, Cervantes decided to prepare for his return by making a legally validated statement concerning his term in captivity. The attempted defamation of his character by Blanco de Paz had compelled Cervantes to want to clear his name of any possible taint once and for all. It certainly was a most unusual step to take but one he deemed absolutely necessary for his return. We should not forget that he had left Spain an unwilling fugitive from justice. But, having fled in disgrace, he had no wish to return home in dishonour. Cervantes' response to the slanderous accusations of Blanco de Paz was the now famous *Información II*, and it is the source of much that is known about him while a captive.[28] Twelve witnesses testify to the truth of the deposition that is made up of twenty-five questions relating to his lifestyle, customs and conduct in prison. To Cervantes the document was crucial: he clearly recognized its importance in a society increasingly dominated by concepts of honour and the importance of one's ancestry and where valid documentation was deemed indispensable. Having been dispossessed of the letters of recommendation written by the now deceased Don John and the Duke of Sessa, the affidavit would have to serve as a passport to a worthwhile post on his return to civilian life. He knew the temper of the age and he understood the importance of keeping the family name free from scandal. In the event, the affidavit did little; it possibly redeemed his good name but did not provide him with a livelihood.

Two weeks later, on 24 October 1580, Cervantes, wishing no doubt for a pirate-free return and carefully guarding his affidavit, set sail with five other freed captives for Spain. His precarious life as a captive was over, and yet things in Algiers could have been so different for him. The offer to become a *turcople* (a Christian newly converted to Islam) was made more than once. It is possible that Hasan Pasha, himself a convert to Islam, harboured this desire for him, too. And had Cervantes acquiesced he would have joined a vast body of men and women who simply took the easier course of action.[29] Ironically, one such was The Gilder, the one who had betrayed Cervantes' second escape bid and who was to die three years later on the feast of St Jerónimo, the last day of September and the day of his betrayal.[30] Such acts of betrayal did not dim Cervantes' view of true Christian virtues, especially those of valour and fortitude. Witnesses repeatedly attest to the depth and constancy of Cervantes' Christian principles while remaining the most unwilling captive of his day. In much of the documentation from the Algiers period of his life, the phrase 'desiring to serve God and His Majesty' recurs time and again.

And when all seemed lost he found himself a free man. Redeemed at the eleventh hour from what surely would have been the oblivion of Constantinople, his sense of disbelief mixed with the pure joy of a freedom regained could easily have spilled over into tears. Freedom would at least mean food and clothing, for, according to the documented report of Francisco de Aguilar, a Portuguese ransomed at the same time, Cervantes throughout his captivity got neither, and so he was compelled to borrow. He thus returned, landing at the port of Denia in Valencia with substantial debts.[31]

When Yaffer Pasha replaced Hasan the Venetian in August 1580, he claimed to have introduced a more lenient regime and actively encouraged the release of ransomed prisoners, saying that he 'had not come to line his own pockets'. And when, in January 1581, a new three-year truce was signed with Spain, life for captives remaining in Algiers improved, but by then Cervantes was looking for work in mainland Spain.[32]

4

THE CAPTIVE'S RETURN
(1580–6)

Astrologers predicted that the year 1580 was going to be a bad one. There were flu epidemics in Rome, Madrid and Paris, a third spectacular moon eclipse in January and widespread fears among the Portuguese of calamity when their king, Cardinal Enrique, died, supposedly after seeing a comet. As Cervantes made his way from Valencia to Madrid, he knew that Philip II was in Badajoz, awaiting the call to enter Portugal as its new king. But not even the monarch was immune to flu and, after a particularly nasty attack, believing he was near death, Philip II drew up his will. His recovery was hastened by the news that the Duke of Alba with an invading army of 32,000 Spanish troops had been successful. The annexation of Portugal would be a relatively brief episode – some sixty years – in Iberian political and cultural history, and few, it seems, suspected the problems yet to arise.[1] Journeying by horse and carriage, Cervantes had time to reflect on recent events. No doubt intrigued by Hasan Pasha's final act of leniency towards him, he surely felt relieved to have severed all ties with the Orient. And so, armed with his affidavit, Cervantes went to court and became a royal petitioner. There he met Mateo Vázquez, the king's secretary, and, grateful that his good name had been salvaged, he probably felt cautiously optimistic.

This stands in vivid contrast to Hasan Pasha who was returning to Constantinople in disgrace. Algiers was in economic ruin; plague and famine had killed more than five thousand in January and February 1580, and the janissaries, the cream of the Turkish army, were up in arms clamouring for a change of ruler.[2] Despite the crisis in Algiers, Spain could not rest. Rumour had it that Uluch-Ali was preparing to launch his armada and attack Fez in Morocco to bring it under Turkish control. Counter-rumours were spreading that Spain was making ready to launch an all-out attack on Algiers. At such moments the work of spies and agents was at its most frenetic, not helped by alarmist propaganda sent out by the French, who tried to undermine the efforts of Spain at every turn.[3] Indeed, on 23 January an accord between Spain and the Turks was signed, which declared peace for three years. But no sooner had Giovanni Margliani, the chief negotiator acting for Spain, returned to Italy than Spanish secret agents working in Constantinople reported that a possible attack by Uluch-Ali's armada in the Mediterranean seemed likely.[4] Although the second secret truce between Spain and Turkey was still intact – it was to end in January 1581 – pirates from Algiers went about their business as usual. Against this backdrop of intrigue and rumour Cervantes returned to his homeland.

By the time Cervantes had arrived in Madrid the Duke of Alba had taken Portugal. Philip II was now king in all but name, a world ruler of dominions so vast that the sun – so ran the popular saying – never set upon them. To the Spanish authorities burdened with the annexation of Portugal and unrest in the Netherlands as well as threats of attack – despite the recent accord – from Turkey, not to mention the growth of Protestantism and the machinations of the French secret service, Lepanto and what it meant to Cervantes carried little weight. Despite this, Cervantes was confident that his case merited a special hearing. But it was clearly not the moment to harass the court officials with requests for a suitable post based on services, no matter how honourably discharged, of a decade earlier. If Don John and the Duke of Sessa had still been alive his case might possibly have stood an even chance. But with only Mateo Vázquez's voice at court, Cervantes' prospects of securing a suitable post were slim. The secretary, who had the crucial task of processing Philip's papers when they came in, would report the contents of correspondence verbally or by means of a summary written on each paper and, where relevant, would state the advice offered by himself or by ministers.[5]

Cervantes, however, was in dire straits. On his return he had found his parents ageing fast and financially worse off than ever. His two sisters were still not free from emotional squabbles, especially Magdalena who had now met Pérez de Alcega, a nobleman and a potentially good catch – he had been deputy controller to Philip II's fourth wife, Anne of Austria, who died in October 1580, and thereafter controller in the royal household. He reneged on his promise of marriage, however, and, although he paid the welcome sum of 100 ducats, it was only one-third of the amount promised as an out-of-court settlement.[6] The liaison left her disillusioned and poor, and it is no wonder that soon she turned to a life of piety; she found in the Church the solace and love she once sought in the company of men. For his part, six years later Alcega married the daughter of Juan de Ledesma, the secretary to the Council for the Indies. The dowry Alcega received was very large, but he was to die six months later, still in debt to Magdalena.

Even Doña Leonor's submission of Cervantes' certificate to the Crusade Council – set up to help towards debts incurred for ransoms – brought little joy to the family, and Rodrigo junior, who Miguel had not seen since his release, had already re-enlisted and had marched into Portugal to secure the throne. In short, Cervantes returned to a household as much on its knees as the nation's economy. His parents were penniless and Spain was in the grip of the worst economic decline of the age. Philip II had already survived two bankruptcies, in 1557 and 1575 (the third in 1596 was settled in 1597), but how many saw the inevitable trend? Too busy with events of the moment, Cervantes, with no time to convalesce after his imprisonment, once again left home. He needed money: the debt of ransom together with five years of borrowing in Algiers had returned with him.

A sonnet to welcome his return written by Gálvez de Montalvo suggests further proof of the renown of Cervantes before his unwanted exile. Reunion with Montalvo enabled him to catch up on literary events in Madrid and that included a meeting with López de Hoyos. It is quite possible that Cervantes discussed with both men the writings he had undertaken in prison. We do not know whether Hasan Pasha would have allowed Cervantes to take with him to Constantinople his poems and stories begun in Algiers, but we do know that Cervantes had already written the first half (Books I–III) of La Galatea and that further books (IV–VI) were written on his return from captivity.[7] A number of fellow captives claim that he wrote in prison and what he wrote were poems, so it seems probable that drafts of the text date from his time in Algiers. Furthermore, given that in the prologue Cervantes refers to his 'occupation of writing eclogues', which are short pastoral poems, some argue that La Galatea is not prose but poetry.[8] The good news for writers was that in 1579 the first theatres in Madrid were opened. The demand for new plays provided would-be dramatists, Cervantes included, with the opportunity that both writers and the public sought. The timing was right. It was a challenge that he could not resist. Sadly, most of what he wrote for the stage in this early period of his writing has been irretrievably lost, although he never lost his passion for the genre.[9]

The reunion with López de Hoyos would have been a happy one, because both shared the tolerance of humanist thinking which the works of Erasmus (1467–1536) kindled in Spain and which Cervantes had breathed in Italy. Undoubtedly the most renowned scholar of his age, Erasmus, a contemporary of Machiavelli, was also the leading moderate of the Reformation, although he never joined the Protestants. His educational mission and his hopes for religious reform through a return to the fundamental texts of Christianity appealed to a tolerant-minded Cervantes as it did to López de Hoyos. Materials devised by Erasmus for use in schools in the teaching of Latin and Greek found widespread support, and, when we evaluate Cervantes' early school-ing in Andalusia and later education in Madrid with López de Hoyos, we can sense the importance of Erasmus for whom eloquence was per-haps the foremost objective of educational philosophy. Without eloquence, the informed and moral person, so Erasmus believed, could not be an effective, persuasive presence in Christian society.

Although a mere fragment of what Erasmus stood for in early Renaissance Europe, his insistence on grammar, rhetoric, the rules of poetry and the inculcation of style are major issues tackled by Cervantes throughout his literary career.[10] Eloquence, the power to persuade, was certainly his trump card while in Algiers; how else was he able to organize his escapes? Eloquence, in its fullest sense, is aptly illustrated in the knight errant's discourses. Yet Erasmus may have influenced Cervantes in another way, too. Amid all its assets, *Don Quixote* is a compendium of proverbs. To what extent, we may ask, is the text indebted to the *Adagia* of Erasmus? For of all his varied works, probably no other work of his had a greater direct impact on European culture than the *Adagia*. Indeed, both authors hint that proverbs derive from that time of ancient harmony and understanding – the Golden Age – which occurred long before the cataclysm of our first parents. Proverbs are simply the vestiges of that ancient philosophy which was destroyed by the calamities of human history, especially modern.[11] It is commonly accepted that Erasmus influenced Cervantine thought; why not also in literary precept, style and technique which were crucial aspects of Erasmian texts?

Although impossible to gauge, Cervantes' debt to Erasmus explains at least in part his deep gratitude to López de Hoyos who, as we recall, described Miguel as 'my dear and beloved pupil'. Apart from contacts with his literary friends, little is said or known of Cervantes' reaction to his return to Madrid. Clearly, the transition from dungeon life in Algiers to the salons of the capital was as great as that between the cultural freedom of Renaissance Italy and the traumas of captivity in an alien society. In an age of great changes, eleven years proved too many to be away. Nevertheless, he still believed that the king and country owed him something, a royal favour, some recognition of his services. And so, having caught up on literary news, he made his way to Thomar in Portugal and to his first petition at court. Among the hordes of petitioners, what could a maimed and somewhat obscure man such as Cervantes expect? Not much and, without the influence of the king's private secretary, nothing. Unluckily for him, Mateo Vázquez at the time was out of favour because Philip II believed that he had violated royal confidence during the annexation of Portugal. When Antonio Pérez, the king's first secretary, the wealthiest and most powerful civil servant in the land, lost his position, the king gave the post to Juan de Idiáquez. Mateo Vázquez, thereafter, was never to emerge from the shadow of the king's mistrust.

Another reason why Cervantes went to the king's court was to present his case for a soldier's pension. A legitimate claim that he had made for a pension had been refused by the Council of Castile. Indignant, he saw no alternative but to go in person to petition. Whatever else took place in his meeting with Mateo Vázquez, one thing is clear: he did not surrender his affidavit, for that was submitted a decade later when he applied to go to the New World. A clear setback was the discovery that Philip II had agreed to fill posts both in Portugal and in its colonies with Portuguese citizens. Although this helped to placate many of the king's new subjects, it was a policy that put paid to any hope of a plum post in administration for a Spaniard. But not all was lost for Cervantes, as the king was desperate to know what was happening in North Africa. On 21 May 1581 he authorized the payment of 'fifty escudos to Miguel de Cervantes for a royal mission to Orán' and a further fifty on his return. It was the nearest Cervantes came to employment as a spy, and so for a brief period he joined that large but faceless network of undercover agents and informants who infiltrated the courts of both the Spanish and Turkish empires. Cervantes, advised by Vázquez, probably saw his task as a stepping-stone to more important commissions. He left Cádiz on 23 May and returned in late June to Lisbon where Philip II now held court. It is curious that he should so willingly venture forth to a region from which he had so strenuously striven to escape; and to go there carrying papers signed by no less a person than the king. Besides, the sum offered, one hundred escudos, although much better than any regular soldier's pay, could never have bought his freedom if he were captured again. It seems that he knew no fear or perhaps he believed that no risk was too great in the service of the king. And yet his assignment was typical of ex-captives sent, at delicate moments in state affairs, on fact-gathering missions to areas known to them. He left at the beginning of the peak season for piracy in the Mediterranean.

To earn the hundred escudos Cervantes' task was to consult Don Martín of Córdoba in Orán and with officials in Mostaganem. Philip was sending his eager vassal to gather information about the movements of the Turkish fleet and to ascertain the loyalty of the Portuguese fortresses in North Africa, as some Portuguese colonial officials were openly hostile to his annexation of their homeland. The two lions that the general of the garrison in Orán allegedly sent to Philip II possibly mirror those accompanied by the curious Don Diego de Miranda – who may be a fictional counterpart of Don Martín – that Don Quixote encounters in *Part Two* of the novel. To date, however, nothing has come to light about such a possibility in what is undoubtedly an intriguing episode in the novel.[12]

By far the most urgent aspect of his mission was his visit to Turkish-controlled Mostaganem, a city to the east of Orán and one of the military enclaves closest to the Spanish fortress town. Mostaganem had been the site of one of Spain's worst military disasters in 1558 when 8,000 of her troops were taken captive. Its mayor, known as the alcaide, was an informer in the pay of Spain. It was to him that Cervantes was sent to learn about the movements of Uluch-Ali and his fleet. A convert from Islam, the mayor was called Don Felipe Hernández de Córdoba and thus linked to the noble family from Andalusia. With the return of Uluch-Ali to Istanbul in August, however, Cervantes had served his purpose, and so, when he returned to Lisbon in late June, the king and the secret service, burdened with weightier matters, had no further interest in him. His short-lived affair with the world of espionage and secret diplomacy fizzled out. His report to the court has never been found and is very possibly lying under the mountains of unclassified documents still housed in Spanish archives.[13] Cervantes duly received his fifty escudos in July and stayed on in Lisbon where the king had taken up residence. Having established that Uluch-Ali had no plan to launch an armada against Spanish interests, Philip II set about answering the endless requests, complaints and grievances, especially from a devastated Portuguese nobility still reeling from the disbelief of annexation. Worse, the king was facing opposition on two fronts: from Don Antonio, pretender to the Portuguese throne, and from the Azores, a crucial outpost for shipping to and from the New World. Earlier attempts to take the Azores had failed, news of which strengthened Don Antonio's desire to mount a rebellion. Philip II knew that France and England also opposed his rule and would therefore secretly assist any rebellion against him. So what seemed a simple matter of outposts in the Atlantic took on much deeper significance. Philip II decided to attack the following summer, 1582, thus avoiding a costly winter campaign, and gave orders for the greatest naval armament ever seen in Spain.

Don Antonio sought Elizabeth of England's help, but she refused her ships, so he turned to France, offering Brazil and the Azores as bait. France agreed while simultaneously signing a peace treaty with Spain. However, Philip II's spies saved the day, warning him of the French fleet, some seventy vessels and 15,000 men, that had set sail to besiege the island of San Miguel. The Marqués de Santa Cruz arrived and routed the French. His fleet, which included Rodrigo de Cervantes, returned to Lisbon in August amid great festivities. But Spain's naval success did nothing to further Cervantes' personal career or ambitions. Eighteen months had passed since his return and rumour now had it that Philip II would return to Madrid. Given that Cervantes collaborated with a poet friend Pedro de Padilla on a collection of ballads, published in March 1583, it is probable that he returned to Madrid in late summer the year before. His days as a petitioner at court were over, but his admiration for the city of Lisbon remained throughout his life and resurfaced in his novel *Persiles and Sigismunda*, published in 1617, one year after his death. Furthermore, what he had learned of the courtier's life, with its falsehood, fickleness and hollow pleasures, also finds its way into his first novel, in which erstwhile courtiers, disguised as rustics, discuss Neoplatonic theories of love. The convention of shepherds and shepherdesses who flit through the Arcadian landscapes philosophizing about the origins, nature and growth of love appealed to a would-be writer who had seen his honest endeavours to serve the Crown fall foul of intrigue and political infighting. Cervantes was later to claim that he had no sense of shame and that he 'was not made for palaces because he didn't know how to flatter'.

But other solid reasons exist that explain his failure as a court petitioner. Recent research proves that the court was the great marketplace for royal patronage; Cervantes was not alone in his desire for a royal privilege or office. The modern historian, Rodríguez Salgado, shows that Philip II received thousands of letters annually requesting employment or favours. For example, for the month of May in 1571 he received 1,200 petitions. On one occasion Philip II complained to Mateo Vázquez that in one day alone he had signed 400 documents. It was not for nothing that the secretary revealed in the 1580s that he 'sought to make himself if not invisible, at least utterly inconspicuous in order to fulfil Philip's vision of the ideal adviser'.[14] The relationship of Vázquez to the monarch has been carefully recorded and makes for compelling reading. It emerges that the secretaries – and Philip had eight personal secretaries – became the lynchpins of Spain's vast organization, acting as intermediaries between king and council. Although they had no vote, secretaries would attend meetings, summarize conciliar discussions and decisions, transmit information, undertake the preliminary sifting of material and, most importantly, see the king. Hence Cervantes was wise to seek the aid of Vázquez but unwise not to seek that of others, too. For all his knowledge of the ways and wiles of courtiers he failed to appreciate the court as both an institution and an ethos. Philip had no real choice but to protect himself from the ever-increasing hordes of petitioners. Clearly Cervantes

had not the stamina to do what Antonio de Guevara – the most influential courtly writer in the sixteenth century – advised an aspiring
courtier to do, namely to 'visit, serve, suffer, make himself visible and
persevere'. And such actions would only bear fruit if the aspirant had
already gained access to the king's chambers, something Cervantes,
despite the successful mission to Orán, could not manage. When Castiglione wrote that the perfect courtier should love and adore the
prince he serves over all humans, using all his will, virtues and arts to
please his master, he was stating the principles of court etiquette.
Every courtier realised that personal virtues and worth were far less
important than the ability to flatter, even enchant, the king or the heir
to the throne.[15] Cervantes had not the constitution to become what
one anonymous author, writing in 1493 about royal favourites, had
called 'palace dogs'.[16]

To illustrate Cervantes' resistance to the ways of court, we can
compare his efforts with those made by Ruy Gómez de Silva when
seeking military office for his brother in Italy, a petition not dissimilar
to that of Cervantes. Gómez de Silva not only made a personal request
to Philip but urged another secretary, Gonzalo Pérez, to help him persuade the council to recommend his brother. Gómez de Silva had been
a childhood friend of King Philip II and in his career had risen to
become chamberlain of the royal household and later great master
of the household of Don Carlos, the king's son; if he had to resort to
lobbying, what chance had Cervantes' solitary request of success?
Indeed, his great hero, Don John, had once employed similar tactics
when trying to build up a rival party to that of Philip II. As Rodríguez
Salgado asserts, 'It was always necessary to appeal to a wide range of
individuals and institutions to procure offices and concessions.'[17] If
cooperative secretaries proved invaluable for ambitious aristocrats, it
was also true that no secretary could survive without noble support.
On this point, too, Cervantes' application, despite his father's claimed
hidalgo (noble) ancestry, would have failed. Flattery and deceit were
not in his armoury; yet his study of Machiavelli should have shown

him the dangers of court procedure long before. It was around this time that he submitted to Antonio de Eraso, the secretary of the Council of the Indies, his first petition for a post in the New World. Written in February 1582 but not discovered until 1954, it also mentions his writing of *La Galatea*.[18] Although Eraso did not find him a post overseas he did sign the licence for the publication of *La Galatea*, dated 2 February 1584. Hence it is clear that between his return from Lisbon and the date of the royal licence – the novel was first published in 1585 – Cervantes spent some of his time writing. Luckily, the genre that he had chosen while in captivity had been given a new lease of life with the publication of Gálvez de Montalvo's *El Pastor de Fílida* (1582). The model in Spain for such works was that of Jorge de Montemayor, whose *Diana* ran to twenty-six editions between 1559 and 1600. Although pastoral romance is rarely read nowadays, *La Galatea* marked Cervantes' first serious attempt at literature and initiation into the world of the professional writer, something of a novelty in the 1580s. Even though Cervantes, through the canon's voice in *Don Quixote*, claims that 'nothing is concluded' in *La Galatea* and that the reader 'should wait for the second part which is promised', this does not mean that his first novel should be dismissed as incomplete and therefore not worth reading.

Despite the phenomenal success of the pastoral novel in sixteenth-century Spain, Cervantes shows in the prologue to his contribution to the genre his awareness of the danger of writing pastoral dialogues at a time when poetry was out of favour. Compared with prose and drama, poetry is still out of favour, so much so that nowadays the reading public tends to view the bucolic theme as a bore. The despair of youths, often courtiers in disguise, traipsing woodland vales lamenting over the grief caused by love attracts little interest in today's world of soap operas and blockbusters. In fleeing from courtly life, however, writers of pastoral novels had a royal model in Charles V, who, in 1556, turned his back on the palace and retired to Yuste monastery in remote Extremadura, seeking in contemplation and in nature spiritual solace. Love, generally unrequited or as a potentially spiritualizing force, is certainly the all-encompassing theme of pastoral novels, and in this *La Galatea* is no exception. In particular, the question of the moral justification of courtly love is examined. Yet, underpinning the text is another vital concern, that of the art and science of poetry as an ideal in itself. Cervantes had a great deal to say about the role and function of poetry, and he began here. In so doing he had little choice but to cross swords with what he would later term 'lesser poets', and by lesser he generally meant those whose concept of poetry was devoid of the classical ideals associated with the ancients. The outcome was a literary feud that in turn was to spawn further disappointments and pessimism leading ultimately to his increasing isolation. When in his prologue he claims that *La Galatea* was written for the 'interested and careful reader', he was excluding from such a category his literary opponents.[19]

His way of tackling the problem of mediocrity in literature was to produce – or at least to attempt to produce – the best in each genre he tackled. To succeed in this there were certain hurdles to clear. To begin with, any Spaniard writing in the wake of the Council of Trent (1545–63) walked a moral tightrope; literature had to be imbued with a Christian – that is, a Roman Catholic – ethic. Given that the setting for pastoral novels was Arcadia, the home of Pan, the confrontation with the world of pagan rites and ceremony was inevitable. In *La Galatea*, both Nísida and Blanca, to name but two, use the disguise of pilgrims to flee their home to go in search of Timbrio. Cervantes refers to the use of disguise in his prologue, but it was more than a literary convention, for, in 1590, Philip II issued a decree aimed at ensuring that the pilgrim's garb was not to be used as a 'cloak for vagrants and malefactors'.[20] Admittedly Nísida and Blanca are not villains, but neither is the novel escapist literature. In fact nothing Cervantes wrote could be termed as such.

Not all saw through convention, however. It was no real surprise that in the Portuguese edition of the novel, published by Bartolomeu

Ferreira in Lisbon in 1590, all allusions to paganism were expunged.[21] There is no record of Cervantes' response to Ferreira's action, but the fact that Ferreira expurgated his text clearly indicates the slippery, if not immoral, path others thought Cervantes had taken.

If Cervantes' first problem was ethical he also faced a second: how could he teach a moral lesson and simultaneously entertain his reader? When we visit the prologue to La Galatea to seek answers, we find a self-effacing claim to love poetry and a desire to please. This is of course only half the story, for his prologue is a deliberate smokescreen intended to conceal his true motives. Cervantes has a hidden agenda that is further developed much later in Voyage to Parnassus, a text that has considerable affinity to the pastoral. This agenda is concerned with the religious theme that is central to the genre and which is employed to launch a covert attack on vulgarity and vulgar poets, illustrated in Telesio's paganistic burial of Meliso, 'a shepherd-poet'. Described in Book 6 as 'an ancient priest', an epithet which, according to Márquez Villanueva, clearly refers to a pagan or heathen, the ceremony at which he officiates highlights Cervantes' subtle but discernible literary attack.[22] Cervantes intended his novel to be more than the fruit of his dialogue with prior texts.

The wearing of garlands, the lighting of the funeral pyre, the use of incense and the incantation of prayers in which the wind seems to conspire smack more of paganism than orthodox Christianity. That said, this rustic burial place for Meliso is special because it is sacred to those who are true poets, a truth confirmed by the supernatural appearance of Calíope, the mother of Orpheus, who is seen to rise from the funeral flames. Her song is dedicated to the praise of contemporary poets. More to the point is the praise showered on Meliso; his virtues reflect ideals to which Cervantes aspired and possibly prefigure the sort of epitaph he would have preferred for himself; such as the 'integrity of his blameless life, sublime inventiveness, strength of mind, the pleasing dignity of his speech and the excellence of his poetry and above all his heartfelt diligence in adhering to his sacred religion'.

What is the religion referred to here if not that of dedication to the highest of literary ideals?[23] From the outset the novel sets us challenges, for it is much more than a conventional eclogue in line with the series of pastoral novels published in Spain in the wake of the *Arcadia* (1504), written by Jacobo Sannazaro.

In its favour, the pastoral novel discusses love and its effect on the inscrutable workings of fate. Love, fate and providence – heaven's will? – are realities Cervantes believed not only influenced but appealed to every human heart, and he was to write about them throughout his career. Although poetry was out of favour, he chose the bucolic theme to show how the genre offers ample scope to creative minds to extend their limited horizons of the treatment of love; in particular, love as a spiritualizing force, which operates through pain and heartbreak, and is presented in a way that ennobles the language while entertaining the reader. Montemayor's claim that 'those who suffer most [from love] are the best', added to Cervantes' reasons for writing bucolic literature – that the themes could be developed further than they had previously been – mean that his contribution to a much maligned genre merits our reading. But the reading has to be careful, for his text – which at the very beginning describes a brutal murder, an event never before seen in the hermetically sealed universe of fountains, glades, weeping willows and oaks – is clearly unconventional: the stabbing of Carino by Lisandro breaks with all the rules of the pastoral novel. Despite a discourse by Tirsi in Book 4, which fused Neoplatonic concepts of love with Christian theology and thereby affirmed the sacred nature of matrimony, Tirsi's proposed plan at the end of the text to kill the Portuguese shepherd chosen not by Galatea but by her father to be her husband registers a further contravention of the canons of bucolic literature.[24] His intention to murder paves the way for a sequel that, although promised, was never to materialize.

Sixteenth-century readers would have known those rules and would have felt the literary earthquake a murder provoked; many modern readers coming to the genre through Cervantes would not know that tradition and would not find such a murder, no matter how morally reprehensible, in any way extraordinary. And, when Darintho claims that rustic life is 'a war on earth', we again see how the rules of pastoral literature, where nature is the handmaid of the Lord, are broken. The outrage of an assassination immediately follows the laments of Elicio and Erastro, two friends who are both in love with Galatea. Amid idyllic settings where sheep graze in serene harmony with nature the two friends cannot conceal their painful dilemma of loving a paragon of beauty and virtue, Galatea. Their abiding love for her creates all sorts of morally and socially compromising situations. But they are not alone: others are similarly struck by Cupid's arrow and suffer heartache. Their pressing personal circumstances and their varied social backgrounds differ little from what we are to find in certain episodes in Don Quixote, Part One, (1605) and the Exemplary Novels (1613). For biographers, however, a central issue is the question of what La Galatea reveals of Cervantes' everyday life.

Despite the idealized settings found in the pastoral genre, we know from Spanish reform writers (arbitristas) that, from the middle of the sixteenth century onwards, urban lawlessness was endemic. The hordes of bandits and vagrants roaming the cities, especially in Seville and Córdoba in the south, in Madrid and Toledo in the centre and Valladolid in the north – all places familiar to Cervantes – were seen as a 'parasitic drain on the nation's resources'.[25] While the low incidence of crime outside the great centres of population bore witness to the continuing vitality of peasant agriculture in New Castile, it also provided writers with a natural setting for their views of an ideal, possibly perfectible, society. Yet the latest studies prove that the descriptions of rural life in such novels are no more than urban myths. The image of a stable, traditional, rural existence is far from what Cervantes knew and experienced. The unchanging village as a vision of order, harmony and serenity simply did not exist.[26] His imminent move to Esquivias, and later his travels in the employ of the Crown, were to demonstrate that truth to him.

It was in direct response to the spread of crime that the government issued a number of decrees in 1530, 1552 and 1566 by which condemnation to the galleys became the mandatory sentence for thieves, cut-throats, accessories and receivers and for 'anyone who harboured criminals or resisted the justices'. Although such a sentence grew out of, at least in part, the military need to man the galleys – needs that increased by the decade – Cervantes could not have forgotten that he, too, had resisted the justices. Had he been caught he may well have ended up as a galley-slave. Seen in this light, the episode in *Don Quixote* where the knight sets free the chain gang of galley-slaves on their way to the port takes on new significance. '"Slaves?" asked Don Quijote. "Is it possible that the king actually enslaves anyone?" "That's not what I said," replied Sancho, "except that these are condemned criminals going to serve the king in his galleys, whether they like it or not."' A closer picture of the social reality known to Cervantes is found in his picaresque novel 'Rinconete and Cortadillo', a reality explored later in 'The Colloquy of the Two Dogs', published in 1613, and described so vividly by Quevedo in his prose writings, too.

Little of what we know to be the major events in his adult life up to and including royal approval of the text is touched on in his first novel. There are points of contact, however. Timbrio does 'escape' to Naples, Turks do attack villages along the Catalan coast and there are amorous liaisons. But these similarities are minimal. Is therefore his pastoral novel a mere literary exercise in which he decided to show the world his knowledge of Renaissance literature and of contemporary literary fashion as well as his obvious skill at characterization and story-telling? The disputes between lovers, in particular the protracted debate between Lenio and Tirsi, are clearly based on Neoplatonic theories current at the time, but in the weight given to jealousy is there not a throwback to Cervantes' possible relationship with Silena in Naples?

Clearly there are themes and attitudes presented in his first novel that will appear, albeit modified and honed, throughout the rest of his writings. The heartaches of Elicio and Silerio find a counterpart in episodes in *Don Quixote* in much the same way that the exploits of *Persiles and Sigismunda* have their parallels in certain of the plights of disaffected courtiers or disguised shepherdesses that inform *La Galatea*. In this continuity of theme we see his faith in the social usefulness of poetry and in the notion of López Pinciano, one of the greatest literary theorists of the age, of the poet as a 'bridge' between heaven and earth. Cervantes, like Meliso, was forced to flee to that sacred valley – one's inner sanctuary, Mount Parnassus in the later work – because this was his only support. For genuine poets, *Calíope's Song* is a message of hope and consolation. But Cervantes had no time to stay with Calíope, Telesio or Meliso. Circumstances did not permit him to enjoy for long the aura that surrounded a writer; his father died in 1585 and one year later he was struggling to survive in a relatively hostile environment as a government agent.

Between the earliest of Cervantes' poems printed in the homily to Elizabeth of Valois in 1568 to those found in *La Galatea* he had undergone considerable development. The text itself is proof of his learning and poetic art and of his impulse to experiment. It is clear that in those intervening years Cervantes had applied himself to serious humanistic study and had somehow managed to continue his education. His love of learning, noted by his teachers, reflects his love of life, despite the setbacks that life threw at him incessantly. But it was in such setbacks that he gained the experience necessary to write about the things he wrote to the standards he unquestionably attained. The five years' apprenticeship as a soldier were the perfect preparation for the horrors of Algiers, in much the same way that extensive wanderings around Spain as a child and teenager prepared him for the trials and labours of a soldier's life abroad.

Cervantes was asked to write laudatory sonnets by other writers of note – Padilla, Montalvo and Juan Rufo – more importantly he renewed his friendship with Pedro Laínez, now living in Esquivias, and with Francisco de Figueroa. Sadly for Cervantes, López de Hoyos died in 1583. He left nothing in his will, not even one of the nearly five hundred books he owned, to his erstwhile 'beloved disciple'. Amid external threats to political stability in Spain Cervantes continued his literary pursuits and must have been pleased to receive the sum of 120 ducats, paid in two instalments, for his novel. With the 100 ducats already earned from his mission to Orán, this period proves to be one of his most prosperous so far and paves the way for him to decide to become a professional writer, a brave decision at any time but especially then. Not that he would be able to live entirely from his writings; even the most successful playwright of the day, Lope de Vega, continued to work as a secretary to his patron.[27] Of the 'twenty to thirty' *comedias* Cervantes claims to have written only two are extant, *Numantia* (?1583) being his most famous.[28] Based on the legend of the citizens of Numantia, who destroy their own city rather than surrender to the Romans, the real issue of the play turns on the theme of the just war and the construction of a national identity. The publication of Diego de Valera's *Corónica Abreviada* in 1482 had resurrected the theme of Numantia, and his text was immensely popular in the first half of the sixteenth century.[29] Indeed, between 1482 and 1567 his abridged history was reprinted fifteen times and inspired several ballads. It was the subject to tackle if you were a budding writer. In the reign of Philip II few themes could have been more relevant. It was crucial to sixteenth-century political ideology, and as such Philip II could not escape its vortex.[30]

What is significant is the choice of theme. Cervantes certainly knew what his public wanted and he made sure they got it. His friendship with two professional actors, Getino de Guzmán and Tomás Gutiérrez, helped to launch his career as a playwright. By no means a fortune, the forty ducats earned in 1585 for two plays published by Gaspar de Porres no doubt encouraged him further. He needed to earn in order to pay personal debts accrued during captivity. Despite his combined earnings from publishers for prose and drama he still owed the Trinitarians for his ransom. The noble attempt in August 1582 of Cervantes' mother, 'to license Juan Fortuny to transport to Algiers from Valencia goods to the value of 2,000 ducats, the profits of which will be used for the ransom of Miguel de Cervantes', despite an extension of the licence two years later, came to nothing.[31] Not until November 1584, some four years after his release, was the ransom debt finally settled.

Around this time, amid relative success, he met Ana Franca de Rojas and fathered an illegitimate daughter, Isabel. Given that Ana Franca together with her husband Alonso Rodríguez were 'taverners to the court' and ran an establishment frequented by theatre people, it is more than likely that Cervantes met her there. In the absence of more tangible proof, scholars inevitably speculate wildly about the liaison; she was twenty, by all accounts pretty, he thirty-seven and a celebrity. Her father, a wool merchant, had died young, and so at the age of fourteen Ana Franca was sent out to work in her uncle's house. When the uncle married, Ana Franca was destined to meet his wife, Damiana, who immediately warmed to her, so much so that when her husband died three years after their marriage she gave one hundred ducats to Ana Franca as a dowry. Armed with this no mean sum, Ana Franca soon met Alonso Rodríguez who, seemingly, had his eyes fixed not on the delectable Ana Franca but on her dowry. A marriage of loveless convenience ensued, a recipe for extramarital affairs. By contrast, Cervantes cut an appealing figure, a writer who was in the news, a soldier and ex-hero, whose life had been truly adventurous and very different to the supposedly dull and illiterate Asturian trader she had married.[32]

But their affair fizzled out before it had really started for reasons that we can only guess at. Although the speed of events must have confused her, she was left the mother of their daughter. Was their affair a mistake, an error of judgement which in the plays of the day led to unimaginable tragedies? Cervantes, despite his tolerant, humanistic outlook, is not always benevolent to those characters of his who miscall their lustful aberrations love. A study of his play *The Labyrinth of Love* exemplifies the absurd machinations and ruses the lovers Rosamira and Dagoberto concoct to conceal the truth. In his relationship with Ana Franca, Cervantes would certainly not go to the same lengths as his fictional characters to conceal his love, but he concealed it nevertheless. And whereas Rosamira and Dagoberto's love was just, his for Ana Franca was clearly illicit.

His immediate concern was Ana Franca's pregnancy and how the true paternity could be concealed from her spouse. The reality of fatherhood forced a decision that cut short an illicit affair which obviously had no future. Spain's prestigious Order of Santiago refused membership to innkeepers, taverners, painters and practitioners of other 'vile' and 'lowly' trades.[33] Indeed, accounts of the period show that inns were notorious for their 'filth, vermin, noise and their dishonest clientele and owners'. Unfortunately, the bad reputation of inns and innkeepers spread to those who ran taverns, too. In Chapter 2 of *Don Quixote, Part One* Cervantes describes an Andalusian innkeeper 'as crafty a thief as Cacus' (Vulcan's son and a thief). The selfsame reference to Cacus is found in the 'Postscript' to the semi-autobiographical poem *Voyage to Parnassus*. Strictly speaking, a tavern in early modern Castile was a place licensed by the local government to sell wine; prices and profits were fixed and the tavern-keeper was required to keep accurate liquid measures and a stock of 'good' wine. The success of tavern-keepers varied enormously: in a populous area profits were to be made, and in all probability Ana Franca made a good living from her trade on account of a prime location.[34] Yet several Spanish writers at the time complain of tavern-keepers who regularly 'baptize', that is, add water to their wines. Both Cervantes and Quevedo attack the practice, which indeed became the norm after the introduction of the *millones* tax in 1590; watering the wine was the usual way to cut an eighth off the measure. Profitable or not, tavern-keeping was viewed as a menial task, close to the bottom of the socio-economic scale. The family of Ana Franca de Rojas could not, as that of Cervantes could, boast of a mention by the court chronicler Juan de Mena; in status and in name she was out of bounds to Cervantes.

The issue is not whether Isabel was his child, but why he married Doña Catalina de Palacios Salazar Vozmediano so soon after the liaison with Ana Franca and just one month after Isabel's birth in November 1584. Given that 19 November is the feast of St Isabel, it is probable that she was born on or near to that date. The affair with Ana Franca that occurred in January or February of that same year was clearly something that Cervantes preferred to keep a secret from his wife-to-be. To harbour such a secret was not the best way to enter a marriage, however. The problems so carefully outlined in his play *The Labyrinth of Love* seem to be ever nearer home as one accompanies Cervantes from Ana Franca to Catalina via Isabel. Those early biographies of Cervantes, which in the main tend to be hagiographies, do not discuss such issues. From today's viewpoint, however, such indiscretions are much less reprehensible and for some may even enhance an individual's worth, both in human and in moral terms. Nevertheless, after what must have been a very short engagement Cervantes, with secrets intact, married a girl half his age.

He had met Catalina in Esquivias, a town just off the main route linking Madrid and Toledo, where he had gone to arrange the posthumous publication of the poetical works of Pedro Laínez, a close friend of his who had died six months earlier, leaving behind a young widow, Juana Gaitán. When he arrived, he found Juana remarried to one Diego de Hondaro, the son of a businessman, something her contemporaries, especially to other noble families in her area, found somewhat shocking so soon after de Lainez's death. Not all, however, felt the same way. One of her trusted friends was Catalina de Palacios Salazar, a neighbour who was also recently widowed and who had been left with three children to support, one of them Cervantes' future wife, also named Catalina. Unfortunately for her, she inherited from her late husband, Fernando de Salazar Vozmediano, a catalogue of debts.

To compensate, however, she was left with smallholdings of olive trees and vineyards. If Cervantes had secrets, so did the mother of the girl he was so shortly to marry. There is frustratingly little documentation about the events leading to his marriage. What is known is that after only a few months of courtship they were married in the local church, the Holy Mary of the Assumption, on 12 December 1584. The officiating priest was Juan de Palacios, a maternal uncle of Catalina's. Cynics claim that Cervantes married out of personal gain, and there may well be a grain of truth in what they say. Although he did not know the limits of his wife's patrimony or the extent of her debts until after the wedding, he did have strong personal reasons for becoming a respectable husband. To evaluate his motives we have to reconcile the facts of his situation that led up to his marriage with our knowledge of his conduct in Algiers. We know that in captivity he was unselfish, scrupulously moral and prepared to die to save his friends and collaborators from Hasan Pasha's wrath. With regard to marriage, no doubt both he and Catalina saw personal benefits from it; most couples do.

Presumably Cervantes could have offered good reasons to explain his decision. Hard on the heels of his disillusionment with courtly life that preceded his short-lived affair with Ana Franca, he arrived in the tranquil backwaters of Esquivias. Thanks to a decree issued by the government of Philip II, we have a precise record of the geography, settlement pattern, occupations and population figures for Esquivias in 1584. Of incalculable value to urban and social historians, the Prudent Monarch ordered such information to be gleaned for all Spanish towns. From the census then taken it emerges that Esquivias was the home to noble families that had fallen on hard times; names such as Salazar, Ugena, Vozmediano and Cardenas appear and even a Quijada, a man of the church and distant relative of Catalina's. Is this name the origin for Cervantes' famous knight? Certainly the basic diet followed by the locals of Esquivias and catalogued in the text approximates to what Don Quixote generally ate; even the description of the bleak

Castilian environment in which only poor wine and oil are produced resembles the landscape that was the home to the foolhardy knight. With its village community, rural concerns and measured pace Cervantes would have experienced a welcome change from the frenzy of uncertainty he had known as a soldier, captive and court petitioner.

If there was one place Cervantes could nurture his muse, it was here in the heart of Castile and not far from his birthplace in Alcalá de Henares; here he could find a haven from court but remain reasonably close to it.[35] Did he perhaps believe that with Catalina he could erase the error of his illicit affair with Ana Franca and, more urgently, help both himself and Ana Franca to conceal the truth about Isabel? In the event, it seems that Alonso, Ana Franca's husband, accepted the daughter as his own. In other words, he was kept as much in the dark about the affair as was Catalina, although both in time were to discover the truth. But what did marriage offer Catalina? It offered her a man with a reputation, a glamorous past life, fame as a poet in the limelight of Madrid, not to forget his good looks, especially his *gracia*, that indefinable quality bordering on charisma which his closest friends claimed he possessed. All this would have appealed to a young girl in mourning from the loss of her father earlier that year. 'A woman that listens is lost,' the old proverb says, and in that briefest of courtships it may well be that his art of conversation – the occupation he missed most in captivity was 'civilized conversation' – despite his acknowledged stammer, may well have won her heart. Attractive and literate, yet vulnerable, easily touched by her elders and probably encouraged by the example of Juana, she would have found Miguel a prize catch. And so it was that they married. Their union has baffled biographers and readers of Cervantes ever since.

And yet in *La Galatea* there is a possible clue to Catalina's acceptance of marriage. We read that Rosaura, when she first saw Grisaldo, 'was beside herself' because 'the sight, the conversation, the worthiness' of the man made such a deep impression on her soul that he soon won the keys to her heart.[36] From the scant records we have of their

117

marriage it is more than possible that Cervantes had a similar effect on Catalina. Indeed from the lively and entertaining dialogues held between an astonishing array of couples in his text it is probable that Catalina may have been privy to an extraordinary courtship. Having married her, Cervantes may have believed that the traumas of jealousy associated with the alleged love affair in Naples were well behind him. Nevertheless, its poison was still to afflict several of his more famous creations.

The usual thing for a village girl like Catalina would have been to marry a man from within the community; in fact there were strong parochial pressures to do so. Such pressures did not arise out of xeno-phobia but out of one basic reality: when a local girl married an 'outsider' she took her dowry with her. This was not the case with Cervantes because he married into the community and stayed in his wife's home. Nevertheless, for her to marry an 'outsider' carried with it a possible stigma reflected in this proverb from León: 'One who goes afar to marry is deceived or is going to deceive.'[37] The question remains, however, did Cervantes deceive himself?

We know from the census that the Salazar Vozmediano family were of 'noble' stock, something, as we have seen, that cannot unequivocally be claimed of Cervantes' own. We know that during and after the Reconquest the Crown could, and often did, confer noble status, normally after some feat of 'service' to the king. By the reign of Charles V, privileges of nobility were openly sold to whoever could pay for them, as a means of increasing royal revenues. *Hidalguía* (noble status) was desirable because it conferred social prestige, immunity from direct royal taxation as well as certain legal privileges, such as the one Rodrigo de Cervantes, the writer's father, invoked when threatened with debtors' gaol. Domínguez Ortiz, the eminent Spanish historian, divides Castilian nobility of the Habsburg period into no fewer than five categories, ranging from powerful grandees and fabulously rich aristocrats to the impoverished but independent peasant struggling to survive.[38] We have already seen the struggle for survival that characterized Rodrigo's life; all trace of wealth had disappeared long before Cervantes was born. With regard to the Salazar family it is clear that similar conditions applied and that the household nestled precariously close to what Domínguez Ortiz calls the class of *labradores* (independent peasant farmers). This category of *hidalgo* usually owned no more land than he could work himself, but some of them became quite well-to-do, hiring labourers to work in fields under their supervision.

By definition, the *labrador* took a personal hand in the running of his farm, regardless of its size. If we now consider the role assigned to Cervantes by his mother-in-law, it is plain that the family were clinging on to the bottom of the five categories listed by Ortiz. This can be confirmed by comparing the findings of a census of 1558 for the town of Monleón in Salamanca with what we know of the situation in Esquivias. The population of Monleón was ninety-three, of whom five were nobles. Of these, two owned no property in the village; a third owned small flax fields, two meadows, two vineyards and a garden; a fourth nobleman owned only a few olive trees and one vineyard in addition to his house. Only one of the five called himself a *labrador* and owned 100 acres of land, one meadow, three enclosed arable fields, the house in which he lived and a house he rented out; he farmed with one pair of oxen and owned a dozen cows.[39] Although four beehives, a cockerel and forty-five hens were part of Catalina's substantial dowry, no mention is made of farm animals in the estate which Cervantes was to administer. Had there been more it would have been recorded. When Fernando de Salazar was alive it is probable that the land owned had been rented out to *jornaleros* (day-labourers), of which there were about a hundred in the town. Despite the coat of arms that adorned the imposing entrance to the Salazar family home, it is clear that enormous differences existed between members of the so-called nobility. Arguably, the family Cervantes married into could be ranked as *labrador*, although economically it stood side by side with the more humble commoners of the town.

Catalina had inherited land that was hers to use until her brothers came of age. As part of her dowry Catalina inherited some eleven and a half acres divided into six parcels of land that produced almonds, olives and vines; one piece was a small orchard and, given that it was called 'Pear Orchard', we can assume that is what grew there. In the light of this, it seems unlikely that Cervantes married for money. Such holdings were small and, according to David Vassberg, 'vineyards were the property of small peasants'. Indeed, land for orchards and viticulture had a far more egalitarian distribution than any other. In the early modern period, when the economy was largely geared to local self-sufficiency, vineyards and gardens had a far wider importance than they do today. The dowry tells us that the orchard 'was adjacent to the stream that came from the fountain and next to the alley that led to the church'. This is in keeping with sixteenth-century practice in which orchards were invariably situated in or near villages and typically on the banks of a stream or river. Such plots of land were intended to meet household or local market needs.

Little mention is made of the specific nature of Cervantes' administrative duties and nothing at all of the types of contracts, rent prices or yields expected from the lands owned by the Salazar family. Nevertheless, the family could not have escaped the effects of taxation, inflation, natural hazards or the problems of land utilization that characterized agricultural life in Golden Age Spain. Nor could it have escaped the gradual change from oxen to mule. Although this crucial technological change – as dramatic then as the change from the horse to the tractor and the motor car was in the twentieth century – is never mentioned in biographies of Cervantes, it would have had a direct bearing on farming practice and on land tenure in Esquivias. Because fields were becoming increasingly dispersed it was a crucial consideration when new lands were being brought into cultivation. The consequences of this one change in farm practice were far-reaching and relevant to every town and village council. [40]

Cervantes' recently widowed mother-in-law had no choice but to seek in her daughter the help she needed to bring up her two young sons, Francisco aged seven and Fernando aged three. Catalina, a faithful daughter, would have responded willingly, but all would have looked to her husband for guidance and financial support. Having five mouths to feed in a household of debts, it was obvious that earnings from writing would not suffice. Young Catalina lived in a house where she was simultaneously wife, daughter and sister. Clearly this was no easy task, yet the issue of divided loyalties is never mentioned; it must, however, have surfaced occasionally, especially when money matters came to the fore. In Seville there is record of a loan of 204,000 maravedís that Cervantes received from Gómez de Carrión on 2 December 1585 and therefore almost one year after his marriage, of which, on the 30th of that same month, he paid back 187,000. He was able to do so because he borrowed the same amount from Diego de Alburquerque and Miguel Ángel Lambias. Curiously, there is no mention of why such a large sum was borrowed or what it was for, although it is possible that it was used to pay debts. There is no record to state that either creditor was ever repaid, but the lack of any litigation suggests that they were.

Eight months later (and twenty since the marriage) Cervantes received the dowry, although he was slow in his turn to produce the one hundred ducats – the conventional contribution made by the groom – that he had promised Catalina. In fact twenty-one months passed before he handed over the money, a delay that has made some scholars conjecture that it was a payment for an agreement to separate.[41] Somewhat controversial, such a view may not be far from fact. Cervantes quickly uncovered a great deal about his new family, but how much did the Salazars know of his? More to the point, were they aware of his impoverished background? In a courtship of a few months one can be economical with the truth. Understandably Cervantes had no wish to imitate his wretched father, rushing throughout his married life from pillar to post seeking financial security.

Cervantes' situation was somewhat different in that he had no offspring and his wife had a home. It would have been easier for him to move to earn a living, no matter how personally inconvenient, than for the household to endure what his brothers and sisters had endured years before. Possibly, too, the newly-wed was already growing tired of adapting outwardly to those who could not share his literary interests. And, although rarely mentioned by commentators, there was always the potential for conflict arising from the generation gap. In employment away from home he could see a hidden bonus, that of the opportunity to read and to write, activities his new family could hardly be expected to share.

Whatever the situation was at home no one, not even in a backwater like Esquivias, was unaware of the impending crisis between Spain and England. It was known that Elizabeth was persecuting the Catholics at home while supporting the Protestants in France and in Scotland. She encouraged the revolt in the Low Countries and openly abetted the work of pirates, including those of Hawkins and Drake, making the latter an admiral after his exploits in the New World. Indeed Drake, ever since 1577, had been ransacking cities in Chile and Peru as well as in Puerto Rico and Santo Domingo, returning to Plymouth laden with silver. And yet Philip II dragged his heels. Some claim that he secretly admired Elizabeth. His three proposals of marriage to her demonstrate more than mere admiration, however. But, despite his earnest wooing of the Virgin Queen, his proposals foundered on the religious question.[42] Even when Pope Pius V excommunicated her and when the Catholics of Ireland and Scotland were pleading for his help, Philip II did not budge. But Santa Cruz, the greatest Spanish seaman of his day, did. He strongly urged the king, in January 1586, to launch an all-out attack on England, a plea he had previously advanced three years earlier. The Spanish monarch at last had begun to listen to Santa Cruz's advice, which soon became official policy, endorsed when Drake attacked Cádiz in April 1587.

It was love for his religion as well as pride that persuaded Philip II to intervene. He was determined to act and remove the Protestant threat once and for all. He possibly envisaged a repeat of Lepanto. If so, was not now the moment for Cervantes to plunge into the healing waters of action, to go to his second defence of the *patria* in the noble service of the king? A major decision was taken, one that would keep Spain's most famous author almost twenty years in what he later termed 'the silence of oblivion', during which time very little of his was published.[43]

We also know that in the month Drake attacked Cádiz the city of Toledo celebrated the transfer from Flanders of the relics of St Leocadia, the city's patron saint, and that the entourage had stopped in Esquivias on its way to Toledo. Given that on 28 April Cervantes, now in Toledo, duly signed over 'all powers' to his wife, consensus has it that he accompanied the entourage there from Esquivias.[44] Whether the transfer of relics served as an excuse to flee the home is debatable, but it was a timely convenience for him to pay tribute to a saint and execute his next, more permanent move, for he had heard the news that commissioners were needed to oversee supplies for the Armada and that there were vacancies in Seville. To the surprise of everyone Cervantes went to Seville – whether directly from Toledo is not clear – leaving his wife to administer the property, supported by Gaspar de Guzmán, a nephew of Cervantes and the one charged to tell Catalina of her husband's intentions.[45] Why did he allow his nephew to act on his behalf in matters of his estate, a task that Cervantes' mother-in-law had put trustingly into *his* entire care? The word trust is apt, because censuses of the period indicate that widowed women often continued to operate the family property and did so with the help of their children and/or hired workers. Catalina senior took the easier option, making the assumption that her son-in-law would settle down into his new home environment and revive the household's flagging income. How disappointed she must have felt when she learned of the document brought to them by Gaspar de Guzmán that proved, in her eyes and probably in those of her daughter, Cervantes' apparent abdication of responsibility.

The question arises as to how calculated this move was. There is no written evidence to show that his move had been pre-planned or that he had been biding his time until an opportunity arose to flee the nest. Despite the lack of documentation, there are those, such as Américo Castro, who believe that in marriage Cervantes was a skilful hypocrite. True or not, there is no denying that after only twenty-eight months of cohabitation Cervantes, in effect, moved out of the family home and became, like his unfortunate father before him, an itinerant on the highways of Spain. Had a gulf of misunderstanding arisen between the couple? Had Catalina discovered the existence of her husband's bastard daughter? Or to take a notion from Shakespeare's *As You Like It*: 'Maids are May when they are maids, but the sky changes when they are wives.'[46] In his flight – desertion? – to the south, Cervantes saw a way to support the household. For reasons strikingly similar to those of the Bard when he left his wife and family to travel south to London, Cervantes is convinced that he would serve his family best by removing himself from the roost.[47]

In a curious and little known work that discusses Cervantes' life as a military administrator, *Cervantes: Administrador Militar* (1879), it is indeed affirmed that 'dire financial necessity' drove Miguel to the 'colourful but oddly dangerous south of Spain'.[48] After all, what could Esquivias, a village in La Mancha under the jurisdiction of Toledo, offer him? Five of its 175 families were Morisco – William Byron makes the undocumented claim that there was a *converso* branch in Catalina's family tree – but more significant was the presence of thirty-seven noble families, whose details were recorded in the register compiled in 1584. Except for the poorest, most households managed to keep body and soul together but achieved little else. None, so it appears, grew rich from their holdings; even those of noble lineage found life a struggle. This we now know was also the situation of the Salazar family. Besides, there was more reason for concern: Catalina's mother was elderly and ill at the time and needed daily nursing. In the interim Catalina's two younger brothers were growing apace and saw in their sister a second mother. And we should not overlook the death in 1585 of Cervantes' father. It was clearly a factor, but little is said by commentators of his passing and of the psychological effect it had on his sons. When Cervantes laconically admits years later that 'other things took his attention', he was presumably referring to the increas-ing pressures of home life in Esquivias and that may have included the loan owed to his creditors. Demands at home clearly militated against all opportunity to write. Luck was against Cervantes, for it was about this time that Spain's most popular dramatist, Lope de Vega, labelled by Cervantes as 'that monster of nature', was sweeping all before him and was adulated by both the general public and, more importantly, by theatre managers.

In the prologue to *Persiles and Sigismunda* Cervantes, referring to Esquivias, points somewhat ironically to its 'illustrious lineages and . . . its very illustrious wines'. In plain words, the wines were of a higher category than the gentry. Catalina's inheritance fell short of her needs, even if the wine from her meagre vineyards was of superior quality. The fact that she had to sell land soon after her marriage proves that the household was struggling. The debts left to her widowed mother surely precipitated the sale of what would have fetched more had her property been located nearer to Madrid, Valladolid or Toledo or been sold twenty years earlier when Spain's economy was relatively buoy-ant. As administrator of her estate, much of Cervantes' work involved deferring payment of debts against it. It was he who had instigated the sale.

From the evidence to hand, it is clear that for Cervantes his idyll in the country was over. No matter how preoccupied he had been, his situation in Esquivias would have demonstrated that. He may well have remembered the common adage *pecuniam obediunt omnia* (all things obey money). He had no wish to imitate his father, and so, once money problems began to bite, he acted swiftly, for he was never one to procrastinate. Moreover, it was not only the household in Esquivias that needed money. As the father of Isabel, Cervantes was also obliged to meet her needs. We have also seen his impatience, a known character trait, that helps to explain his promptness of action. His departure from Esquivias is therefore the result of a cluster of factors to which we can safely add unrest in Spain and disquiet abroad.[49] In the light of such happenings, is there more behind the famous opening of *Don Quixote, Part One*, 'In a place in La Mancha, whose name I don't want to remember . . .'? Is Esquivias the place he no longer wants to recall?

It is ironic that in *La Galatea* the spring of the greatest suffering is that of separation, whether enforced or not. To be separated was a fate for lovers worse than death itself. How could Cervantes write so poignantly about the woes of separation that besieged so many of his beleaguered characters and yet in real life be the very instrument of its cause? His separation from the family home in Esquivias was to be a lasting reality, as his wife and her mother came to know all too well. The notion that Cervantes secretly missed his young wife is rarely raised, but that does not prove it did not occur.

The several sallies of his sorrowful knight, followed later by the incredible journeys of *Persiles and Sigismunda*, strongly suggest wanderlust; the impulse to travel, to seek adventure and to serve in a quest could never have been satisfied in a sedentary rural existence. Like his inimitable hero he was forever on the move, a man of action, always engaged in something and yet simultaneously within him was a voice crying for security and permanence. In short, whatever the real cause of his departure, we know that he moved south to take up employment for the Crown. Whichever role he had envisaged when returning from Italy, it was clearly not happening in the outpost of Esquivias. Rural community life had reduced the tempo and scope of his own and, more importantly, the exciting and challenging unpredictability of his life before his marriage was absent. Things, probably for both parties, had not matched expectations. His family's debts had to be met, and to be able to meet them he had to move out.

5
PRECARIOUS YEARS IN ANDALUSIA
(1586–90)

It is all too easy nowadays to forget what journeys by road then entailed; the trip to Seville from Esquivias took ten days by horse and coach. The route passed through Toledo, Ciudad Real and Almodóvar del Campo on its way south, a route that Cervantes came to know as well as any muleteer. On such and similar journeys every third day was a rest day. Ten days in which to take stock of the decision to leave behind a young if not vulnerable wife and a sick mother-in-law in order to try his luck as a government agent collecting oil, wheat and barley in support of the war effort against Protestant England. His yearned return to Spain had not brought the rewards that his credentials once promised. Thanks to his connections he had obtained the post of commissioner and begun a career that compelled him to examine social, ecclesiastical and civic institutions and the manner in which they impacted on the realities of everyday life for millions of Spaniards in Habsburg Spain. It would prove to be a fraught existence and no less burdensome than his life as a soldier and a captive.

His missions taught him that Castile was a rural society with over 80 per cent of its population living in villages or small towns and that they owed their livelihood to crops or livestock. Even the great cities of Castile were parasites on the agro-pastoral economy, for there was little industry. From the outset, it should be said that the society he lived in and describes so vividly in his diverse works depended to an unprecedented extent on the changing laws governing property and land use in sixteenth-century Castile, an area much bigger than that of today.[1] Administratively, Castile included all of peninsular Spain except for the kingdoms of Aragón and Navarre. Over such a wide area conditions varied considerably, and it is precisely these local and regional differences that he was to meet on a daily basis when he lived in the 'silence of oblivion'.[2]

He would have known of the stream of reforms ushered in by Philip II during the summer of 1586, which continued until the launch of the Armada in May 1588. Apart from much-needed measures to improve the recruitment system and the procurement of munitions, a major aspect of such reforms was to find a 'way to organize provisioning without so many complaints against the purveyors and their officials'.[3] It was this aspect which had direct effect on the activities of Cervantes. The Prudent Monarch instigated schemes to enable the cities of Andalusia to agree to provide fixed quantities of their harvests and to empower town councils to buy the grain and act as guarantors of payment. More importantly, the king wanted municipalities to establish official grain quotas in accordance with the capacity of each village. New biscuit-baking ovens were set up in Málaga and Lisbon. The victualling requirements of the Armada called for twice the amount of wheat normally procured by the Castilian military commissariat in Andalusia in an ordinary year, a quantity itself considerably increased since 1580, and three times the amount of wine, in addition to all the provisions brought from Sicily, Naples and other parts of Castile. These demands were all the more difficult to meet because the 1587 harvest was poor and the fear of embargo or English interception inhibited grain shipments from the Baltic. The price of biscuit – the single largest expense in the operation of the galley-ship – quadrupled between 1529 and 1587.[4] Ultimately, the failure of the Armada arose not because of procurement but by the erosion of supplies by delay, wastage and fraud, with dire consequences for several commissioners.[5]

Known to Cervantes, but overlooked by biographers, were the enormous differences in the life experiences of 'average' Spaniards, owing to traditions and customs that arose as a result of the Reconquest.[6] Land was owned by the Crown, the Church, the nobility, the military orders and the peasant, and for each class different rules and regulations often applied. Any misunderstanding of such differences led to aggravations and recriminations; an important achievement of Cervantes was the role he played in reconciling these various interests and yet obtaining the quotas he set out to collect. In this interplay of conflicting interests, he showed his mettle and won the support and admiration of his superiors, while some of his colleagues were dismissed, imprisoned or even executed.[7] Just as in Algiers, Cervantes, while a civil servant, employed his powers of persuasion to cope with a thankless task. He came to know intimately a world of contrasting social orders from the seemingly anarchic world of life in towns and big cities – especially Seville – to the almost medieval parish existence of life in an Andalusian village. Consequently, he had to be aware of his social context, and his grasp of the historical moment in which he moved was to help him not only as a civil servant but also later as a writer. His astute observations of major socio-politico-historical happenings constitute the backbone of that subtle synthesis – a blend of historical fact and poetical truth – which inform his major works.[8] His literary achievements, which owe much to his forgotten years away from the court in Madrid, grew out of a social and historical reality he knew better than most of his peers. To understand Cervantes, to place him and his works in context, we, too, have to penetrate that reality. His early travels on the roads of Spain followed by his work as a Crown agent help to establish his context, but it was the laws and decrees promulgated by the War Office and various royal councils that formed the social realities which his office forced him to deal with.[9] Subject to the same government edicts as his contemporaries, he was yet instrumental in enforcing them in the villages and townships he entered.

We know little of what he knew of local and regional politics, and his experience of accountancy and budgets and the procedures that go with them was clearly limited, but his knowledge of both was evidently sufficient for him to assist in an enterprise of national importance on which the king was staking his reputation. Given that the Armada was a military campaign and that Cervantes had spent over ten years 'at war', if we include his time in Algiers, he must have believed that he had the necessary credentials.[10] His willingness to serve his king, country and God never came into question. Moreover, in his easy sociability he struck a deep chord in his associates; a certain affability that was innate rather than acquired. His natural charm and sense of fair play would be sorely tested and had to compensate for occasional 'errors' in accounting.[11] All too often he would have to smooth over the grim resistance of local authorities to meet his quotas. He also understood that the provisions he collected went to keep soldiers such as his brother alive, a powerful incentive, as he knew that soldiers all too often suffered shortfalls. The zeal he had already displayed against the infidel at Lepanto was to resurface in his post as purveyor for the Armada.

Before starting his government post he spent four months in Seville in the opulent home of his boyhood friend Tomás Gutiérrez, a retired actor who owned one of the most fashionable hotels in the city and was responsible for the contact that landed Cervantes his commission. Several of the hotel guests were noblemen, captains, viceroys and governors in transit to or from the New World. In Seville the talk was about the rising power of the English, Drake's daring raids on Spanish shipping and Elizabeth's growing opposition to Spain; but most of the gossip would have centred on Spain's offensive, their massive *Armada Invencible* for which he was now to collect provisions.

In a ruler as manifestly powerful as Philip II, the desire for retribution took on added significance when news broke of the Treaty of Nonsuch in August 1585, which committed Elizabeth to provide aid to Philip's rebellious subjects in the Netherlands. With the recent success of the annexation of Portugal to his credit and with the diplomatic truce of 1578 with the Ottomans still in force, Philip II, aware of the sharp increases in remittances of silver from the mines of Peru and Mexico, could now turn his attention from the Mediterranean to the Atlantic. His decision to do so proved to be a key event in the history of naval warfare and a decisive moment in the historic shift in the balance of power. In what historians term the 'Atlanticization' of war, the conflict with England was to alter for ever the framework of association, not only between Castile and the rest of the peninsula but between Spain and the so-called Mediterranean kingdoms.[12]

Drake's raid on Cádiz, which followed hard on the heels of Mary Queen of Scots' execution, had been the last straw. Indeed, after Drake's raid on Galicia in 1585, Zúñiga, the senior adviser to Philip, drew up an important strategic assessment, the drift of which advocated the conquest of England.[13] Outside her borders Spain flaunted military supremacy, but at home, as Drake's daring had proved, she was almost defenceless.[14] If we accept that for Spain the most significant military operation of the first half of Philip's reign had been the suppression of the Morisco revolt in Granada, which may be seen as the continuation of the feudal wars of the Reconquest, the king's present task was, by comparison, gargantuan. In the shadow of the campaign against England he was compelled to revolutionize his nation's military organization, so he created the Council of War and the Secretariat for War. The need to rationalize the administration had grown ever since the annexation of Portugal; fighting wars was one thing but to manage the bureaucracy it entailed was another, and Philip took every measure to galvanize the huge machinery of state to prepare for the invasion of England. Just as the entire nation had united to clear the land of the Moors – a campaign of almost eight centuries – and had united to defeat the Turk at Lepanto, so once again Spain was being urged to unite behind an enterprise common to all. Álvaro de Bazán, Marqués de Santa Cruz – whom Cervantes describes in 'The Captive's Tale' as 'that thunderbolt of war' – was chosen by Philip to lead the Armada, and he envisaged some '94,000 men and some 510 vessels of 110,000 tons, 46 galleys and galleons' racing to British shores to bring the Virgin Queen to her knees.[15] Flushed by his success in the Azores (1582) the stalwart marquis had urged the king as early as 1583 to invade England.[16] Gradually, the conquest of

Protestant England was seen to be the sole means of guaranteeing imperial security. Despite his seventy-three years, the campaign envisaged by Santa Cruz, had it gone to plan, would indeed have proved 'invincible', as the Vatican suggested it would be. This stupendous fleet was greater than the entire Christian force at Lepanto and twice the number that had conquered Portugal in 1580. But the proverbial slip between cup and lip was to prove its – and the monarch's – undoing. Such an undertaking required men, supplies, equipment, armaments and support. The war effort, which in the event included the feeding of over 30,000 soldiers for some eight months, required the highest organization and diligence. How seriously anybody took the plan we cannot say, but it is clear that it was not acted upon. The blueprint as it stood was a logistical impossibility, and Philip had no choice but to scale it down. A special junta set up late in December 1586 was instructed to find 7 million ducats for the following year to meet the expenses of what some chroniclers began to call the Enterprise of England and which included costs for the regiments in Flanders. In other words, the Armada was to be a shared strategic effort. From the summer of 1586 until the eventual launch in 1588, Philip rushed through a spate of reforms – the division of the secretariat of war, the expansion of the War Council, the appointment of military governors in Galicia and Andalusia – and he also created a new office for recruitment. It was a mammoth task, and every able-bodied Spaniard was expected to play his part.

Drake's fireships in Cádiz harbour had destroyed some 10,000 tonnes of goods, an attack which Elizabeth claimed she had not ordered. Now no more than an item on the calendar of events in Andalusia for the year 1587, the loss of so much food was sorely felt by the Seville Commissariat. Cervantes, because of his work, knew better than most what the loss entailed. Seville was the main centre for the provisioning of the galleys, the North African garrisons, the Indies fleets and the Atlantic galleons. From Seville, purveyors and commissaries radiated outwards, sweeping up local supplies and preparing the way for the passage of troops from Italy and Germany into Portugal. As much as one-third of Spain's domestic military budget was spent by the various purveyors based in Seville and its outports. To exemplify the type of operations in which they were involved it has been estimated that military purchases in Seville 'rose from 3,000 to 4,000 ducats a year in 1576–7 to between 600,000 and 1 million in the 1580s and 1590s, the equivalent of one-quarter to one-third of the demand generated from the New World'. In brief, military demands placed a real strain on the agricultural production of the region and on wheat in particular.[17] Wheat and barley were requisitioned at the *tasa*, the legal maximum price, and other produce at a price adjudged to be fair by the purveyors. Both procedures entailed large losses to the producers and were in effect covert forms of taxation. Data for the years between 1582 and 1600 demonstrate that, for eleven out of those eighteen years, the wheat *tasa* was exceeded. Moreover, there were several complaints of underpricing made by foreign merchants whose goods were requisitioned, and thus it became necessary to grant exemptions in order to induce shippers to continue to come to Spanish ports. These conditions were aggravated by non-payment. In December 1584, that is, not long before Cervantes joined the commissariat, 'no less than 454,000 ducats were owed for supplies, transport and labour contracted between 1574 and 1582 by the purveyor in Seville'.[18] These debts had still not been paid off by September 1586, the year Cervantes began his tours of office. Credits were being traded at 25 and 30 per cent discounts, but, when payment was eventually made, the treasury refused to pay more than the discounted price. Such practices served to militate against the policy of fair play that Cervantes as a purveyor endeavoured to pursue.

Supported by Diego de Valdivia, the head of the commissariat in Seville and a friend of Gutiérrez, Cervantes' primary task was to collect foodstuffs. Empowered to confiscate goods, to intercept merchandise in transit, to impose fines, to send dodgers to prison, to search properties and force doors and locks if need be, his modern image is very much that of a tax-collector-cum-policeman. He was given funds to pay muleteers, coachmen, scribes, messengers and day workers, but he had no right to pay the farmers who produced the supplies; they were paid by a different arrangement, although Cervantes had to write their bill of exchange. Once in his possession, he had to weigh the grain, store it or transport it to be milled. Although able to dispose of considerable amounts of money, he received no salary until after the conclusion of each mission. This meant that he had to finance himself for several months before receiving payment that, if it came, came late and sometimes less than the sum agreed on. A far cry from poetry and courtly circles, it was an onerous task but one, as later reports confirmed, he did to the best of his ability. His innate patriotism saw to that.[19]

His first assignment, undertaken in September 1587, was to Écija. Known in former times by the Greek name of Astyg or Astir, it was referred to colloquially as 'the frying pan' of Andalusia. Home to a population of 8,000, it was at the time the only place in Spain that produced cotton. Designated a town in 1402, in the reign of Henry III (called 'the Mournful' by historians), it could boast of six parish churches, twelve monasteries and eight convents, twelve fountains, as well as several hospitals which Philip II had converted into one. A strongly held tradition has it that St Paul had once preached there. A line drawing of 1567 shows Écija as a walled city with four town gates and an Arab quarter. It was a tightly knit community, watered by the river Genil that flows into the Guadalquivir. The eleven-arched bridge that spans the river gives way, at either end, to some of the richest farmland in Spain. Famed for its olives, oil, barley, wheat, wines and honey, its rural setting and lifestyle must have closely resembled those described in pastoral novels. It even boasted silk and weaving, but it was for oil and wheat that Cervantes was sent. Yet, in carrying out the king's orders, he was drawn into a situation that spiralled out of control. Sent to collect wheat for an enterprise of national importance he was dragged into a dispute with the Church – the biggest landowner in

Écija – for he insisted on collecting wheat from where it was readily available. Cervantes knew he had to use tact because recent harvests had been poor and, what was worse, the townspeople had not been paid for a previous requisition. Resistance to collectors was therefore to be expected, and when Diego de Valdivia, Cervantes' superior and assistant to Antonio de Guevara, the leader of the entire commissariat, refused the townspeople their request for more time Cervantes had no option but to take available wheat from granaries and that meant from the richer landowners, including some prebendary canons. His motives were just, but the Church saw his action as an attack and reacted bitterly. Within one month of Cervantes' new job, the deacon of Seville had him banished from the fold. A harsh decision, especially when by law every Spaniard had to be a member of the Church. He took little consolation from the fact that both Charles V and Philip II had suffered excommunication twice.

With news of his excommunication posted to the doors of the parish church, and possibly to every church door in the diocese, Cervantes, with a job still to be done, promptly appealed against the decision, no easy matter in the circumstances. After Écija he went to La Rambla, another community that was being asked to give foodstuffs twice in the same year. Denied unfettered access and amid local uproar he asked Diego de Valdivia to intervene. Breaking Diego de Valdivia's promise not to burden the villagers, the chief commissioner in Andalusia left Cervantes, yet again, to fend for himself; in the bickering that ensued he had no alternative but to send several villagers to prison. In an aside to Sancho, his master Don Quixote once tells him that 'there's no peasant who keeps his word if he finds it doesn't suit him'.[20] Cervantes was to learn the cunning of rural communities but was clearly tolerant of peasants, who were at once his victims and his persecutors. He then moved on to Castro del Río, the town where later he would spend his first spell in an Andalusian gaol.

A watercolour of Castro del Río dating from the mid seventeenth century shows the town built on a hill overlooking the river Guadajoz.

An ideal location for a fortress, the town was constructed around a Moorish castle. Divided into two parts, one on top of the hill, the other at its foot, its population was protected by a wall that had two main gates. The gate to the north connected the castle to the main town via an arch. With a delightful parish church, several hermitages, a Carmelite monastery and a hospital founded in 1577, Cervantes would have found a thriving community living in a Moorish citadel that had been extensively repaired in the mid-1460s. Similar to Écija in its fertility, the region around Castro del Río, with some 1,500 inhabitants, was famed for its orchards, olives, livestock, wheat and barley, and it was the latter two commodities Cervantes went to requisition. [21] It was also a town where the farmsteads (*cortijos*) were owned by absentee landlords, mainly the nobility who lived in Córdoba, so the cliché that Andalusia was dominated by the large estates of the nobility found adequate proof here. Typically, too, there were sizeable ecclesiastical lands in the town, a fact that was a source of concern to taxpayers because these privileged estates were exempt from many forms of taxation. Whether this entered the purveyor's calculation or not no one knows, but after assessing the situation with the local constabulary and town elders Cervantes decided to ask the Church to give most, and the result was a second excommunication. He also made the mistake of having the town's sacristan, who resisted the requisition, hauled off to gaol for non-compliance.

Whether instructed to or not, he acted wisely in consulting the local dignitaries (councillors, constabulary, landowners and church officials) mainly because of Philip II's known policy of selling township status. As the need for more finances increased, the monarch extended the sale of municipal government to even the smallest towns and villages. In fact, between 1581 and 1600 more than 400 populations were involved, forty-four of them within the jurisdiction of Seville alone.[22] Such sales resulted in the mass transfer of control over communal lands and the village economy from annually elected village councils to proprietary 'village tyrants'. The effect was to undermine the corporate dominance of the cities over their hinterlands and with it the security of their food supplies. Whether Philip foresaw it or not, such a sales policy was to have a major effect on city life in the seventeenth century. The street urchins and the peasants portrayed by Murillo in the mid seventeenth century are graphic reminders of the effects of such a policy. In his playlet *The Election of the Councillors of Daganza*, Cervantes clearly draws on his own dealings with aldermen and local dignitaries and, while poking fun at men with ambition but who clearly lack the intelligence to match their aspirations, he also attacks aspects of official administration led by Philip II.[23]

An important spin-off of these missions was a knowledge of Spain and of the daily lives of its inhabitants that few contemporary writers could equal. In his official capacity he had to strike up contacts and contracts with all strata of society; the theme of his conversation was not the latest play or poetry competition but the state of the harvest, the quota and the value of commodities. In brief, money and military matters dictated his life on the roads of Spain. How he turned his contacts with officialdom into the brisk and often cheeky exchanges between colourful characters in his works – seen particularly well in his playlets – is therefore all the more commendable. His knowledge of routes and wayside inns is demonstrated in the lively conversations between Sancho Panza and Don Quixote as they journey to the villages and towns of Andalusia and of La Mancha. The inns of Spain were notoriously bad and attracted more undesirables than honest citizens. Above all, the food, if provided, was often extremely poor.[24] Municipal ordinances prohibited innkeepers from selling foodstuffs; that was a privilege reserved for those who held monopoly concessions from the local government. Such a system militated against overnight stays for travellers, and so, in 1560, Philip II allowed inns to provide food and drink. But not all did so: many towns and villages retained their monopolistic ordinances and travellers throughout the seventeenth century continued to complain about restrictions. Not alone in his criticisms, the famous French traveller Barthelémy Joly, who journeyed extensively in Spain between 1603 and 1604, describes the wretched conditions in Spanish inns.[25] In fairness to innkeepers, their main priority was to supply food and a resting-place for animals; providing for humans was very much a sideline. In some of the inns visited by Don Quixote the food served was very unpalatable; but not all inns were bad; in several of the *Exemplary Novels* there are examples if not of wholesome company at least of better food.[26]

After four months on the road Cervantes had still not received his pay. For his labours he bore the stigma of a double excommunication, had incurred the wrath of farmers despite his attempts to act justly – something which cannot be said for many of the agents at the time – and he was left without any income. The quartermaster claimed that he had no funds to pay salaries – which would have been grim news indeed – and Cervantes had to wait. It was not to be the only time that his lawful earnings would be paid in arrears, and the delays he and Rodrigo had suffered when soldiers in Italy had resurfaced.

One happier encounter Cervantes made during his first commission was a visit to Cabra to renew contact with Andrés and his son Rodrigo, whom Cervantes now enlisted as his assistant, and both went to La Rambla and to Córdoba gathering foodstuffs for the Armada. Documents show that Rodrigo assisted Cervantes until April 1588 and that he 'represented Cervantes in connection with certain church documents to do with [Cervantes] having arrested a sacristan in Castro del Río', but thereafter Rodrigo disappears from the scene.[27] Later documents prove that he went off to become a soldier in 1602 after which he receives no further mention.[28] After work in La Rambla and Córdoba Cervantes returned to Seville on 10 January 1588. His respite in Cabra was now behind him and he had to await further instructions. The news that Lope de Vega, Spain's rising dramatic genius, had been exiled from the court of Madrid for eight years and from the kingdom of Castile for two years for libelling a former mistress, Elena Osorio, would have brought him no consolation.[29] The most popular and prolific of all Spanish playwrights, he had been Cervantes' major rival when both men were competing for theatre space. Lope de Vega decided to go to Valencia and could be said to have relocated the centre of Spanish theatre with him. Cervantes had been wise to turn his attention to other matters. Despite his work as a civil servant, Cervantes, at the start of 1588, found himself without money. How could he continue to requisition without the means to support himself?

Many claim that Philip II's overriding objective with the Armada was not to conquer England but to stop English interference in his affairs.[30] In addition he wished to compel Elizabeth to withdraw from the Netherlands, from the Indies and from support of the Portuguese pretender. If he could force the Virgin Queen to concentrate her forces for her own protection and, if possible, reduce her fleet or a part of it to permanent coastguard duties that would involve her in heavy defence expenditures, his enterprise would have been worth while. The panic that swept through England every time there was a whisper of a concentration of Spanish shipping helped his cause. Cervantes would have remembered how rumour of a Spanish attack had occasionally swept through Algiers, inducing a similar sense of panic that sometimes led to dire consequences for the captives. Rumour could be a powerful ally in times where an uneasy peace overlay frantic and often clandestine negotiations. Every month that passed was costing Philip 700,000 ducats, and the diversion of resources from Seville to Lisbon was disastrous for the Indies trade. With clear overtones of Machiavelli's statecraft, the Venetian ambassador's words of advice to Philip II, 'vigorous preparations for war are the surest way to secure favourable terms of peace', encouraged the Spanish monarch to launch his fleet in an all-out attempt to parade a massive show of strength.[31] In this Philip clearly shows his debt to a society that had been founded on display and spectacle. If he could convince the enemy that his Armada was as powerful as rumour made it, he might succeed without firing a single cannon. Besides, such a show of military power would perhaps galvanize dormant English Catholics to rise up against Elizabeth. And if fighting took place it would be on land,

and Spain would undoubtedly win. Such diplomacy made sense to a man reputedly 'as afraid of war as a child was of fire'.[32]

Although spring was considered the best season to launch a fleet, the inevitable delays associated with such a mighty enterprise took their toll, and when summer had passed Philip II suggested September. Agreement was reached to set sail in January – Santa Cruz had opposed the date but was outvoted – and high expectations of a victory to surpass even that of Lepanto filled the air. However, more delays meant that more months of waiting ensued, and, amid these frantic preparations for war, the death was announced on 9 February 1588 of the Marqués of Santa Cruz, the most able Spanish seaman of his day. His loss was followed nine days later by the beheading of Mary Stuart. After such a long incarceration the cruel death of Mary outraged Catholics everywhere, especially those in Spain who were very fond of their Catholic 'sister'. Elizabeth's inhumane conduct made Philip II and his subjects doubly determined to bring her to justice.[33] There are those who claim that Philip wanted to hand Elizabeth over to the Pope, who then would have passed her on to the Inquisition. The restoration of Catholicism in England clearly animated the Spanish monarch's campaign, but there were other factors, too.

The Duke of Medina Sidonia, who seems to have been totally inexperienced in naval warfare, was chosen as the new leader of the fleet. Nicknamed 'the Duke of Tuna', on account of the wealth he acquired from the tuna fisheries in Andalusia, a major base of which was Cádiz, Philip's choice carried the logic of the wounded. The Duke was aware of the damage that Drake's fireships had done to the port and of the panic that the attack inevitably provoked. Who better, therefore, than he to retaliate and from Seville, now in its prime and by far the most opulent city in the Iberian Peninsula? The Duke's sincere pleas of incompetence fell on deaf ears. This was because Philip's enemies were goading and ridiculing him. In March 1588 the ministers of Henry III of France 'announced publicly that his fellow monarch and chief rival Philip II was mad'. The grand chancellor assured his awed dinner guests in Paris that while Philip's councillors debated state affairs his eldest daughter, Isabel, was 'signing documents and in control of government'.[34] Philip was not unaccustomed to malicious rumour spreading from France; more painful to his innate pride, however, was the taunt that he, the ruler of half the known world, was at the mercy of a woman, Elizabeth, the mistress of half an island.[35] The love that had made him pen three petitions of marriage to Elizabeth had, with the raid on Cádiz, turned to an all-consuming rage. Philip therefore placed all his confidence in the Duke of Medina Sidonia, a choice criticized later by several historians.

In support of his choice, Philip could argue that it was the duke who, in his capacity as captain-general of Andalusia, had given advice on the best way to raise provisions, had led troops in 1580 to receive the submission of the Portuguese Algarve and who had been involved in very delicate diplomatic relations with the Barbary States. He had also been the one who had voiced the need to control the North African coast and who had deliberated on such vital strategic issues as the advisability of dispatching a flotilla to New Spain in 1587. Furthermore, the Duke of Medina Sidonia was one of the richest noblemen in Spain; he had money and a following, and Philip II badly needed both. It is known that the duke contributed some 8 million maravedís of his own money towards the costs of the Armada. But in the appointment of the 'Duke of Tuna' there was yet one major trump card that Philip knew he could play. His chosen leader had valuable contacts with England and was known to be a great protector of the English merchant colony in Andalusia. Proof of this was seen in the contact he made with the Earl of Leicester over the purchase of tin and copper for artillery for his estates. Philip compelled the duke to break off all negotiations with such 'manifest heretics', and he did so – although six years later we find that he still has agents in England who buy wheat for shipment to Spain.[36] According to some, the real reason why Philip chose Medina Sidonia was because the duke was married to Ana de Silva y Mendoza, the illegitimate daughter of the king's alleged liaison with the Princess of Éboli. This liaison is discounted as absurd in a recent biography of Philip II by Henry Kamen and played down by Spanish historians partial to the king, but at the time the affair and its consequences seem to have been common knowledge.[37]

In fairness to Philip, whom else could he have chosen to lead his fleet? Few had the Duke of Medina Sidonia's varied administrative experience or his wealth and personal influence. The fact that within three months he was able to put the fleet to sea was no small achievement. Granted that Spain's war effort in the Atlantic depended, *inter alia*, on the grain, men and the shipping of Andalusia, he was the right man to choose to mobilize the region's resources. Whatever foreign observers may have thought about his choice of leader – chosen five days after the unexpected death of Santa Cruz – Philip never withdrew his confidence from his reluctant leader. Medina Sidonia's reluctance to lead the attack against England and his deep fears of the outcome are clearly expressed in his letter to Philip, who, in his reply, written in his own hand, rejects all talk of incompetence, lack of experience, sea sickness or the ill-preparedness of the fleet. What the Duke of Medina Sidonia was not privy to was the letter Philip sent in secret to the Duke of Parma in which the king set out his conditions in the event of a peace being struck with the enemy. In essence Philip wanted Catholics in England to be able to practise their religion freely and for Elizabeth to return the towns and cities 'lost' to Spain in the Low Countries together with compensation for damages. In such demands we see clear signs of Philip's absolutist rule in Castile.[38]

By the time the Duke of Medina Sidonia sailed in May with a fleet far smaller than first planned we learn that Cervantes' two hasty excommunications had been repealed in February and March and he was already into his third mission in Écija, where he somehow had restored harmony and goodwill with the townspeople. This is indeed remarkable, for near the end of the reign of Philip II records show that the *corregidor* (Crown official and leader of a municipality) of Écija noted that many fields of the area were no longer planted and blamed this on the high cost of labour. This arose out of inflation but more accurately arose out of the system whereby the king had imposed the *tasa* without regard for wages. It is often overlooked that many of the hired labourers in Andalusia at the time Cervantes was on his rounds were migrant workers, belonging to what were termed poor *labradores* who had to spend over half the year working in the south. As the economic situation worsened many became homeless vagabonds.[39] Concern about labour unrest, price inflation and the implementation of the *tasa* must have given Cervantes many a headache. On this occasion he seems to have coped, a feat that reminds us of his skill and competence, character attributes not often mentioned when his life as a civil servant is discussed. However, as often in his life, success was often tinged with sadness, and on 1 May 1588 he learned of the death of his mother-in-law.[40] The fact that she excluded him totally from her will suggests that relations between them had soured, maybe because he had not sent one penny home to his struggling wife, who was left lonelier than ever. But he was too poor to return, even if he had so wished. Besides, how could he possibly send what he himself had not received?

In June he received a payment of one month's salary but was still owed ten months' wages. While in Écija he discovered that a good part of the grain collected the previous year had fallen foul of the grubs. His endless journeys on the back of a mule or horse, his protracted negotiations and unsought disputes about payments and quotas were all nullified by weevils. The setback provided him and the townsfolk with one more reason for the bickering and wrangling to continue, and so they did until April 1589 when Cervantes' first series of commissions came to an end. Meanwhile the Armada had floundered off British coasts, beaten more by mismanagement and bad weather than by the superior forces of the enemy.

There is no record to show that either Cervantes or Medina Sidonia were aware of the little-known report of Don Francisco de Bobadilla sent on 20 August to Philip's minister of state, Don Juan de

Idiáquez, in which the several deficiencies of the Armada as a fighting force are spelled out.[41] It did nothing to deter Philip, who saw in the duke a commander able to launch the campaign which, once under way, would be handed over to Parma and his troops. If Philip had any premeditated strategy, this was it. In their hasty deliberations, after months of procrastination and setbacks, little thought was given to contingencies. Conditions in the North Atlantic are very different from those in the calmer eastern Mediterranean. The known unpredictability of weather in the English Channel were to scupper Philip's best-laid plans and intentions. Even with favourable weather conditions and knowing what Bobadilla knew, success was scarcely possible; the fleet departed undermanned and under-equipped. Recent research shows rather that the Armada was at such a decisive disadvantage in firepower, in both weight of shot and range, that 'it was probably incapable of winning the sea-battle on whatever terms it was fought'.[42] It is now clear that the two fleets were equipped precisely for their chosen tactical roles, the English to keep the action at long range, the Spanish to close, batter and board. With what we already know of Cervantes at Lepanto it is clear that Spain's tactics had not changed with the changing conditions. And yet, when it came to close combat as witnessed in the final day-long engagement off Gravelines, it was not the English but the Spanish fleet that was shattered by the close bombardment.

The helpless Parma, commander in the Low Countries, was forced to flee, and several Spanish vessels sank off the Irish coasts; it was the winds of God, not English cannon or cunning, which caused the campaign to fail. Such is the official Spanish explanation and, with regard to the weather and tides at least, it finds support from records in the Meteorological Office in London.[43]

Successive violent storms and the timely launching of fireships off Calais certainly caused disarray among the Spanish fleet. Link these events to the English fleet's knowledge of local conditions in and around the Channel and we discover the cause of the loss of the bulk of the fleet which led to the English victory. Besides, as hindsight shows, ultimate success depended on Medina Sidonia 'joining hands' with the Duke of Parma. It did not happen, and so no invasion of England took place. Chance had played a role in the enterprise, a factor that Philip and his advisers seem not to have considered. Had Philip read Chapter 25 of Machiavelli's *The Prince* he would have found ample instruction on the influence of 'fortune' on war and statecraft.

While captured Spanish ensigns were on show in London over Traitors' Gate and at Paul's Cross, the despondent Medina Sidonia was met on his return with jeers from street urchins. Although it was Philip who had given priority to precedence over military valour, it was the unfortunate duke who suffered the shame. He had not lost face with the king, however, who immediately dreamed of a second Armada. Philip's desire for revenge was a natural reaction, but one wonders whether his tightly knit and well-established spy network had mentioned in their regular dispatches that the rage in the 1580s in England – and allegedly the most influential play in sixteenth-century England – was Thomas Kyd's masterpiece of revenge, *The Spanish Tragedy*.[44] Such irony would not have been lost on Cervantes, who had left Seville in May 1590 to go to Madrid. He no doubt, too, would have winced at the folly of such a dream in a century that had seen little else but the spectre and misery of conflict. But empires are posited on wars, and so long as Philip II kept at the helm the nation would follow.

Formerly censured by Spanish historians for his role in the defeat, the Duke of Medina Sidonia is now treated far more leniently, if not justly.[45] He was a reluctant pawn in the widening arena of Spanish military administration in an age when the interconnections between war and the development of government were being defined. War as a social and economic phenomenon severely affected those state institutions and finances that were relevant to the activities undertaken by Cervantes when in the employ of the Crown. As his two poems about the Armada show, he eagerly followed the events that surrounded the Duke of Medina Sidonia's campaign against the English. As an ex-soldier, who had seen action on the waves he, more than many around him, knew the enormity of the task faced by the duke and most probably sympathized with his reluctance to step into the shoes of Santa Cruz. His subsequent despondency at the outcome – there is no excuse for what heaven decrees – was typical of a patriotic Spaniard. Even the adversaries of Spain shared Philip's belief that God would decide the outcome.[46]

Amid galloping inflation, surging labour costs, shortages of essential materials, such as timber and hemp, and the ruin of crops in the south caused by freak storms, there was something prophetic in the sung proclamation in Seville Cathedral on 4 May 1589 of the gift to the city of an alleged thorn from Christ's crown. To a monarch whose inscription on a medal struck in 1580 read *non sufficit orbis* (the world is not enough), the defeat of the Armada was humiliating, deepened by the political unrest in Catalonia, Aragón and in Portugal in that same year. The euphoria that had surrounded the monarch with the annexation of Portugal in 1580 – an event sung by the soldier-poets Fernando de Herrera, Alonso de Ercilla and by Francisco de Aldana, whose verses were widely circulated at the time – turned to the disillusionment of crisis management. Philip was now compelled to make hard strategic choices. Projects such as the invasion of China and the repeated efforts of the Portuguese to conquer Sri Lanka were, as Parker explains, jettisoned. 'Within Europe', he continues, 'his failure to provide substantial and sustained support to Tyrone's rebellion in Ireland ranks as perhaps the greatest lost strategic opportunity of the 1590s.'[47] When Pope Sextus V refused to pay the 500,000 ducats he had promised to put towards the cost of the failed Armada, Philip quickly dropped all thought of a second. But Elizabeth now ordered a counter-Armada, and so hostilities between both nations were to continue. The king's inability to defend his subjects' interests at home – understandable when we consider how his resources were fully committed elsewhere – led to severe losses. English assaults on Spain's mainland in Cádiz in 1587 and again in 1596 and in Corunna in 1589 were damaging, but far worse were the losses at sea caused by English pirates and privateers who plundered ships returning from India, Africa and the Americas. Although peace was struck with England in 1604, Spanish losses from piracy continued. The Dutch began to trade and loot in Africa, South America and eventually in Asia, a fact that caused the colonial administrations of Castile and Portugal to invest heavily in defence. The burdens of kingship began to tell. 'Uneasy lies the head that wears the crown' was a truth Philip II knew to his cost.

The cracks in the absolutist state were already visible, its stresses brought on by the burdens of war. Military law, prerogative government and 'alien' commissioners – one of whom was Cervantes – were seen to threaten customary and statutory rights and local interests.

At every level the desire to evade or the attempt to exploit fiscal and military levies and purveyance led to tensions and confrontations, setting communities against each other and reactivating long-standing conflicts of authority and jurisdiction. Life as a commissary was proving ever more stressful, but typically Cervantes persevered. He carried out his several duties until May 1589, after which all traces of his whereabouts disappear. And when he reappeared in June he was unusually well heeled. He settled his account with Tomás Gutiérrez and left his elegant premises. On the same day he settled the bill, some thirty-five ducats, of a certain Doña Jerónima de Alarcón, but no one knows who she was or how he had met her. The common reason given for his new-found affluence is success at gambling. Cards and dice-playing were the major pastimes of Spaniards and not only of soldiers and travellers. Anyone who has read Cervantes' works will know of his knowledge of what were then current forms of gambling and of the tricks and malpractices of those who were most skilful in them; it is a theme often used in Spanish picaresque novels, too. Cervantes' understanding of low life, especially in Seville and earlier in Naples and Algiers, was comprehensive. According to Astrana Marín, there were three hundred gambling houses in Seville in the late sixteenth century. It was during this time that Philip issued a general decree aimed at what he termed good governance in his capital of Madrid; among several issues of public behaviour was his prohibition of card- and dice-playing at court. Concern about these activities was nothing new, for as early as 1519 a text entitled *The Cure for Gamblers* had been published that went into several editions, thus proving its popularity. The royal decree reveals the extent to which gambling had gripped society. Rodríguez-Salgado informs us that Philip's young wife, Elizabeth of Valois, 'often had to borrow money from her officials and pawn her jewels to cover her debts'.

Having paid Doña Jerónima de Alarcón's bill Cervantes disappeared for some seven months. When he again turned up his proposed course of action is a surprise: an application for a post overseas. Was this a sudden decision or the result of a carefully weighed option? The document, dated 21 May 1590, follows the eighteen entries that show Cervantes on his rounds from 12 February until 3 May after which mention is made of his salary 'for the fifteen days he spent in collecting and storing olive oil in Carmona'. Was it the considerable discrepancy between work done and salary given that occasioned the seemingly sudden petition to go overseas? Whatever the cause, the petition's contents clearly point to a Cervantes who was ill at ease.[48]

6

THE VEXATIOUS LIFE OF A GOVERNMENT
TAX COLLECTOR (1590–8)

Long winter journeys followed by the scorching heat of summer, the seemingly incessant squabbling of farmers and labourers, the unchristian behaviour of the clergy, the delays in salary payments, a life on the back of a mule or in a cart and, to cap it all, aspersions cast on his honesty had conspired to sap Cervantes' morale. The demands of his job occupied him day and night, and he had then to write up every transaction in an atmosphere which, at best, was tense on account of the frauds, thefts, percentage cuts and bribes which hunger or greed create. And so, when an alderman openly accused him in January 1589 of having requisitioned an amount greater than that recorded, Cervantes, who successfully refuted the charge, had had enough. No one had worked more exhaustingly for the Crown, but even he had his limits. On 21 May 1590 he submitted a petition to the President of the Council of the Indies asking to be considered for any one of four vacancies in the Americas: chief accountant in Granada (Nicaragua); the governorship of the province of Soconusco (Guatemala); paymaster in Cartagena (Colombia); or chief magistrate in La Paz (Bolivia). His petition included an account of his career to date and how 'His Gracious Majesty had never yet granted him one favour'. It was a document of the kind every servant of the monarchy needed to draw up to gain preferment: a statement of the petitioner's merits supported by the testimony of witnesses who could vouch for the authenticity of the claims. The affidavit drawn up in Algiers in 1580 is similar to that which Cervantes was now presenting. All such applications depended totally on the ethos of service, which was nothing less than the confidence in the ennobling effects of duty to the Crown. A remarkable but little-known illustration of this is the application in 1588 of Jerónimo de Quadros, a Portuguese soldier and adventurer based in Ormuz. He was a commander of one of a string of Portuguese garrisons in Laristan on the mainland of Persia, one of the most exposed and obscure corners of Philip II's domains, overlooked by historians now and neglected at the time. Although the document never reached its destination – the so-called tyranny of distance as well as administrative inertia saw to that – the harrowing account of heroic service compiled by de Quadros shows both the nature and the extent of the competition faced by Cervantes whose application did reach its desired destination.[1]

But there was another reason for Cervantes' petition. Up till the 1550s outstanding military exploits were a necessary prerequisite for recognition by the Crown in its allocation of office and of the status of nobility. With the installation of Prada and Alva in 1586, preference was given to those who had served in administration in the field or in the commissariat. Prada had been Don John of Austria's staff secretary and secretary of state and war in Flanders, whereas Alva had been an inspector and purveyor of the galleys.[2] To both men, the distinguished service, competence and loyalty of Cervantes, recognized by Don John of Austria, would have weighed heavily in his favour. Hence Cervantes' confidence must have run high because his petition showed the two most essential criteria needed for selection and personal advancement: his military exploits and his most recent work in administration, the criterion that was proving the most persuasive. Little wonder then that he goes on to say how he would be content with any one of the four posts available 'because he is able, competent and worthy', and he clearly believed that his credentials would bring him one of the four prizes sought.

The petition was signed Cervantes Saavedra. Curiously, apart from being the first time that he uses this surname – one rarely used by his immediate forefathers – he was to use it subsequently as the name under which several of his works were published, including 'The Captive's Tale'. Its use suggests that he may still have harboured fears about his duel with Antonio de Sigura; whatever other purpose Cervantes intended with the use of his double-barrelled surname it did not succeed. Scrawled across the bottom of his returned petition came the laconic response, 'Look for something over here.' Excluded from high office, he made amends in the governorship he awarded to Sancho Panza for his loyal service to his master, Don Quixote.[3] In literature Cervantes could rectify the disappointments and injustices of real life. His application for a post in the New World, that realm perceived as a 'species of new creation', was clearly found wanting and so he remained a reluctant commissary.[4]

Cervantes must have known that competition for such posts was fierce and were sought by men who had influence or who could pull appropriate strings. The strings he once could have pulled no longer functioned. Besides, how could he attempt the job of magistrate or that of a provincial governor? Possibly the other two posts were more in keeping with his more recent experience, but a job dealing in money, as his missions in Andalusia had already proved, did nothing for him except to create problems. The seemingly unkind decision to keep Cervantes in Spain brought for him yet another disappointment. A contemporary, Mateo Alemán, a former Treasury official and author of a very successful picaresque novel, *Guzmán de Alfarache* (1599), went to Mexico only to die in obscurity. Would the same fate have befallen Cervantes? At the time there were only two locations in the New World worthy of a writer: Mexico and Peru.

The advice to seek a post at home should not be taken as a total snub. The secretariats and the treasuries provided openings for educated applicants. Sources reveal that between 1589 and 1662 the 'number of officials in the secretariats of war increased tenfold'.[5] Had Cervantes followed the example of his eminent grandfather and studied law he may well have landed a post. The legal revolution that took place in Spain during his lifetime left an indelible mark on Spanish culture. The spectacular increase in litigation – clearly present in the lives of Cervantes' grandfather and father and present in his life, too –

shows the nation at odds with itself. The vacancy of chief magistrate in La Paz clearly demanded an applicant who had some sort of legal training, and this he lacked. That said, Cervantes' rejection resulted from a bureaucratic decision that discounted his previous loyal service to the state. Therein lay his disappointment, because in the development of Castile as a major power in the early modern period the relationship between war and bureaucracy is generally considered as a reciprocal one that extended across a wide range of contacts, yet in his case such reciprocity failed. Neither on his return from Algiers nor after his stalwart service as a commissary was Spain prepared to reward him with a post he deemed appropriate. And yet recent research proves that the non-legal sector was 'one of the most open and socially accessible areas of administrative service' and not limited to graduates.[6]

One also wonders if Spaniards seeking posts overseas at that time took the geography of such places into account. Cervantes apparently was prepared to go to any one of the four regions that are vastly different from each other. The sight of richly laden galleons that returned regularly to Seville proved more than enough to satisfy any adventurous or desperate spirit, and at this point he was both. And he was not alone. The Second Poor Law of 1565 had been nothing less than a licensed begging system: Spain was becoming a nation of beggars and Cervantes well knew the sting of poverty.[7] Emigration to the Indies was often seen as an opportunity for the dissatisfied to make their fortunes or, at the other end of the scale, an escape for the lawless and penniless.[8] What provoked Cervantes' petition was not the ideology of evangelization which lay at the heart of Spain's colonizing process or a view of the Spanish empire as a 'universal monarchy' but deep personal frustration and all that this entailed.

Any enthusiast of Erasmus would have been aware of the objections to the scale and extent of the Spanish Empire overseas. Such men as Domingo de Soto (1494–1570), Diego Covarrubias y Leyva (1512–67) and the humanist bureaucrat Fernando Vázquez de Menchaca (1512–69) numbered among the most influential of those who were anti-imperialists, and all spoke out against expansion.[9] That spirit of conquest, which even as late as 1590 seemingly ruled the age, was to wind its way into *Don Quixote*. Perhaps in the outcome of this novel we can foresee the decline also of the Spanish imperialist dream – the difference being that the dying knight sees the error of his ways long before Spanish monarchs were compelled to by a series of disasters culminating in the humiliating Spanish War of Succession which ended in 1714.

Another aspect of Cervantes' application for a post in the New World is whether he would have gone for ever. There were some who returned almost as rich as the galleons in which they travelled; the return of the *indiano* (a Spaniard returning rich from the Americas) is not an uncommon theme in Spanish literature. Indeed, the main character in one of Cervantes' most acclaimed short stories, 'The Jealous Old Man from Extremadura', is such a character. Cervantes' willingness to tackle the unknown is to be admired. Noble service to the Crown, a by-product of that all-contagious 'spirit of conquest', was no longer the measure of one's worth, however. He probably believed that five years in the thick of Algiers constituted the best apprenticeship and recommendation for the Americas. But officials had to be bribed, and they duly allocated such posts to court favourites and those who were well heeled.

By the time the reply came to him in June, he was already back on his rounds in Andalusia requisitioning grain for the Spanish fleet. A document dated 27 August 1590 shows his accounts for wheat taken during the previous three years. In it there appear the irregularities in deliveries of grain that soon were to embroil him in a protracted confrontation with the Treasury.

An intriguing question often passed over by commentators is whether, had Cervantes been offered a post, he would have taken his wife with him. Until he had received the official reply the question may well have weighed on his mind. What is also intriguing is the timing of his application. As early as the previous autumn it was known that there were vacancies abroad. Why did he wait so long? Could it have been connected with his bastard daughter's education or with his mother-in-law's terminal illness? He filed his request only three weeks after Catalina's passing. Did her death, which was not unexpected, make his decision more urgent? The fact that his wife joined the Order of the Most Holy Sacrament later that year adds something to the mystery. The order emphasized chastity, so clearly she and her husband were intending to lead separate lives, which they did. Apart from sporadic meetings to do with the wider family circle – funerals, marriages, baptisms or ordinations – their conjugal life finished when he obtained his first commission in Andalusia and did not resume until nearly two decades later. He knew this and so did she; to her chagrin his continued absence from the family home proclaimed the fact to her family and friends.

To all intents and purposes she was living the life of a widow, and she knew it. Published records show the startling number of widows in Castile.[10] Prominent among the reasons given to explain this were the country's imperial obligations, which demanded a constant supply of manpower to fill the armies and to conquer and colonize the New World. These were indeed factors, but to judge from the reproofs of moralists it appears that bigamy and desertion of one's family were not uncommon. Would Cervantes have joined that rather numerous army of deserters? Spanish commentators tend to speak of Catalina's patient and submissive nature; some go so far as to imply her martyrdom. Her mother, a true widow, certainly foresaw her daughter's plight and left Cervantes out of her will. All in all, his application to the Indies leaves more questions than answers; true, it shows a man discontented with his lot, a man willing to ditch everything he knew and once had valued in the Old World – his wife and family included; it was, however, a world that had treated him all too harshly. Had he gone to the Americas his humanistic outlook would have been severely tested. From his writings we can see that he would probably have been appalled at the barbaric treatment of the natives. Not for nothing arose the Spanish proverb 'more elastic than a conscience in the

Indies'. The extraordinary work of Bartolomé de Las Casas reveals the enormous problems and dangers faced by those who genuinely supported humane ideals in an alien environment.[11]

His true response to the rejection may be gauged from in the advice given to Sancho: 'there's no high office that isn't obtained by some form of bribery'.[12] Cervantes was not prepared to stoop so low. His high-mindedness had carried him through Algiers and thus far in his work for the government. Wisely or not, he believed in honest endeavour, in personal worth.[13] But he was not to taste the riches – sometimes described as a poisoned chalice by historians – offered by the Indies.[14] Did he know that the secretary to the Council of the Indies was Juan de Ledesma, a friend of the family of Nicolás de Ovando, the man who had deceived his sister Andrea? Probably not, because it is thought that it was Magdalena who carried the petition for her brother to Madrid. The rejection of the application might seem less surprising in this light. Neither the Americas nor mighty Spain held a place for the veteran of Lepanto. Had a meritocracy ruled in Madrid the biography of Cervantes would speak much more of his prosperity and success.

So the government agent continued to toil. In August 1590 he submitted his signed accounts for all the grain requisitioned over the past three years. They showed a shortfall, with the result that *he* now owed the Exchequer. This was bad news because the government had discovered irregularities in the requisitions of other agents working in Andalusia for Antonio de Guevara, who was in overall charge of food supply for the Armada. In the accounts submitted by those to whom Antonio de Guevara's other agents gave provisions enormous discrepancies were found and thus an inquiry was launched. This was serious, because after the Armada Philip had ordered the state to examine the reasons why the campaign had failed and especially why so much foodstuff had to be thrown overboard. In the witch-hunt that ensued prison sentences were given to a number of Antonio de Guevara's agents, four of whom were hanged.[15]

Although Cervantes admitted the shortfall he was able to explain its cause: he had made an error in his calculations. He submitted his request for what was owed to him but received only half; his protests against the amount annoyed the authorities, who then asked him to attend in person to explain his arrears. Lacking the funds to go, he asked Antonio de Guevara's secretary, Juan Serón, to appear for him and he did so. It is probable that Cervantes had, on occasion, used government money to pay his own way. Besides, any money he owed the authorities was docked from his salary as a matter of course. The fact that he was not charged with fraud shows that his arrears were not deliberate but the result of financial need. The inquiry brought requisitions to a stop and so he found time to write.

A document dated 12 March 1591 shows that Cervantes filed another request for his salary and that he received due payment, some 110,000 maravedís. This was an astonishing volte-face when we consider the inquiries into fraud and deception, even embezzlement, at that time still in progress. A new chief commissioner was appointed, Pedro de Isunza, whose primary task was to weed out and imprison the fraudsters. Isunza's appointment did not affect the position of Cervantes, who then returned to his work requisitioning wheat and oil. His travels took him to Granada, Baeza, Estepa and Montilla. His assistant was Nicolás Benito, who inadvertently was to embroil him in a dispute that involved the government taking proceedings against Isunza; the matter – Isunza was unjustly accused of selling grain seized by Benito for personal gain – was to drag on for years.

Documents discovered in Simancas show how extraordinarily hard Cervantes worked on behalf of his king. Unaware of the case against Isunza and, by implication, against himself, he was unflagging in his efforts, despite not being paid, but when in May 1592, his commission over, he returned to Seville, he was to spend most of the rest of that year trying to keep the lawsuit at bay. While insolvent and awaiting new commissions he agreed to write six plays for Rodrigo Osorio, one of the finest and most popular actors of the age and at this time a successful theatre company manager, for which he would receive fifty ducats each. But he would only receive such a sum if, in Osorio's view, each play was 'one of the best ever staged in Spain'. It is generally accepted that Cervantes agreed to this, but opinions differ as to why. Was he driven by the need to establish himself and earn money or by the belief that his work would match the stipulation? As the plays were never written, we will never know how Osorio would have found them. The suit against Isunza saw to that. To clarify and defend his position, Isunza demanded the presence of Cervantes in Madrid. In helping his superintendent, however, he realized he would be helping both their positions. It worked, for the day after his statement the decree against Isunza was suspended – but not without a setback: a warrant issued by a magistrate named Francisco Moscoso of Écija caught up with Cervantes on 19 September 1592 in Castro del Río, the same town in which he had once been excommunicated for putting a sacristan in gaol. He was charged with having illegally seized 300 bushels of wheat and was ordered to make restitution and pay court costs within two weeks. Moscoso had made no investigation of the charge and he had 'tried' Cervantes *in absentia*. An appeal was made to Isunza, who duly procured his release, and this timely intervention led the War Council to dismiss all charges against Cervantes, whom Isunza described as his 'devoted servant' and as 'honourable and highly trustworthy'. It seems that Cervantes spent less than one week in the local prison. Another unwelcome spell behind bars proved to him how all too easily, despite the best of honest intentions, his present job could land him in hot water. At least he had found an ally in Isunza, who by now was a very sick man and mercilessly hounded by Moscoso, who pursued his suit until Isunza's death in 1593.

Isunza was replaced by Miguel de Oviedo, who immediately commissioned Cervantes to gather wheat for the Spanish navy. He employed him because he viewed Cervantes as 'competent, experienced and trustworthy'. High praise indeed from a source close to the investigation of the scandal associated with other commissaries in the region, although it is impossible to know to what extent Oviedo is merely parroting the opinions of his predecessor.[16] But the terms used approximate closely to the view that Cervantes had of himself and had already put forward in his application for one of the posts in the Americas. He was no doubt pleased that at least one person in official-dom had recognized his talents and virtues. Unfortunately, 1593 was another bad year for farmers in the south of Spain, and the over-stressed commissary was faced with a further tour of duty trying to extract from famished farmers the little they had harvested. A reduced crop had pushed the free-market price nearly 25 per cent above the government rate. Amid the clamours of reluctant labourers, Cervantes learned in October 1593 of his mother's death at the age of seventy-three. Death must have come suddenly, for she left no will. Little is said of the passing of Doña Leonor de Cortinas, and less is known of her son's reaction to it. The last time he had seen her was when he went to Madrid to defend Isunza. 'I was brought into this world', laments Don Quixote, 'to show what real misery can be, to serve as target practice for the arrows of evil fortune.'[17] In this Cervantes and his sorrowful knight were one.

Events change circumstances, however, and he would have sensed that with each death mortality was dividing him more and more from his past. Even now his personal situation was far from rosy: although he was owed money he had debts and his workload was both arduous and precarious because, despite the War Council's decision, a few minor officials in Seville remained sceptical of his innocence. In fact, some still disputed a number of his previous transactions. And more sadness followed: within days of his mother's death his uncle Andrés, the mayor of Cabra, also died, and Cervantes had suddenly lost two lifelong supports. If we include the death of Isunza in June that year, Cervantes had good reason to wonder at the workings of fate. Delay in the news of the deaths in his family prevented him from attending either funeral. What would have stayed with him were undiminished memories of how his mother had served her husband and how she had moved heaven and earth to marshal funds to meet the ransom bill, even lying to the Crusade Council. She appeared ten times in all before six different notaries, and on six of these occasions she abstained from mentioning her husband and on the other four she declared herself a widow: her sole motive in so doing was to soften the hearts of the Council so that they would grant funds to save her children. Ten times she made her way to the Council's offices and on the occasion that she was granted sixty gold escudos she claimed that 'both her sons had served in galley ships in Flanders and in Italy and that one son had had his hand cut off and that the other son had one arm maimed'.[18] To date no evidence has come to light of Rodrigo's maimed hand, and Cervantes, as we know, never served in Flanders, but when it came to the raising of funds Leonor proved adept at shuffling the facts. Even her attempts at business had as their sole purpose their longed-for freedom. When she was finally able to submit 300 ducats (this includes the fifty given by Andrea, her daughter) for Cervantes' release, she would have realized that a successful outcome was by no means certain. Cervantes would have eagerly approved of the fiction concocted by his mother to muster funds for his release, and without her efforts he would have sailed away with Hasan Pasha.

But Cervantes had little time to brood on personal circumstance. With public outcry against commissioners mounting, especially after the scandal of the affair with Antonio de Guevara, the king decided to change the system and to deal with the local landowners, councils and constabulary directly. Oviedo's operation was wound up and so, after seven years' toil, Cervantes' life as a commissary was over. In June 1594 his accounts were approved and he was a free man. He had very little money, but he could return home, unlike so many in the profession, with honour. This he did, and by June we find him in Madrid enlisting the aid of a friend, Agustín de Cetina, to find him work. Cetina had survived the Guevara scandal and was working as a member of the Royal Council of Auditors. Through him Cervantes, after three months without gainful employment, became a tax collector in the

159

kingdom of Granada. His principal task was to collect 2.5 million mara-vedís in tax arrears. A clear but amusing picture of the type of official the tax collector was and the type of existence he suffered is to be found in the playlet *The Divorce Court Judge*. The authorities demanded that all tax collectors appoint guarantors so that, in the event of fraud or theft, the Treasury would not lose out. Having obtained the customary guarantor – a Francisco Suárez Gasco – to the tune of 4,000 ducats, Cervantes, unable to find another, was compelled to pledge his and his wife's personal fortune. Although probably suggested by Cetina, Gasco was not a wise choice for he had been suspected of, although not charged with, trying to poison his wife.[19]

His acceptance of such a post so soon after the trials of his career as a commissary points to financial necessity, for already in September 1594 he was in Guadix in the Kingdom of Granada, the oldest diocese in Spain, to render the first of his several visits to the towns and villages in the region. Once again he had to submit accounts, but this time he was dealing in currency destined for the Treasury. His pay was to be drawn from the taxes collected, a value-added reason to be dili-gent in his task.

This turning point in his career is worthy of consideration. Despite his frustrations and stints inside prison he had been a relatively suc-cessful civil servant. In an age when so many in his profession were loathed for corruption, his tours of office were distinguished by his honesty, trustworthiness and his knack with people. What is not men-tioned, however, is his knowledge and understanding of taxation. His experience and innate virtues made him the right man for the job and the Treasury sorely needed such men because Philip was desperately short of finances. As a result, nothing mattered more to his adminis-tration than the collection of the arrears that could be used to offset his increasing debts. It was no secret that, amid growing opposition to his fiscal policy, Philip's government relied more and more on returns from tax collectors. For forty years Castile had shouldered most of the support of the monarchy and strongly opposed the imposition of

Lithograph after a painting by Eusebio Zarza, dated
1864–6, of Cervantes in his youth

Alcalá de Henares, the birthplace of Miguel de Cervantes. Coloured drawing by Anton van den Wyngaerde, 1565

IRELAND

ENGLAND

DENM

ATLANTIC

London ● ● Amsterdam

LOW COUNTRIES

OCEAN

Brussels ●

Mühlberg ●

Paris ●

FRANCE

Corunna ●

Santander ●

Turin ● Parma
Tren
Genoa ● Ve
Luca ● Bologna
Florence ●

PORTUGAL

Perpignan ●

Valladolid ●

Lisbon ●

Madrid ● ● Alcalá
de Henares
● Toledo

● Barcelona

CORSICA

SPAIN

● Valencia

BALEARIC ISLANDS

Menorca

Rome

Seville ● ● Córdoba

Ibiza ● Mallorca

SARDINIA

Cádiz ●

● Granada ● Cartagena

M E D I T E

Tangier ●

Algiers ●

Trapa

Alcazarquivir ●

Melilla ●

Binzert ●

Orán Mostaganem

Tunis ●

MOROCCO

La Golett

Tri

- - - - - - - -   Extent of the Holy Roman Empire

Habsburg dominions
(Spanish branch)

Habsburg dominions
(Austrian branch)

Turkish possessions

EUROPE
AT THE END OF THE 16ᵀᴴ CENTURY

openhagen

PRUSSIA

POLAND

GRAND DUCHY

OF

LITHUANIA

AUSTRIA

Vienna ●

● Budapest

HUNGARY

THE

OTTOMAN

EMPIRE

BLACK SEA

Ragus ●

Constantinople ●

INGDOM
NAPLES

CORFU

sina ●

● Lepanto

● Smyrna

● Modón

MALTA

CRETE

Famagusta ●
Nicosia ●

CYPRUS

A
N
E
A
N

S
E
A

SPAIN UNDER PHILIP II

Corunna

ASTURIAS

Santander

BASQUE PROVINCES

NAVARRE

Bayonne CERDAGNE

ROUSSILLON

Laredo

GALICIA

PYRENEES

Perpignan

Vigo

Pamplona

ARAGON CATALONIA

Valladolid

Tarazona

Monzón

Toro

OLD CASTILE

Saragossa

Barcelona

Segovia

Salamanca

Ávila

Guadalajara

Madrid

Alcalá
de Henares

ARAGON

Yuste

Toledo

VALENCIA

Valencia

Thomar

CASTILE

Almeirim

EXTREMADURA

Lisbon

PORTUGAL

Badajoz

NEW CASTILE

Setúbal

Córdoba

MURCIA

ANDALUSIA

ATLANTIC OCEAN

ALGARVE

Seville

Granada

Cartagena

MEDITERRANEAN SEA

GRANADA

Algiers

Cádiz

Tangier

Ceuta

MEDITERRANEAN

Orán

X
Alcazarquivir

NORTH AFRICA

Valencia

LA MANCHA

Ciudad Real

Albacete

Badajoz

SIERRA MORENA

Alicante

Baeza

Ubeda

Murcia

Córdoba

Jaén

La Rambla

Castro del Rio

Carmona

Montilla

Espejo

Baza

Cartagena

Seville

Ecija

Cabra

Marchena

Guadix

Huelva

Loja

Granada

MEDITERRANEAN SEA

Alhama

Ronda

Málaga

Motril

Almeria

Cádiz

THE ANDALUSIA OF CERVANTES

The future Philip II as a young man, by Titian, 1551. Philip (1527–98) came to the throne after his father Charles V abdicated in 1556. Under Philip's rule Spain became the most powerful nation in Europe.

© Prado, Madrid

Left: Sultan Suleiman I (1494–1566), by Hans Eworth, 1549. Under Suleiman the Magnificent, as he was known, the Ottoman Empire reached its greatest extent.

Right: Fernández Alvarez of Toledo, Duke of Alba, by Willem Key. A grandee of Castile, the Duke (1507–82) was favourite of and principal adviser to Philip II. He suppressed the rebellions in Flanders in 1566 and Portugal in 1580.

© Prado, Madrid

Right: Undated portrait by an unknown artist of Ana de Mendoza y La Cerda, Princess of Eboli (1540–92). She was the sister to Ruy Gomez de Silva, better known as the Prince of Eboli, who led one of the two competing factions at court which vied for power shortly after the accession of Philip II. Rumour, widespread at the time, was that she had an affair with Philip II.

THE FOUR WIVES OF PHILIP II

Mary of Portugal (d. 1545)

Mary Tudor (1516–58), by Antonio
Moro (Antonis van Dashort Mor), 1554

© Prado, Madrid

Elizabeth of Valois (1546–68), by Alonso
Sánchez Coello, 1560

© Kunsthistorisches Museum, Vienna

Anne of Austria (1546–80), by Alonso
Sánchez Coello, 1571

© Kunsthistorisches Museum, Vienna

Philip II and Elizabeth of Valois. Philip married Elizabeth, daughter of Henry II of France, in 1559 as part of the Peace of Cateau-Cambrésis. She died in childbirth in 1568.

Left: Don John of Austria (1547–78), by an unknown artist, dated 1571. The half-brother of Philip II and leader of the Christian forces against the Ottomans at Lepanto in 1571, he died prematurely from typhoid. He was the 'soldier of the age' and the Christian commander whom the Turks most feared. It was Don John who had written the letters of recommendation that Cervantes was carrying when he was taken prisoner and which made his captors in Algiers consider him such a great prize.

© El Museo Naval, Madrid

Facing page: Don Carlos (1545–68), by Velázquez, dated 1626–7. Philip II's eldest child died in mysterious circumstances in 1568, aged twenty-three. His short and tragic life is the subject of a play by Schiller and an opera by Verdi.

© Prado, Madrid

Above: Ali Pasha, leader of the Ottoman forces against the Christian Alliance at Lepanto in 1571. Ali Pasha was decapitated after the Ottoman defeat. Detail from *The Battle of Lepanto* by Andrea Vicentino, 1571

Facing page: A depiction of Don John of Austria as a clown, known as *El Bufón*, by Velázquez, dated 1632–5

Tapestry depicting the conquests of Tunis (1573) and La Goletta (1574), by Cornelio
Vermeyen. It is generally accepted that both Cervantes and his brother Rodrigo took
part in these campaigns.

Algiers in the mid sixteenth century

Fray Juan Gil of the Trinitarian Order ransoming Cervantes in 1580, by H. Müde. Note how the artist shows Cervantes without his left arm, whereas the evidence suggests that, while he lost the use of his arm after injuries sustained at Lepanto in 1571, the arm was not amputated.

Cervantes' signature on the document concerning his captivity and rescue, known as *Información II*. This is a sort of affidavit, drawn up by Cervantes and signed by twelve bona fide witnesses, consisting of twenty-five separate questions about his conduct in Algiers.

An engraving of a Spanish galleon by Crescentio Romano. The galleon was used as both warship and trading vessel in the sixteenth and seventeenth centuries and formed part of the Spanish Armada of 1588.

Above: Sir Francis Drake (1540–96), by Marcus Gheerhaerts the Younger, 1591. Drake was a major thorn in the Spanish side, atacking their shipping, colonies in the New World and even sending fireships into Cádiz harbour in 1587, causing enormous damage and delaying the departure of the Armada by a year.

© National Maritime Museum, London

Facing page: An undated portrait of Charles Howard of Effingham, 1st Earl of Nottingham, by Daniel Mytens. Among many other achievements Howard led the English delegation to Spain in 1605, which came to ratify the peace treaty with England signed in 1604.

© Greenwich Hospital Collection, National Maritime Museum, London

Engraving attributed to Fabrizio Castello of El Escorial, a monastery and palace in central Spain. Built between 1563 and 1584 by Philip II in thanksgiving for his victory over the French at St Quentin in 1557, it encompasses a mausoleum, library, college and art collection.

Watercolours of Moors from Granada, one male and one female, wearing traditional dress

Portrait of Cervantes as a *barquero*, or
boatman, by Pacheco

© Museo de Bellas Artes, Seville

Above: Engraving of Philip III (1578–1621). Crowned king in 1598, his rule was dominated by his favourite, the Duke of Lerma, who was effectively the power behind the throne. It was during Philip III's reign that Cervantes wrote most of his major works.

Facing page: Philip II in old age, by Juan Pantoja de la Cruz, dated 1595. Portraits of Philip II in later life generally show him dressed simply in black; he had no need to carry outward symbols of kingship to convey his royal majesty.

Above: Philip III on horseback, by Velázquez, dated 1620–9. This painting bears comparison with that of the Duke of Lerma opposite.
© Prado, Madrid

Facing page: The Duke of Lerma on horseback. Born Francisco Gomez de Sandoval y Rojas, 5th Marquis of Denia, 4th Count of Lerma and Duke of Lerma from 1599, he virtually ruled Spain as Philip III's favourite until his downfall in 1618. In this portrait by Peter Paul Rubens, painted in 1603, Lerma appears as a victorious warrior adorned with the symbols of the office of General of the Spanish Cavalry.
© Prado, Madrid

Lope de Vega (1562–1635), painting attributed to E. Caxés, dated c.1620. Regarded as the founder of Spanish drama, he is reputed to have written around 1,500 plays of which hundreds survive. His other works included epic poems and pastoral romances. He and Cervantes famously fell out, with Lope de Vega saying that there was no poet as bad as Cervantes or anyone so stupid as to praise *Don Quixote*.

additional taxes, so any revenue coming from the other kingdoms was particularly welcome and officially encouraged. While Cervantes went on his rounds, the debate over the fiscal obligations of Castile that had begun early in the 1590s continued, eventually spilling over into the nature and function of monarchical government. It was to plague the last years of Philip II's reign and was an issue that Cervantes, in his new role, could not avoid. Spain was facing financial ruin, and the collection of taxes was one of a number of measures deemed crucial to stabilize the regime.[20]

As is generally known, the agricultural situation in Spain grew progressively worse in the last decades of the sixteenth century. An increasing number of subsistence crises produced a malnourished population that was highly vulnerable to plagues, drought and famine. Strange as it may sound, the Castilian peasant spent much of his time worrying about the weather, either praying for rain or that the rains would cease. Given that the population was growing rapidly, Spanish farmers knew that decreasing yields severely affected the precarious balance between supply and demand. Not all parts of Castile experienced the same conditions, and the rain that was beneficial to one crop might be disastrous for another. Yet another danger, apart from the whims of weather, was the locust. Records show that such plagues affected Andalusia in 1508–9, Old Castile in 1541 and 1556 and again in 1573–4. Of specific interest to the commissary work of Cervantes was the locust plague of 1585–6 that devastated Extremadura, La Mancha and Andalusia.

It is easy to forget that, despite the gold and silver from Mexico and Peru – which accounted for some 11 per cent of total revenue in 1554, rising to only 20 per cent by 1598 – most of the rest of the national income came from taxation paid directly or indirectly by the Castilian peasant, described by one French historian as 'a marvellous beast of burden'.[21] That vast imperial venture of the Habsburg empire was propped up by a rural society. It has been estimated that between 1494 and 1598, the year Philip II died, the total royal revenue increased ninefold. It is fair to add that such increases were offset by the fact that over the same period the population doubled and there was a fourfold price increase.

Behind the splendid façade of imperial Spain these happenings affected the lives of millions of her citizens. By the end of the sixteenth century, over half of the peasant's harvest went to enrich the rest of the population. This being so it is surprising that the vast superstructure held up for so long. Even with the death of Philip II nothing changed to improve the lot of those who produced. Spain could take heart from the fact that her colonies were now producing sufficient for their own needs, thus ending what had been, for the shrewd few, a very lucrative trade in wine, oil and grain from the mother country. And such trade went on not only in the Americas but also the Netherlands and Spain's other possessions, notably in Italy and in North Africa. Providing for such a vast overseas markets meant that shortages occurred locally, thus causing prices to soar. Profits for some were so high that agriculture became a good investment, attracting capital that otherwise might have been invested in trade and manufacturing. Many wealthy commoners were able to buy titles of nobility, and so they insisted on maintaining the traditional privileges of the medieval system. This led to the phenomenon of *latifundismo* in Andalusia, the region most affected by the American trade. But when the bubble burst at the end of the sixteenth century – as it had to – Spain went into a spectacular decline.

Cervantes would have also known about the *alcabalas*, a sales tax, as well as the exemption from it of certain towns, the restoration of primary jurisdiction to the towns of the Military Orders as well as the creation of seigniorial jurisdictions that were having widespread effect on populations and their distribution. It was to lead to extensive migration from the cities to the towns in the next century.[22] It was the sales tax that affected his work most directly. In theory it comprised 10 per cent of purchases, but in practice 'only half, or one-third, or even one-fifth of this 10 per cent was collected, depending on the goods or property involved and the place and time of the transactions'.[23] And this substantial reduction was the result of the system of agreement between the Treasury, his employer, and the taxpayers for the payment of a fixed sum. Once the overall sum had been fixed it was divided among the forty districts of the eighteen provinces of the kingdom of Castile, and each was allocated a quota. This was then reapportioned by the district council of each of its trading sectors and then passed down to individual traders. Discussion and dispute would accompany each level and did not stop when commissaries arrived to collect government dues. Cervantes would also have been very aware of the tax called *millones* (the millions) approved by the Cortes, the National Assembly of Castile, in April 1590, which amounted to over 8 million ducats to be paid over six years and, for the first time ever, included payment by the nobility and clergy. Fortunately for him municipal councillors were entrusted to collect this tax and thus bore the brunt of the bitter resentment and hostility. Recent research shows, however, that such officials used all sorts of means to evade the direct tax so that it became indirect, and thus a fraud on society. This explains why the Treasury came down hard on anyone suspected of cooking the books. The work of social historians tells us that it was common practice for tax collectors to stretch the rules and regulations under the guise of concessions in order to produce a more favourable balance for their own accounts.

No collector was unaware of the famous decree of 1594 that improved the lot of farmers in debt to money-lenders and which authorized them to sell part of their crop as bread and not only as grain. Cervantes knew as well as the government did of the economic depression that, from the 1580s, had hung over Castile, especially in central areas. The proctors in the National Assembly were constantly denouncing the nation's plight, and such complaints gave rise eventually to the *arbitristas*, or reform writers, whose schemes and projects, intended to restore Spain to its former greatness, offer today's students such invaluable documentation. The scheme of the *arbitrista* in 'The

Colloquy of the Two Dogs', who called for 3 million Spaniards to fast one day a month and to put the money thus saved towards the king's taxes, provoked laughter but is not as idiotic as the source from which it came is held to be. The four patients in the Resurrection Hospital – alchemist, poet, mathematician and reform writer – are all deemed to be mad, the outcome of syphilis. But Cervantes was well aware of the chaos of Spain's economy, and his suggestion, through the voice of the *arbitrista*, merits consideration.[24]

In his role as a tax collector Cervantes was unable to avoid the consequences of droughts and famines, but his worst enemy was plague. Towards the end of his government career Cervantes would see the consequences of plague which began in the Basque provinces in 1596 and raged throughout the peninsula until 1602.[25] In fact plague is the dominant feature of catastrophic mortality throughout sixteenth-century Castile, and a violent outbreak of the same disease hit London in 1603.[26] Travellers were especially vulnerable, but when plague accompanied poor harvests no one was safe. Both came to a head in 1598, so that Mateo Alemán could write that Castile marked the dramatic meeting point of 'the famine travelling up from Andalusia' and 'the plague travelling down from Castile'.[27] This was the final straw for a peasantry already crushed by poor harvests, burdensome taxes and rising prices, a sorrowful aspect of life's reality faced by Cervantes on a daily basis.

Another crucial matter for Cervantes would have been the great fluctuations in cereal prices during the second half of the sixteenth century. Violent swings in output caused by adverse weather conditions led to deficient harvests, which meant price increases owing to sharp reductions in supply. By the end of the century it has been estimated that the total burden of the dues, taxes and rents absorbed half of the peasant's harvest. Cervantes also had the bad luck of working in Andalusia in the years when the trade with the Americas began its decline. After a long spell of almost continuous growth during the whole of the sixteenth century (except during the recession of

1550–62), the upward trend of Spanish trade with the Americas was interrupted until 1622. Cervantes was to witness this decline that began towards the close of Philip II's rule and which was to continue beyond his death in 1616 under the rule of the Duke of Lerma, the *válido* (favourite) of Philip III.

A map drawn of the towns and villages visited and revisited when Cervantes was a commissary and later as a tax collector would demonstrate the relentless nature of his duties and of his unflagging energy. The fact that so many taxpayers had good reason to give less than their quota did not help his cause, however. Records show that Cervantes was authorized to collect 2,557,029 maravedís from various townships within the kingdom of Granada. This was no mean sum and demanded precision both in the collection and in the drafting of the accounts.[28] With the displacement of the Moriscos from the kingdom of Granada after the Second Rebellion of the Alpujarras in 1568–70, the agricultural economy of the region and eventually of the nation was decimated. In 1571 Philip II confiscated the real estate of Moriscos who had participated in the rebellion, and their lands were allocated to some 12,524 families from northern Spain and Andalusia. At royal expense these new settlers, mainly from mountainous areas, were brought in to populate around 270 villages out of some 400 that had existed in Morisco times.[29] But those from the north failed to achieve what their Muslim counterparts had done for centuries. Given that, traditionally, in Spain there had been two types of farming economies based on very diverse farming practices, it is not surprising that the new settlers could not adapt to a totally new environment; the transition from grains to vines, olives and fruits that needed irrigation techniques not known in the north proved too much, and within a few years much of the old Morisco arboriculture had been abandoned. Dryland farming was – and still is – the overwhelmingly predominant type of agriculture in Castile.

When the amounts collected eventually reached Madrid he was charged with a deficit of over 79,000 maravedís. Careful scrutiny of the sums received and then sent to the Treasury show that the auditors erred and not he. Unaware of this, Cervantes surrendered to a merchant banker, Simón Freire de Lima, the sum of 7,400 reales in exchange for a letter of credit. A wise move, otherwise he would have had to cross the wilds of the Sierra Morena carrying a small fortune; in an age when bandits roamed the region it was prudent to carry a bill of exchange.[30]

Having arrived in the capital to submit his accounts, he waited for the money from Freire only to discover in May 1575, after several frantic months, that amid claims of bankruptcy Freire had absconded taking 60,000 ducats. This was disastrous, especially in the light of what had happened to his ex-colleagues while in the employ of Antonio de Guevara. The last thing he sought was association with another financial scandal. During what proved to be a fraught-ridden affair there was a brighter moment for Cervantes when he won a national poetry competition organized by the Dominican friars of Saragossa to celebrate the canonization of St Hyacinth. His prize of three silver spoons awarded on 7 May 1595 later featured as part of his daughter's dowry. In that same month Juan de Palacios – the priest entrusted with Cervantes' wife's estate – died, and so now Cervantes was truly the head of the family.

With no time to enjoy his success as a poet, Cervantes, aware that he and his wife would have to foot the entire bill if Freire failed to pay, went directly to Seville to hunt down the culprit only to find that other creditors had beaten him to it and had already impounded Freire's goods. He remonstrated that money owed to the Treasury had priority, but to prove the point he had to return to Madrid to obtain written authorization from Philip II. This was granted on 7 August 1595 by Bernardo de Olmedilla, a judge in the employ of the king.[31]

From the date of Olmedilla's authorization until September 1597 Cervantes' whereabouts and activities are a mystery, although it is clear that he was more than preoccupied with Freire's bankruptcy. Inexplicably, however, Cervantes had failed to submit a final account of all his transactions, an oversight that made the Treasury and its officials doubly determined to recover the shortfall. Consequently they summoned his immediate appearance, while at the same time making known their intentions to Suárez Gasco, his guarantor in Madrid, who had agreed to underwrite a sum of 4,000 ducats. This was no mean sum, but it was only agreed to after Cervantes promised to forfeit to Suárez Gasco his goods and those of his wife. Cervantes' promise shows the extent to which he was willing to go in order to secure the post. Aware of the perils of falling foul of the king's men, Gasco asked for an immediate respite of twenty days and sent notice of the summons to Gaspar de Vallejo, one of the presiding judges in Seville. Exasperatingly, Gaspar de Vallejo fixed Cervantes' bond at the full amount of the initial assignment, over 2.5 million maravedís instead of the 79,000 deficit. No one could guarantee such an amount, and so in September 1597 Cervantes, instead of being sent to Madrid, went undeservedly to prison.

The royal prison of Seville was opened in 1569 and could hold more than 1,500 inmates. It is also the place, so runs the tale, where *Don Quixote* was conceived. If so, consensus has it that it was as the embryo of a novella, a short story, not more. Whether he began to write the text inside prison is altogether a different issue. Who can say? Stranger things have happened. Ideas, concepts, outlines of novels and poems can arise anywhere, and we do know that he did write when a captive in Algiers. Nevertheless, Seville prison was not designed for men of ransom and there were no concessions for self-declared members of the nobility. The prologue to *Don Quixote* tells us unequivocally that the Muses best flourish in the best conditions, and these are not found inside a crowded prison where 'every discomfort has its niche and every mournful sound its home'. Contemporary accounts of prison life point to an institution where bribery and corruption ruled the day. A comment from Tomás, the innkeeper in the short story 'The Illustrious Kitchen Maid', indicates what Cervantes thought of the ministers of justice: 'those [whose palms are] not greased squeal louder than cartwheels'.[32] He had good reason to view the presiding judge, Gaspar de Vallejo, in the same light. But Cervantes, imprisoned not because of deliberate fraud or embezzlement but because of an error of the Treasury, would not offer one penny to Gaspar de Vallejo, whose livelihood depended on 'gifts' from the inmates.[33]

Documented is the fact that, while behind bars, Cervantes appealed to Philip II, who replied in December 1597, requesting his presence in Madrid within thirty days to settle the bill. But Gaspar de Vallejo, through spite or incompetence or both – for opinions vary – misinterpreted the king's letter and thus would not release him. Whatever view we take of Vallejo's action, the outcome for Cervantes remained the same: another incarceration. Those who believe that Vallejo's action arose out of malice use it as proof of that reversal of absolutism which historians tell us began after the defeat of the Armada. If it is true that the monarch's authority weakened as a result of the tensions that arose for the government in Castile between the centre and the periphery, it is very possible that Cervantes was made to suffer for it.[34] Without going to Madrid Cervantes could not pay the debt. And his creditors Gasco and Catalina would not pay one maravedí until they saw him in person. Distressingly, the impasse dragged on for several months during which, some argue, he had time to write. Several of the colourful low-life individuals who fill the pages of *Don Quixote*, the *Exemplary Novels* and numerous characters in the *Interludes* would have been found in Seville.

While Cervantes was still in prison, Treasury accountants queried the commissions he had completed for Isunza in 1591–2. Cervantes claimed that if he were released he could answer their queries. Fortunately for him, and despite their later efforts to question his involvement in his defence of Isunza, Cervantes never did go to the Treasury to proffer any explanation. The matter simply fizzled out and should never have been resurrected. Besides, Cervantes had more than enough to contend with inside a prison where he was unlawfully detained. It is not known whether he was freed in January or in the spring of 1598, but few can doubt the pyschological blow of his incarceration. After all, he was now in the fiftieth year of a life that had been both restless and precarious. It is no real surprise that the concept of justice and the relationship between crime and punishment should become a recurrent theme in *Don Quixote*.

When Pedro de Urdemalas claims in the play of the same name that 'one's office is as good as the end to which it aspires', he of course was referring to his decision to become an actor. The end to which Cervantes as a civil servant aspired was certainly not imprisonment, yet that was the unfortunate outcome. Such gross injustice came on top of calamitous years of famine, plague, crippling taxation and soaring prices that he had to endure when working as a government official. Those who see in his reaction to life's misfortunes strong evidence of a stoical attitude do have a point. It is a wonder how he maintained his sense of proportion and humour when we know that his duties compelled him to make repeated visits to townships where his presence was often unwanted. With little or no time to write when in gainful employment, his achievement in literature, in quantity as well as in quality, is perhaps of greater wonder.[35]

After his stint in gaol, he began to complete a number of his short stories as well as embark on serious study of the works of literary theorists. But there was something else. In a statement made in 1605 by his sister Andrea she claims that he 'dabbled in writing and in business, and that, because of his skill with people, he had friends'. This is interesting because precious little has come down to us of what his family said or thought of him. It is clear, however, that Cervantes was writing and had a circle of friends. In his works, however, years can intervene between dates of composition and publication. The fact that in the prologue to his *Exemplary Novels* he gives his age as fifty-five suggests that the novellas were being completed around the time of the writing of *Don Quixote, Part One*, that is, c. 1602. Furthermore, the two interpolated novels in *Don Quixote, Part One* also date from long before 1605. The actual date of composition of 'The Captive's

Tale', one of the two, is generally accepted as around 1590, that is, some fifteen years before the publication of *Don Quixote*. How he was able to keep intact work already in draft form or completed remains an enigma. When we consider his life on the highways but more often on the byways of Spain it is altogether a miracle that any of his earlier work survives. Had publication followed directly on from completion of his written work a more chronologically accurate picture of all his writings would have been feasible and the mystery surrounding the genesis of *Don Quixote* would not have arisen. As it stands, however, the time lag between composition and publication serves only to add to the confusion, not solve it.

He still had not produced the works promised to Osorio, one of the finest and most popular actors of the age and now a successful theatre company manager. With the closure of theatres – the death of Philip's daughter in November 1597 induced the king to close all the theatres – any hopes of writing more for the stage proved untimely. Indeed, the theologians and moralists wanted the closure permanent, and they persuaded the austere monarch to agree. For Cervantes, who was thinking more and more of living by his pen, the ability to respond to circumstance and to popular taste was a necessary prerequisite. Lope de Vega had ably demonstrated this virtue for the theatre. For once circumstances came to Cervantes' aid: he was able to concentrate on his prose. The respite, however, was to be shortlived, for, amid the gloom of the royal bereavement, he was to learn that Ana Franca had died in May 1598, leaving their daughter Isabel homeless. Cervantes acted swiftly and enlisted the aid of his favourite sister Magdalena, who was working as a seamstress, to take Isabel under her wing. It was not the only time that he would be indebted to Magdalena.[36]

THE IMPULSE TO WRITE
(1598–1604)

Probably the most significant event in Spain in 1598 was the death of Philip II.[1] Although an invalid for the last two years of his reign, he had ruled Spain over forty years. Now that he was dead Seville made plans to build an honorary tomb on a par with the wonders of the ancient world. Despite Philip II's third bankruptcy the year before, the city of Seville insisted on a last extravaganza for a monarch many saw as the 'incarnation of God on earth'.[2] Cervantes wrote a funeral sonnet that won widespread and immediate recognition and one that he, according to a reference made in *Voyage to Parnassus*, considered one of his best. The tomb, which carried two scenes of Lepanto, was completed after fifty-two days of intense activity, but no sooner had the king been buried than the plague that had been festering since 1596 unleashed itself. David Vassberg claims that some 10 per cent of Castile's total population was wiped out between 1599 and 1601. Eight thousand died in Seville alone. Clearly it was no place for Cervantes to stay. He most probably went north to Esquivias or even Madrid, but we have no documentation to prove this.

Although often read as a celebratory poem, the sonnet Cervantes composed for the dead monarch is rather a burlesque work in which he criticizes Habsburg Spain and the superstructure of Catholic royalty. Critics, citing the testimony of Francisco de Ariño, a contemporary witness to the events surrounding the monarch's funeral, point to Cervantes' cynical attitude with regard to the ornateness of the catafalque that, despite its ostentatious outer trappings, fails to conceal the reality of death within. It was the poet's way of attacking Spanish imperialism which, in order to succeed on the world's stage, conquered Christian idealism. And yet Cervantes well knew that as a soldier at Lepanto and as a commissary for the Armada he had been part of that imperialistic zeal. His sonnet, therefore, offers us an insight into his personal dilemma: his role as an apologist for the dead king and that of an erstwhile soldier who, decades after Lepanto, holds quite other views on spiritual superiority. Whether or not we can go so far as to interpret the sonnet as a work that 'deconstructs the national identity of Spain', the poem is clearly no work of homage to Philip II.[3] Given that throughout his lifetime the war ethic had governed life in the Iberian Peninsula, it can be no surprise that Cervantes, in line with Erasmus, would advocate a trans-national humanism. Both men sought to uphold the ideals of Christianity in what was then an emerging new age of materialism and intolerance. As Cervantes contemplated the tomb he may well have sensed the pangs of disillusion (*desengaño*), the theme that was to afflict Spanish life and letters in the seventeenth century.

In his reflections Cervantes would have remembered Philip II's intense efforts to ensure that Philip III, his sole surviving male heir, received an education worthy of a ruler of such a vast empire. The new monarch's possessions ran from Lisbon to Mexico, from Naples to Manila, Macao, Malacca and Angola back to Madrid. Philip II's messianic imperialism pervaded his court after the annexation of Portugal, only to wane after the defeat of the Armada, so much so that the Spain he left behind was in crisis: demoralized, bankrupt and facing hostilities on almost every front.

If known, he may have pondered the dead monarch's advice to his inexperienced son 'to have more care and awareness than in times past', something that could without difficulty be applied to his own situation. For such advice, prudent to be sure, marked a retreat from ambition, a readjustment to the practice of *Weltpolitik*. The image of Philip II slowly rotting to death on his bed of pain is well known to Spaniards, but less known was his love of flowers, his anxiety about his children, his onerous work-rate, a strong sense of divine election, a gift for exacting obedience and, at the height of his powers, a maritime strategy of unrestrained imperial ambition. Nevertheless, he went to his grave a disillusioned and perhaps an embittered man.[4]

Shortly before he died, Philip lamented to the Marquis of Castel-Rodrigo that others would have to rule for his son, and he was proved right. But how much was the Prudent Monarch to blame for his young son's reliance on favourites? An interesting appraisal of Philip III was made by Vendramino, the Venetian ambassador in Madrid, who claimed that he was 'of a gentle disposition' and that he 'cultivated feelings of generosity very close to those of his father whom he tries to imitate in words and deeds'.[5] There were, however, numerous less flattering observations. While all commentators agreed that the king should be a prudent ruler, not all agreed on the meaning of prudence.[6] Vendramino portrays the new king as both 'very obedient and docile' but one who 'shows little intelligence in matters of state'. He concludes by claiming that 'ever since childhood Philip III had been stirred by a deep religious fervour that bordered on mysticism' so much so that 'he fled the company of women'.

In Spain the transition from one reign to the next was viewed as a natural process and lacked any of the ceremonial and legalistic overtones that characterized the elevation of a new ruler in France or in England. There was no coronation oath or interregnum, for example. The Spanish proverb 'A rey muerto, rey puesto' (A king dies, a king rises) summarizes the process of the transfer of power. In fact Philip III himself stressed the importance of dynastic continuity in a meeting of the Council of State in which, like his father before him, he declared himself 'a militant defender of the true faith'. His subjects were particularly keen to see whose fortunes would rise and fall, a topic already of considerable attention during the last few months of the old king's reign.[7]

The new monarch had inherited from his father a Spain on the wane: three bankruptcies during Philip II's reign had more than alarmed the Treasury; the harvests at home were failing; the plague was biting deeply into all areas, particularly in the south of the country, and Spanish troops abroad were suffering the first of a series of defeats. Imitating his father, the new king had his royal favourites, in particular Don Francisco Gómez de Sandoval y Rojas (?1552–1625) – better known as the Duke of Lerma – who ran the day-to-day administration of the monarchy. So successful was Lerma that his critics labelled him an opportunist and the twenty-year-old Philip his puppet. Furthermore, several historians have concluded that Philip III, because he did not follow his father's leadership style, was weak and inept, and they point to the cost of his marriage to his cousin, Marguerite of Austria – which amounted to almost one-fifth of the annual national income – to prove their point.

Indeed, after Philip III's death in 1621, depictions of him as a weak king, a *rex inutilis* in the parlance of the period, began to circulate widely. Yet modern investigation refutes such a narrow view, which has its basis in the devastating denunciation of the new monarch and of his closest advisers by Francisco de Quevedo. Rather than Philip III's reign being written off as a period of no historical significance, it is now seen as critical to our understanding of the drive to create an absolute monarchy, a process initiated under the rule of his father. The continuation of this process during the reign of Philip III is seen in the reproduction of similar ideologies but more especially in the concentration of power at the centre by creating new institutions and by placing favourites at the apex of the monarchical machinery. And it was the Duke of Lerma who stole the limelight not because he treated the young king as his puppet but as a result of his response to 'institutional needs because he had superior political abilities'.[8]

A special committee created by Philip to examine the location of the court concluded that Madrid was noisy, dysfunctional, bankrupt and overpopulated. It was a significant conclusion, because the presence of the royal court increased demand for every sort of local product and made its location the richest and largest internal market. The fact that Lerma's estates were nearer Valladolid than Madrid may well have influenced the committee's decision, although the final choice rested solely with the new monarch who himself chose the former seat of the Castilian court, Valladolid, over Toledo and Burgos, the other two cities recommended. Hindsight shows that political reasons dictated the move away from Madrid rather than Lerma's economic self-interest or the delicate health of the new monarch as some had rumoured.

In Valladolid the Duke of Lerma could freely behave as the king's protective shield that he believed himself to be. Indeed, the portrait of him by Rubens painted in the new capital – reproduced in the plate section of this book – bears striking resemblance to that of Philip II painted by Titian in 1548. Rubens visited Valladolid in the autumn of 1603 in his official capacity as ambassador of the Duke of Mantua. Although art historians tend to read into their descriptions of historical figures known aspects of the lives of their subjects, there is something regal in the way the Duke of Lerma commands his horse, surroundings and the canvas itself.[9] The battle scenes in the background of the painting are clearly a reference to the Sandoval family's glorious past. The two portraits invite us to compare the epochs and the qualities of leadership that both men enshrined. Despite its brevity, the transfer to Valladolid between 1601 and 1606, which had been proposed by numerous writers and courtiers even at the end of Philip II's reign, was to have enormous repercussions for Spain.

Whatever views one may hold of the Duke of Lerma, he is undoubtedly a significant figure in the life of Cervantes, if for no other reason than it was his government under which Cervantes was to live for almost two decades of his extraordinarily active life. The presence of a court favourite was, of course, nothing new in Spain or, for that matter, in other European courts. In Philip II's court the most influential minister and favourite during the 1590s was Cristóbal de Moura, the king's *privado* or chief counsellor. Philip II was sufficiently conscious of his own royal sovereignty not to allow de Moura to usurp his position or power, as, throughout his reign, he remained a monarch jealous of his personal prerogatives and powers, so much so that he never publicly delegated his authority to any of his ministers. He clearly recognized the dangers to leadership when friendship and politics combine, and so he made sure that he ratified all decisions. But this style of majesty changed after his reign. When personal and political relationships overlap the result is often perceived as corruption or, as Antonio Feros explains, as 'the infringement of private interests on the public good'.[10] With the arrival of the Duke of Lerma on the scene these issues became matters of intense debate especially among political writers, playwrights and thinkers, and Cervantes was not to be excluded. Analogous to such a relationship is that between monarch and subject, master and servant and soul and body, and these in turn became the themes of several books and treatises by various authors, some of which were dedicated to the Duke of Lerma himself.

Having its literary roots in the role of the courtier and therefore in the seminal work of Baldassare Castiglione – whose text *Il Corteggiano* was translated into Spanish as *El Cortesano* by Juan Boscán in 1534 – the whole subject of rule, rulership, service and the public good came under close scrutiny, especially so in *Don Quixote, Part Two*. The reality of the close friendship between monarch and favourite in early seventeenth-century Spain had its slightly earlier parallel in that between master and squire in the novel *Don Quixote*. In the latter case the friendship between them is one that was clearly influenced by previous works on this topic. Much of what Cervantes has to tell us about the urgent issues of his times is commonly veiled but not to the extent that we cannot extract the deeper essence. Whether Sancho ever indulges in the 'politics of intimacy', which is a common accusation levelled against the Duke of Lerma, is open to debate, but for success at court it was a prerequisite. Those servants – counsellors of state? – who were privy to the monarch clearly enjoyed all the advantages that proximity affords. This being so, it was likewise advantageous to keep others, rivals no doubt, away from the royal presence. And so it is no surprise that Philip III's inaccessibility became axiomatic. In this absence from the public gaze he seems to be following the advice given to Prince Hal in Shakespeare's *Henry IV, Part One*, when the king tells the heir apparent not to be lavish with his presence in public but, rather, 'By being seldom seen, I could not stir / But, like a comet, I was wond'red at; / That men would tell their children "This is he"; / Others would say "Where, which is Bolingbroke?" / And then I stole all courtesy from heaven.'[11]

While Don Quixote took centre stage in his noble quest to reform the world, his creator was relegated to the wings. He became more of a recluse – he had to in order to complete the number of works we know he completed – and, although he preferred solitude and tranquillity to the clamour and chaos of courtly existence, he was still preoccupied about his public image and he still sought recognition. The common image of Philip II as 'a black spider in his bleak cell in El Escorial' contrasts vividly with Titian's portrait of him in armour and invites comparison with a Cervantes locked in his study composing his novel while his knight, dressed in armour, takes on the world.[12]

Chroniclers describe the convoys of mule and bullock carts carrying the royal possessions lining the two main roads that led to Valladolid. For several months the locals would have seen cavalcades of wagons and baggage carts make their colourful procession across the landscape of Castile. But this was nothing new; during peak seasons the main roads of Castile were 'choked by caravans of carts and mule trains transporting goods from one part of the country to the other'.[13] As early as 1545 the Emperor Charles V complained of the many places on the road between Burgos and Medina del Campo where it was impossible to walk. The scene that caught his eye must have been cacophonous; Burgos was, after all, the northern hub of Castile's north–south carting network. The agricultural calendar played a major role in the use of roads for land transport. The enormous reliance on the ox and cart created a vast network of itinerant labour; we can only imagine the scene of hundreds of oxen and carts used to transport materials to build El Escorial. Cervantes would have known such scenes intimately and understood the crucial importance of the seasonality of road use. In an age when the village was the *patria chica*, travel to other regions was like travelling abroad. We also have to modify our concept of what constitutes a road: even the major thoroughfares were primitive, and roads were, by and large, nothing but well-trodden paths. Indeed, the city of Valladolid complained to the court about the deplorable condition of several of its thoroughfares. Anyone who thinks Cervantes enjoyed riding on such roads is surely mistaken. In the heat of summer they were dust bowls and often in winter impassable quagmires. According to a map of the principal routes in the Iberian Peninsula drawn by Juan de Villegas in 1546, it is clear that the network was particularly well developed around the major trading centres of the Castilian heartland: Burgos, Medina del Campo, Valladolid and Toledo. The roads from Valladolid to Toledo via Madrid and Toledo to Seville via Córdoba were well known to Cervantes, although Villegas' map fails to show the complex network of local roads linking lesser towns and villages to the urban centres, routes Cervantes the commissary would have had to use for most of his travels in Andalusia.[14]

When the king moved to the new capital it was inevitable that the entire panoply of court personnel and administration would follow, and in a couple of years Madrid would be a shadow of its former glory, much of its population, many of whom depended on the court for work, having been compelled to uproot itself. The serious economic and social decline that befell Toledo after 1561 – the year Philip II decided to plant the capital in Madrid – would now strike Madrid, although not so deeply. Trade routes, commerce and population had left the Imperial City – the popular term for Toledo – to shift northwards to Madrid. Now huge numbers left Madrid to go further north, including, in 1603, Cervantes' eldest sister Andrea and her daughter Constanza de Ovando y Figueroa, accompanied by Magdalena and Isabel. They were joined later by Cervantes but precisely when is not recorded.

By now Isabel was approaching seventeen and had been with Magdalena some three years. To the outside world she was serving her time in domestic service, a typical occupation for a substantial proportion of boys and girls. It was behind this that Cervantes could conceal the true identity of his daughter, but he could not have done so without the initial connivance of Magdalena and Ana Franca. Those employed in domestic service were very often highly mobile. Many rural families took in poor relatives, and Isabel, when her mother died in 1598, was certainly poor. One wonders what Cervantes would have done with his illegitimate daughter had such customs not been in place or if his petition to go to the New World had been successful.

From the summer of 1600, when he finally took leave of Seville, to the summer of 1604, when documents prove his presence – although not necessarily his arrival – in the new capital, the location of Cervantes poses a mystery. So few records of these four years exist that biographers and commentators have been forced to make inspired guesses, although family gatherings probably caused him to pay more visits to Esquivias and its environs. Given that the licence to publish *Don Quixote* was granted in 1604 it is safe to assume that, whatever his location, he had been writing. And as he did so he would have been happy to see that the new century saw Spain intent on peace with France – the Treaty of Vervins signed in 1598 was still intact – relations with England were improving and would soon lead to the Treaty of London (1604) and at long last a peace accord with the Low Countries, ratified in 1609. Amid these positive steps towards peace, Cervantes would have heard of the death of his brother Rodrigo at the Battle of the Dunes in July 1600. Allegedly an heroic death, his career had taken him to Italy, Lepanto, the Azores and to Flanders, but despite his devoted service to king and country he had not risen above the rank of second lieutenant. No one knows why promotion eluded him, and equally as mysterious is the fact that his sisters had to wait over half a century to collect his back pay and then only in part.

Contrary to the ingrained assumptions of English tradition, the defeat by England in 1588 marked not the end but the beginning of the Spanish Armada. Evidence for this is seen in the 1590s, which marked the crucial decade in the formation of the Habsburg monarchy's first permanent naval organization outside the Mediterranean, culminating with the arrival from Spain in Dunkirk in 1598 of Martín de Bertendona with a flotilla of converted warships for incorporation into the Armada. Indeed, in the opening months of the new reign of Philip III, lists of prizes and captives in the three ports of Dunkirk, Gravelines and Nieuwpoort demonstrated the higher profile of the fleet. From these ports Spain was to launch successful raids on the Dutch fishing fleet, which led to the latter's determined land offensive against the Spanish-ruled Flanders ports in 1600. The attack was stemmed outside Nieuwpoort but with a level of loss among the ranks of the army of Flanders that 'engendered an atmosphere of crisis in the Council of State' in Madrid.[15] Among the dead was Rodrigo de Cervantes, lost in action on foreign soil.

Our knowledge of the period tells us that Rodrigo's whole adult life was circumscribed by war or its threat. He was a professional soldier in an age when the war ethic ruled daily life in Iberia, contributing to a crisis in the social order that became increasingly acute in the 1590s. Not only were enemies at home – the Morisco and, after the annexation of Portugal, many Portuguese – but also abroad, in Algiers, Turkey, England, France and in the Low Countries. And of course there were the problems in the Americas. There arose in Spain's consciousness an overpowering fear of invasion from without which magnified and distorted the psychological impact of war. Defence of an empire as huge as that of Imperial Spain depended on an effective machinery of government but also on soldiers like Rodrigo.

The extension of war into the Atlantic in the 1580s compelled governments, not only the Spanish, to construct highly expensive coastal fortifications and the creation of high seas fleets, especially after 1588. It also caused a more general militarization of society as a whole in the interests of national defence. As a result, the impact of war did not fall only on the areas in which fighting actually took place, as Cervantes' role as commissary and Crown agent had proved. In Spain, the burden of billeting and purveyance, the loss of crops and animals, the levying of contributions in money and kind and the stopping of trade by the commissariat proved damaging. There was a plethora of complaints during the 1580s and 1590s precisely from those regions newly affected by fleet purveyance and the passage of troops to the Atlantic ports. By 1598, if a statement in the Cortes is to be believed, the villages of Castile were owed 1.6 million ducats for victualling and billeting expenses, a fivefold increase in just twelve years. Cervantes certainly knew about victualling expenses and Rodrigo would have known all about the problems of billeting and, in particular, of the epidemic of popular disturbances in the 1590s. Protests against high taxes, the export of grain to the army and the depredations of the soldiery characterized peasant rebellions in France, the southern Netherlands and even in Austria and Hungary. Closer to home the Spanish saw the extraordinary resistance of Ávila and other old Castile cities to the *millones* tax and the disaffection of the Portuguese smarting at the pillaging of their empire and of their shipping, which found one outlet in the murder and mistreatment of Spanish soldiers garrisoned in Lisbon.[16]

Life would never have been easy for Rodrigo: soldiers were owed months of back pay and left starving by the incompetence or rapacity of the commissariat. Undoubtedly, the soldier was the real sufferer and, unsurprisingly, it was the military mutiny that characterized popular revolt in the 1590s. Maybe one major reason why Rodrigo did not resign his post – countless did – was the problems associated with soldiers who returned home. Many such were sick, invalid or famished and thus posed severe problems for governments everywhere. Their response is seen in a spate of welfare policies, hospitals – the hospital mentioned in 'The Colloquy of the Two Dogs' illustrates the point – and provision of pensions. Vagrancy was a real problem in Spain and elsewhere, especially during the 1580s and 1590s. The huge numbers clamouring for recompense in the offices of the War Council explain why Cervantes' parents obtained so little and why Cervantes, when a court petitioner, save for one royal commission to Orán, left empty-handed and probably in disgust. The hordes – many of whom were hoaxers – seeking compensation or favours ensured that his genuine petition failed. Besides, Philip II was far too busy with weightier matters to be able to distinguish just deserts from false. The rise and extreme popularity of the picaresque novel can in part be explained by the high levels of vagrancy in Habsburg Castile. With the works of Quevedo in the seventeenth century, the life of the vagrant reaches its peak both in literature and in society. Moreover, Quevedo's prose work entitled *The Dreams* – more akin to nightmares – is an extension of the collapse of social cohesion. The pitiless waste of resources, even the fabulous wealth of the Indies, could not stop the rot. The memory of chivalric Charles V had long since burned out, and it was not revived by the noble-intentioned exploits of Don Quixote. In the decade leading up to Rodrigo's death, to be a soldier was becoming a shameful occupation. The common soldier had to be forced to the wars. Any man with any substance would buy himself out. Is this then the real reason why Rodrigo remained in the services? He simply was unable to buy himself out.

There is abundant evidence of the complaints and bitter protests levelled at soldiers, at billeting and at the military requisition of grains draft animals and carts. So much so that at home Spanish civilians viewed the average soldier as worse than an enemy. David Vassberg, whose studies trace the daily lives of Spaniards in the sixteenth century, shows how this drastic state of affairs arose. What is abundantly clear is that Spaniards considered soldiers a calamity. Indeed, the annual movement of troops across Castile 'left in its wake a trail of destruction and rapine and the coming of a company of soldiers was awaited with the same trepidation as a hurricane'.[17] These are harsh words indeed and show that Rodrigo was wise to soldier abroad where, arguably, it would be easier to endure the ubiquitous hostility of foreign civilians than at home. Research shows that Philip II maintained between 70,000 and 90,000 soldiers in the Low Countries – in what some called *Castra Dei* (God's encampment) – with perhaps as many men again serving in garrisons around the globe. The dangers of abuse resulting from billeting continued long after Rodrigo's death, as shown in Calderón de la Barca's play, *The Mayor of Zalamea* (c. 1640) in which a captain rapes the daughter of the farmer in whose house he is billeted.[18]

If Rodrigo had sought betterment in the army, for the military life did offer prospects of upward social mobility, it never materialized.[19] Accounts indicate that many who had gone to the wars as common soldiers returned as heroes with prestige, wealth and cosy government jobs. The two Cervantes brothers may have sought such rewards, but despite Herculean efforts over long and arduous years neither succeeded, nor did they benefit materially from the wars in which they fought. In this inability of Spain to change the personal circumstances of the majority of its citizens, some political historians trace the seed that gave rise to Neo-Stoicism as the new social ethic. Literary analysts as well as historians – social, urban and political – agree that it was to be one of the principal means by which the traditional social order overcame the crisis of the age. The prominent themes of moral and political discourse about the state of Spain from the end of the sixteenth century onwards were convictions or fears that God had deserted his Spaniards, 'that they had failed the trials of faith and that they were following earlier empires – albeit somewhat prematurely – into ruin'.[20]

Yet nothing was to deter Cervantes from his creative writing. Another spur to which would have been the enormous success of *Guzmán de Alfarache*, a picaresque novel written by Mateo Alemán and published in 1599. It is hard to explain the extraordinary success of this novel – it appeared in twenty-three editions in six years – in which the protagonist leads the life of a rogue while the narrator offers what can best be described as sermons. The hero is really an anti-hero, who lives in a cruel and corrupt world where to survive one has to live off one's wits. When the young Guzmán claims that 'Although I was evil, I wanted to be good', he no doubt was voicing a strong sentiment of Spain's population suffering the bite of rapid economic and social collapse.[21] The home truths presented by Alemán, such as injustice and the ridicule of virtue in a world where immorality triumphs, appealed to a society of which his text was a faithful mirror. And with the wealth of the Duke of Lerma soon to be paraded before their very eyes – he amassed a fortune allegedly worth 44 million maravedís – interest in Alemán's text was destined to continue. Cervantes well knew the realities of which Alemán spoke, but his reaction to them, when he in his turn wrote about them, would be quite different.

So successful was *Part One* of Alemán's novel that before *Part Two* was published in 1604 a spurious sequel appeared written by José Martí. Of interest to us is not the sequel but the fact that Martí's action foreshadows what will happen to *Don Quixote* a little later. No one could fail to ignore Alemán's spectacular success. Through it Cervantes realized that he could extend the length of *Don Quixote*, which had probably begun life as a novella and as such had been favourably received in literary circles. That is why the publisher felt so keen to publish the longer version. Cervantes wanted to offer the public something altogether new, and so he decided not to extend his picaresque short story 'Rinconete and Cortadillo' but present to the world an amusing attack on a genre that had been in vogue for decades but which had been viciously criticized by moralists and clerics. Siding for once with officialdom, he hoped his work would destroy chivalresque novels for ever. And while preparing his text his resolve would have been further steeled by the appearance of yet another novel of chivalry, *Don Policisne de Boecia*, written by Juan de Silva y Toledo and published, the last of its kind in Spain, in autumn 1602. Thus, despite the vitriolic attacks against such poisonous works that had raged for decades, publishers still deemed the genre a profitable product.

There is no record to show when and where Cervantes heard of his brother's death but possibly in Toledo where, on 19 August 1600, his brother-in-law, Fernando de Salazar Palacios, made his will prior to becoming a novitiate of the Franciscan Order in that city. Entrusted with the execution of Fernando's will Cervantes now had access to some money – a good reason therefore to devote himself wholeheartedly to his novel. But the whereabouts of Cervantes thereafter until his next appearance in Esquivias on 27 January 1603, when he attended the baptism of the daughter of friends of the Salazars, remains obscure. A fortnight before this his wife had sold some land of hers for some 10,000 maravedís. What is recorded is that on 10 September 1601 their lordships in the Treasury in Valladolid made known the fact that they had not received confirmation that Cervantes had paid the 80,000 maravedís he had collected from duties he had carried out in Vélez-Málaga some seven years before. The case dragged on – and in this Cervantes may be to blame – because on 24 January 1603 the Treasury officials reported that he had still not paid the outstanding debt. Such officials had elephantine memories when it came to money they believed was owed them but seemed to forget the legitimate debts they owed others, as the case of Rodrigo's back pay proves. But to receive a reminder of a claim for money outstanding, even if ascribed in error, to a man on the verge of completing the first part of what has become an accepted world masterpiece must have been galling. Not only had he to revise, paginate and arrange his material, which included two interpolated *novellas* written several years before, but he also had to compose a prologue, which in his day was never short; and, like his contemporary Shakespeare, all with the aid of a quill pen, the vagaries of which today's world knows nothing about. Arguably, the prologue is the best key we have as to the intentions of Cervantes in writing his masterpiece. Similarly, the eloquent prologue to the *Exemplary Novels* remains the safest base from which to unlock the hidden and mysterious fruit which a careful reading of the stories in that famous collection – a collection woefully unknown to most outside Spain and the Spanish-speaking world – supposedly reveals.[22] Everything had to be prepared for printing, and Cervantes was staking his livelihood on the attempt. Even when he considered the text ready he had to convey the entire work, which ran to some 664 pages of print in the *princeps* edition, on the back of a horse in saddle-packs, praying that no page was lost or stolen in transit.

We do not know of his immediate reaction to the Treasury's unjust claim, but it seems not to have deterred him from his prime purpose. Once free from the strictures of government work, he pressed on regardless. It is no real surprise, therefore, to discover that he kept a low profile. Because he had no need to deal with officialdom there are, during the gestation of *Don Quixote*, very few official documents to be had. Commentators tend to agree that his circle of movement was Madrid, Toledo and Esquivias, well away from the building boom and extravagant fiestas of the court in Valladolid and even further away from the plague-ridden south. If this is true, it may well be, perhaps for the first time since his marriage, that these days in old-fashioned but class-conscious Esquivias brought him the respite for which he had yearned when burdened by his constant tours of duty in Andalusia. It is not difficult to imagine him surrounded by books, pens, inks and papers in much the same way that Don Quixote used to be when absorbed in his reading of prolix novels of chivalry. And, by delving into his wife's family history, Cervantes would have come across the surname of Quijada, probably the prototype of the surname given to his famous knight. Indeed, it is one of the variations Cervantes toys with before hitting on Quijote, a true son of Castile.

If Cervantes did complete *Don Quixote, Part One* in Esquivias, he would have returned to his wife's home after an absence of some seventeen years. It would also account for those 'lost years' for which there is no record of his whereabouts. We know that Catalina went to Valladolid in 1604 to join his family. It would be odd for her to do this if prior contact had not already been made, for nothing suggests that she had not coped well enough without them. Little is known, and little therefore is said, of this belated reunion after leading separate lives for so many years. The eighteen-year age difference remained, but how were the years of separation sealed between them? It could not have been easy, for in any life seventeen years is a long time, especially when you are abandoned at twenty-two. Biographers and commentators pass over this reunion all too quickly, but the event is worth a moment's reflection. She would have known that his return was to write full-time. No mention is made of her younger brother and sister, who by now would probably have been married, thus leaving Catalina alone in the house, ideal for a writer eager to complete what time and opportunity had not allowed him to contemplate for decades. Possibly she would have welcomed his return to a house that was empty and, from her standpoint, rather lonely. Let us not forget that, with the death of Rodrigo, Cervantes' circle of relatives was ever decreasing, so a reunion might have been welcome to both parties. The majority of documents relating to Cervantes and his wife for the years 1600 to 1604 link him to Esquivias, Valladolid, Toledo and Madrid.[23] In Valladolid a childless Catalina would have had to share premises with Cervantes' bastard daughter as well as care for a man who had effectively deserted her after only three years of conjugal life. After having to fend for herself in a backwater, off the major trading and travel routes, she was now to experience urban life, breathe the same air as the royal family and, more importantly, share Cervantes' unexpected fame and glory. She was to witness an explosion of consciousness that led to a prodigious output of creative works, the volume of which alone testifies that even now she very much took second place.

The city of Valladolid was no bad choice for what proved to be a short-term capital. Razed to the ground by a fire in 1561 – the same year that Philip moved to Madrid from Toledo – it had been rebuilt along what were then considered modern concepts of urban living. Boasting a population that had risen from 15,000 at the start of Philip II's reign to in excess of 70,000 at its close, it had been the seat of the Chancery since the reign of Ferdinand and Isabella and had already served, intermittently, as the capital during the reign of Charles V. Strategically located at the centre of a network of communications, its fertile surroundings, greatly improved by a policy of reafforestation the previous century, could certainly offer the delicate Philip III better air than that of Madrid. And within the city precincts it offered the biggest and best of Spain's main squares, with its five hundred porches and two thousand windows. The city's churches, palaces, fountains and shady walks along the river Pisuerga spoke of an opulence that Cervantes' father half a century before had witnessed but could neither enjoy nor share. In fact, Rodrigo would not have recognized the city, for it had lost some 2,200 houses in the great fire.[24]

The new building boom unleashed by the sudden rise in Valladolid's status meant that houses were built rapidly but not well, and those built outside the inner precincts were literally thrown together. The home rented by the Cervantes household was a slum even before it had been completed. Situated in the district that also housed the major slaughterhouse and only twenty paces from the banks of the Esgueva, Cervantes had moved into a very modest second-floor apartment over a tavern on one edge of town. Adjoining the newly built three-storey building was the Resurrection Hospital; despite the name such buildings were often hospices or shelters created to provide food and lodging for the needy. The prosperous years of the sixteenth century witnessed a proliferation of such institutions throughout Spain, and they provided basic essentials to vagrants, beggars, delinquents and criminals, as well as the sick. Strapped for cash and having arrived late, the Cervantes household had settled in the paupers' quarter. The fact that hospices housed those who lived on the margin, including criminals, may have bearing on the Ezpeleta affair that was shortly to involve the whole household.[25]

In stark contrast to the shoddy apartment of the Cervantes household stood the opulent dwellings of those who had moved with the royal entourage and were by now comfortably and safely accommodated in the more fashionable districts around the royal residence. In a society where manual labour was increasingly frowned upon, although there was a greater productive workforce in Valladolid than in Madrid, proximity to the court carried considerable social prestige. El Greco's town plan of Toledo, drawn in the first decade of the seventeenth century, illustrates the inner core of wealth radiating out from the cathedral and city hall.[26] What the city hall was to Toledo the royal court would have been to Valladolid. Modern notions of suburban life as indicative of higher socio-economic groups are misleading when applied to Spain, where social life revolved around the town square, a tradition which Iberian colonialists transferred to Latin American cities and which is still very much in evidence today.[27]

The Cervantes household lived in premises that in total comprised thirteen rooms, and records indicate that the building was home for some twenty people. Cervantes had already received a down-payment for his novel, not over-generous but enough for him to devote himself to his writing, for he knew that his novel was to be published. With a household of women to care for it was no easy matter. He was clearly helped by his sisters, for there is record of Andrea who, in July 1603, 'received 788 reales, the cost of making and repairing shirts for Pedro de Toledo Osorio, the Marquis of Villafranca and for his wife'.[28] All such income – and this was a tidy sum – would have been welcome, for it allowed Cervantes the time and opportunity to persevere. He had a mission, and now, approaching the ripe age of fifty-seven, was, according to Canavaggio, feeling the weight of years and the first onset of the diabetes that was to strike a severe blow a decade later.[29]

The pressures of home life in cheap accommodation were more than compensated for in the contacts Cervantes made outside his home. He rubbed shoulders with the intelligentsia of the city and in particular with Alonso López Pinciano, a native of Valladolid who had published in 1596 what was perhaps the most important theoretical work of its day, a study on Aristotle's *Poetics*. In the scrutiny of books carried out by the canon in *Don Quixote*, it is transparent that Pinciano's text was known and studied by Cervantes. Much of the literary theory the canon displays, his notions regarding the function of literature and the nature of aesthetics stem from Aristotelian principles. What the canon considers good literature is based on premises Cervantes adhered to closely in his own practice of the novel. So fine is the fusion between precept and practice that it is easy to overlook the fundamental literary principles which form the substratum of his writings, especially in his masterpiece. A mark of the genius of the man is the manner in which he weds classical notions of literary theory and invention to create an original work that appeals to many. Cervantes was very much aware and appreciative of the works of theorists. Knowledge of such was indispensable to a writer who boasted that he was the first to write novellas in Spanish. Without a prior knowledge of the principles that governed earlier writers how could he make such a claim or speak about originality?[30]

The publication of Pinciano's treatise, followed shortly by the picaresque novel *Guzmán de Alfarache*, ensured that the century in Spain closed with a literary bang. The timing of both texts coincided perfectly with Cervantes' gestation of his major work. From Pinciano he recognized theoretical principles that his own practice already endorsed, while from Mateo Alemán's best-selling book he concluded that the reading public was still hungry and that such hunger would best be satisfied not by another picaresque novel but by something quite different. Furthermore, the canon's remarks prove that Cervantes kept abreast of literary events and that he was the most avid of readers. We can perhaps see a strong reflection of Cervantes in Tomás Rodaja, the protagonist of 'The Glass Graduate', whose love of reading and learning is a major aspect of that fascinating story. In Valladolid, too, Cervantes met the rising stars of Spanish letters, Francisco de Quevedo and Luis de Góngora. Unfortunately, he was also to enter into a bitter feud with Spain's most popular dramatist ever, Lope de Vega. What was to prove a long-drawn-out literary dispute concerned their individual practice of basic literary precepts. It was never resolved. Both were members of literary academies in which personal antagonisms often tended to prevail. When Lope de Vega wrote in 1604 that there was no poet as bad as Cervantes or anyone so stupid as to praise *Don Quixote*, the feud was already up and running. And, despite Lope de Vega's seeming repentance in 1631, when he claims that Cervantes' verse was made of diamonds, his perverse earlier criticism stuck and has tainted Cervantes' reputation as a poet ever since. The full effect of the damage to Cervantes' self-esteem and his considered reaction to it form part of the motive behind *Voyage to Parnassus*, written a decade later. For the moment, however, Cervantes had eyes only on the imminent publication of what was to become his major work. He had come a long way since *La Galatea*, but with Lope de Vega's cutting remarks ringing in his ears he must have wondered how the world would take to his noble knight and his uneducated, credulous squire.

DON QUIXOTE, THE KNIGHT ERRANT OF LA MANCHA (1604–8)

It was fortunate that Francisco de Robles, the son of Blas de Robles, the publisher who had published *La Galatea* in 1585, had opened up shop in the new capital in 1601. Although he had not been published for some twenty years, Cervantes had visited Madrid on enough occasions to maintain contact with the family-run business and would have learned of the company's move to Valladolid. He had a few sharp things to say about publishers but was appreciative of Francisco de Robles. Having established contact with him, the same merry-go-round for licences, privileges, seals of approval and publishing rights had to be repeated, and in January 1605, that is, six months after his arrival in the new capital, *Don Quixote* was published. Its success was immediate and Cervantes became a household name; he was famous but still not rich. Although no more than 1,750 copies were published – a number modern readers may find surprisingly small – it was atypical in that first runs at the time rarely exceeded 1,000 copies. The reprint – in effect, a revised and updated version of the first and now considered more correctly to be the second edition – also published by Francisco de Robles, ran to 1,800 copies, proof of its popularity. What is often overlooked, however, is the proven fact that such texts were read time and time again. The reprint indeed sold well – but not as spectacularly well as *Guzmán de Alfarache* – and would have done better if two pirate editions had not appeared in Portugal. None the less by the end of 1607 not one copy remained in the publisher's shop.[1] Francisco de Robles had been issued a licence to publish only in Castile, so he now had to gain another licence to publish in Aragón, Catalonia, Valencia and Portugal. Curiously, a batch of copies was sent in February to Peru and two months later another batch to Mexico. Unfortunately, not one of these first editions has ever been found. The fact that copies of the novel were sent abroad underlined the recognition of his success, because in both 1531 and 1543 royal decrees were issued prohibiting the export to the Indies of 'immoral' chivalresque novels such as *Amadís de Gaula*. It was fortunate for Cervantes that in 1555 a petition from the National Assembly in Valladolid which sought to have the ban extended to Spain itself and to include virtually all genres of secular literature never reached the statute books.[2] Nevertheless, probably on account of the unofficial prohibition of chivalresque novels in Madrid, *Don Quixote, Part One* was published without its licence or stamp of approval.[3]

Contrary to popular belief, the success of the novel was not overwhelming or sensational, although its sales were, according to the most recent research, considerable. They were also consistent.[4] Undoubtedly the prime cause for the success of the novel lay in its value as entertainment. Despite the disparaging remarks of Lope de Vega, remarks that prove that the text had circulated in literary academies long before the date of publication, the novel was praised by one and all. Cervantes had been vindicated, but the feud with Lope de Vega was not going to go away that easily.

Whatever the prime reasons Cervantes had for writing his masterpiece, it was seen, read and reread as a fun book, and its inherent humour has never been lost on succeeding generations of readers. In a work so diverse and so comprehensive, later readers may have placed different priorities on the novel, but all readers have consistently appreciated its humour. A study of the interpretations of the novel would itself require several volumes; like the Bible it has a message and a meaning not only for every age but apparently for every reader, too. The abiding appeal of the work is intrinsically related to the fusion of comedy and wisdom, but this is not to say that other elements – social, ethical, philosophical, feminist and multi-cultural – are absent; they are not, but to the sixteenth-, seventeenth- and eighteenth-century reader the novel was seen as 'a good read' because of its sheer entertainment value. Twentieth-century readers tended to highlight psychological, sociological and linguistic elements, but throughout we still laugh at the antics of an inspired but deluded individual or at the attitudes of a down-to-earth materialist. What the postmodernist, third millennium public will make of the knight and his squire remains to be seen.[5]

It is all too easy for the modern reader to overlook Cervantes' acute awareness of the changing tastes of his reading public and of doctrinal demands imposed on fiction – a new concept in sixteenth-century Spain – by moralists and literary theoreticians. For, behind the humour and pathos of the multitudinous events engaged in by the knight and his squire, there blew a controversy that raged far and wide. Until the rapid rise of what can best be termed recreational literature the distinction between poetry and history had been clear cut; poetry could have as its subject-matter things which were not real, whereas history, written in prose, concerned things that were fact. But vernacular prose, used as a vehicle for imaginative literature, was sweeping aside such hard and fast conventions, thereby provoking unprecedented consequences. The Church in Spain vigorously opposed such new trends in writing, claiming that the reading of imaginative fiction undermined the moral fibre of society. The theologian Alonso de Fuentes vividly describes his opposition, asserting that because it may 'spread contagious diseases a ban on the import of infected bed linen from Brittany had been imposed', but no stand had been taken against books which set such bad examples and from which so much evil ensued.[6] The attacks against the lies and immorality of such texts – not only novels of chivalry – were persistent and widespread, and it is abundantly clear that Cervantes and others like him had to face enormous opposition from theologians, scholars and the civil authorities. After all, it was the Church, the custodian of morality, whence the fiercest attacks arose, but it was the Crown that gave or withheld its licence for the publication of new books. The peculiar vetting system in Spain had been in operation since the reign of the Catholic Monarchs and was administered by Crown agents, not the Church, although clerics made up most of the inspectorate. And as all writers knew to their cost – especially to that enterprising new band of professional writers of which Cervantes was an early member – to be published they had to appease their detractors, in particular the vociferous clerics. In other words, Cervantes had to tread a high-tension wire strung between the demands of eminent moralists and the appetites of an eager readership waiting to taste new literature. The fact that Cervantes eventually wrote for a living offers us an important clue to the kind of writer he was and to the sorts of things he wrote, whether or not he was successful financially. He clearly knew what kind of fiction the public enjoyed, and he tried his best to deliver it. He never lost sight of the prime role of literature that, for him, served to entertain *and* to instruct. Indeed, the page-poet in 'The Little Gypsy Girl' reiterates the point in his eloquent discourse on the use and function of poetry.[7]

Juan Luis Vives, one of Spain's most eminent humanist scholars and theologians, had already attacked novels of chivalry, complaining that they lacked learning, goodness and wit. Emanating from such a source – Vives had been a close friend of Erasmus and Thomas More and had joined a circle of pious scholars around Catherine of Aragón – Cervantes would have known of such remarks and taken them to heart.[8] Wisely, therefore, he strove to ensure that the same criticisms would not be levelled against his works. This is why, in his prologues, he lays great emphasis on the exemplariness and harmlessness of his writings: no one, so he claims in the prologue to the *Exemplary Novels*, could be offended by them but, on the contrary, would be able to draw great profit from reading them. There is more than gentle irony in such claims, for, although he goes on to depict theft, rape, scenes of murder, violence, piracy, transvestite disguise and so forth, he is at pains to show that no moral harm befalls the reader. And by moral harm Cervantes specifically means that which arises from doctrinal error. He stoutly refuses to include anything in his writings which could offend Catholic doctrine. Because the censors were so totally concerned with such matters, they were not alert to the other dangers associated with secular literature, and their blind spot played into his hands – although he would never have claimed as much. The prologue to his greatest novel echoes the charges against the lies told by writers of novels of chivalry and is repeated in the celebrated discourse on literature in which the canon, village priest and the knight take part. Whereas the critics of imaginative literature wanted it banned, Cervantes goes on to show the opportunities it offers the writer and in so doing provides us with his response to the controversy between historical and poetical truth. Extolling the scope that fiction undoubtedly allows, the canon claims that the writer 'in a grateful style, and with ingenious invention, approaching as much as possible to truth, will doubtless compose so beautiful and various a work, that, when finished, its excellency and perfection must attain the best end of writing, which is at once to delight and to instruct'; hence, when generations of readers of *Don Quixote* laugh, its author attains – at least in part – what is claimed to be the purpose of writing. In brief, Cervantes has followed his own recipe for success. When he was a schoolboy books were read aloud rather than seen by individuals. But by the time *Don Quixote* was sweeping all before it books were for individual use. This represented an enormous change, a change of which Cervantes was acutely aware. Knowing this, therefore, to what extent does he instruct?

It is in direct response to the didactic aspect of the best of creative writing that controversy raged fiercest and probably where he found most difficulty. And it is, I suggest, in his response to the controversy where the key to his success may lie. In that easily overlooked phrase 'approaching as much as possible to truth' is found the clue to the literary storm that raged around him. For if fiction, which by definition is not fact, can appear to wear the coat of truth, what grounds are there for complaint? After all, when readers approach a text they expect to find realistic plots and true-to-life characters and situations. Cervantes, in a much vaunted phrase, states that in his writing he sought that which had 'glimpses of the possible'.[9] If a thing was conceivable it was prime material for literature, although its presentation should never overstep the bounds of belief or decorum. The earlier references to Erasmus in this book and to his overriding emphasis on eloquence now emerge in their true light, for, when the canon mentions 'a grateful style', 'ingenious invention', 'approaching truth', in a work to 'delight and instruct', the seeds of Erasmus have been sown and bear fruit. The fact that the works of Erasmus were later placed on the Index shows even more clearly how cautiously Cervantes had to step. The subtle interplay of didacticism with invention lies at the heart of the achievement of Spanish Golden Age writers such as Mateo Alemán and Cervantes, and appreciation of this, so characteristic of the age and culture in which both men lived, serves to help us understand the minds of such men and the nature of their success.

Censorship was a fact of life in sixteenth-century Spanish society, but life in Elizabethan England was no different. The Tudor state had laws and fierce powers to impose censorship of printed matter, although in practice it 'seems to have been more concerned with obviously seditious or heretical material'.[10] A curious example, but relevant to our study of Spain at the time, was the suppression of the raid on Cádiz in 1596. Mentioned as a 'famous victorie' in Volume 1 of the *Principal Navigations*, the work of Richard Hakluyt, it did not appear in the edition of 1599. The change no doubt is linked with the fact that the Earl of Essex and his bellicose anti-Spanish policies were falling out of favour at this time.[11] Had Cervantes' works carried the faintest trace of apostasy, his writing career would have ended. He had not forgotten that his name had already been tarnished: ever since his grandfather's suit against the Duke of Guadalajara the family name of Cervantes had not been one to flaunt. Such incidents served to remind Cervantes that he could not afford to cross swords with the authorities, civil or spiritual.[12]

There was another aspect of his writing that proved a bone of contention, and that was the relationship between author and reader and the response of readers to works of fiction. Are readers expected to believe literally what they read or do they suspend belief? The modern reader may have clear-cut attitudes to imaginative writing but not so in Cervantes' day. Who nowadays would believe everything they read in fiction as gospel truth? And yet that is precisely what Don Quixote did, and he was not the only Golden Age reader who did so. The crazy knight had been deceived by the semblance of truth, by the key principle of the era, that of verisimilitude. Given that the knight has an over-active imagination allied to his lack of sleep through too much reading, it is no surprise to learn that his brain has become addled. To the Neoplatonists his conduct confirmed their worst fears about the evil effect all mendacious literature – which is what they deemed secular writing to be – had on its audience. And they had a point, for, if fiction is by definition not fact, how can such writing lead to the good, the beautiful and the true? It is in response to this charge that we see the cunning of secular writers such as Cervantes, who defended their position by claiming that poets never intended to be liars but rather veilers of truth. Feigning was not lying but protecting sacred truths from the great unwashed. In making this response, the supporters of fiction were parroting the Neo-Aristotelian preference for the lifelike lie that rested on a veneer of truth. The difference between appearance and reality was well exploited by Golden Age writers, perhaps nowhere better than in *Don Quixote* and in several of the *Exemplary Novels*.[13] It proved to be a trump card and was used often by Cervantes to explain away the evil deeds perpetrated by his several characters. When, in Chapter 9 of *Don Quixote, Part One*, he introduces Cide Hamete Benengeli as the truthful translator of the continuation of *Don Quixote*, is he not stretching the principle of verisimilitude to its outer limits? For it was widely accepted that Arabs were considered inveterate liars. Readers then and now seem to accept the authorial master ploy that aims at a greater freedom of conscience, a difficult attainment in a society where the Inquisition held sway. Yet if we examine the three times Cervantes broached the Morisco question – Benengeli was a Morisco – is not the issue of freedom of conscience at stake? The fact that Christian captives could hear mass and celebrate Christian festivals in Algiers was not something the authorities in Spain wanted to hear, much less practise in a reciprocal sense. And when the Christian Catalina in *The Sultan's Wife* agrees to marry the Muslim sultan, to what extent was Cervantes pushing his luck with the authorities?

In other prologues to his major works Cervantes again broaches the issue of truth in literature. His claim, for instance, in the prologue to his *Exemplary Novels* that the stories contain some hidden mystery and offer the reader some profit or fruit to be gleaned from reading his works illustrates the point. What is this if not the art of persuasion, the supreme skill of the rhetorician, the epitome of eloquence, perhaps the foremost objective of the educational philosophy espoused by Erasmus and his followers? Without eloquence the informed and moral person could not be an effective, persuasive presence in Christian society. To be virtuous, Cervantes would argue, the individual has to know and be exposed to its opposite.

The fact that his works – and not just *Don Quixote* – are also repositories of wit, knowledge and virtue must owe not a little to the acrid accusations of Spain's most respected and learned cleric. Juan Luis Vives and countless others were seriously worried about the effects secular literature had on its readers, particularly on female ones, and the debate found its way into *Don Quixote*. Like so much in his creative works, Cervantes was able to convert a controversial issue into the very fabric of his story. The criticisms of clerics and the like against the evils and excesses of fiction are no different from those today who complain about the influence mass media has on young minds. In sixteenth-century Spain Vives spoke of the sweet venom that progresses through the body in much the same way that the poison poured into Hamlet's father's ears progressed throughout his body, finally killing him. And in the eyes of the Church, especially after the Council of Trent, it was the reader's eternal soul that was at stake.

Of course, the real basis for the opposition to imaginative literature was Plato's banishment of all poets from his Republic. Possibly the most contentious piece of censorship in the history of literary criticism, it was welcomed by traditionalists who used it to attack the upstarts in secular literature. They also embraced Plato's objections to such writers on both moral and metaphysical grounds. Critics of the new wave in literature argued that readers of literature did not need the spice of fiction to make virtue the more palatable. All that was needed was a return to devotional literature and to the Gospels. And they could point to several texts but in particular to Erasmus' *Enchiridion* or *Handbook of the Christian Soldier*, first published in 1518 and translated into Spanish in 1528, which became one of the most widely read and frequently translated spiritual writings of the age. It became Erasmus' most influential single statement about the life of piety and the philosophy of Christ and of deep significance to St Ignatius of Loyola and to St Teresa of Ávila, both of whom confessed to having enjoyed works of fiction. Furthermore, who will deny that the *Enchiridion* influenced the knight Don Quixote? In Spain, where the translation was reprinted twelve times before 1556, its popularity was unparalleled.[14]

The *Enchiridion* tells us that the good life is everybody's business. Plato had said the same thing, and when Don Quixote sets out to right the wrongs of the world, to fight for justice and truth, to defend the young, aged and defenceless, what was he doing but putting into practice the duties and obligations of a true Christian soldier? When the knight fights – often in vain – for what he believes are good and virtuous causes, he is following the advice found in the *Enchiridion*. And true to the author of that most influential of works, when Don Quixote launches into his exploits what is particularly evident is his lack of deference to clerical direction: he sees himself, despite the occasional presence of the canon and priest, as his own spiritual director. And yet his creator well knew that the Council of Trent had forbidden all chivalric combat.[15] Propelled by an all-consuming spirit of conquest, so typical of his age and so representative of the imperialistic nature of the regime of his day, the wizened knight slowly learns the error of his ways. But did Spanish monarchy learn as much and as quickly? The most Sancho gains is an imaginary island and that not for long. But to what extent is the squire's short reign influenced by Giovanni Botero's seminal work *Della Ragion di Stato* (*On the Reason of State*), translated into Spanish in 1603 by Spain's great historiographer-royal, Antonio de Herrera? The text proved to be enormously influential in Spain, where it stood alongside St Thomas More's *Utopia*.[16]

It is clear from a study of Cervantine writings that he was keen to show that in literature truth was what an audience can be persuaded to believe. That is why he accentuated the principle of *admiratio*, that classical concept which induces astonishment and wonder and keeps the reader glued to the text. In this regard 'The Colloquy of the Two Dogs' serves both to illustrate and to answer the problem of belief in literature. Campuzano repeatedly draws the reader's attention to the story's implausibility, and we know that dogs do not and cannot talk – even both dogs in the story doubt their own seeming ability to speak. Few fall for the suggestion that they might actually be men but have been changed into dogs. And yet we go on reading. Why? Curiosity? Humour? Is it the challenge that such a proposition poses or is it because the dogs actually talk sense? After all, there is nothing in the dialogue except what the two dogs said or are alleged to have said. Cervantes has clearly provided us with a fiction that he somehow makes us believe is true, even though we know that dogs don't speak. His method is the art of persuasion through the medium of language; the speech of the dogs does the rest. Readers would have been aware of the long tradition of animals speaking in literature. The fables of Aesop are an obvious example and form part of the convention that shows that moral satire can spring from the mouths and minds of so-called dumb beasts. The delirium under which the sick Campuzano suffers certainly paves the way for the story to unfold; patients ill in hospital can be prone to all sorts of dementia, hallucinations and phantasmagoria. It is this fact of human reality that provides the semblance of truth which Cervantes employs to release his fiction. Similarly, the dementia that afflicts Tomás Rodaja in 'The Glass Graduate' goes horribly wrong. Given a love potion concocted by his scorned, would-be mistress, instead of falling in love with her it affects his brain and he becomes insane. And, of course, the madness of the knight errant that is brought on him by his excessive reading when alone in his room is a variation of the same theme. In all of these examples taken from Cervantes' own repertoire we can detect the persuasiveness of fiction, even if the moralists did not like it, although how it was achieved was open to debate. In Cervantes' case it was clearly artistic skill that did the work. Using an image from T.S. Eliot, the effect of fiction was like the words in a poem: the words entertain the mind in much the same way that a bone entertains a dog; while the mind chews over the meaning, the poem does its true work elsewhere.[17]

The above account of the forces impinging on writers in late sixteenth-century Spain provides us with matters that were of abiding concern to Cervantes. His works did not miraculously appear out of the void; in those long years in which seemingly nothing was published he was not idle but was constantly busy – and not only with making ends meet. His finished works reveal the extent to which he had read the major texts, theoretical as well as secular – and not only of his contemporaries – as well as also how he kept abreast of literary fashion and tastes. Considering what we know of his lifestyle and of the distractions to which his job as a civil servant exposed him, it is remarkable how he found time to read and digest such diverse and weighty tomes. Those who assert that he found time to read when on the roads of Spain may have a point, but not all individuals are able to read while travelling, and when we consider the state of roads in his day the possibilities for extensive study lessen considerably. This leaves us with the probability that his memory must have been unusually retentive.

Amid the mountains of paperwork that his jobs had demanded, it is astonishing that not more of his writings suffered the same fate as the vast majority of his first cycle of works for the stage. We should perhaps show more appreciation of what has come down to us, and maybe we should be more mindful of Esquivias, for that must be where much of his work was written and housed. In support of this view is the fact that in the inventory of his wife's household goods there is mention of 'several chests and boxes'. This is a significant clue because in the prologue to his dramatic works (1615) it is seen that in such is where he kept his papers.

So much has been written about *Don Quixote* that the study of the critical literature alone is a lifetime's work. It has become a self-generating academic industry; there is no end to what the text provokes in its readers. Yet relatively little research has focused on issues such as who read the text, how it was read and the extent to which the construction of the text either determined its reading or was itself determined by its anticipated readership.[18] That said, modern scholarship tends to focus on the search for possible meanings, even though the fruits of such scholarship indicate that whatever is under scrutiny – whether it is the episode of the barber's basin-helmet or the descent into the Cave of Montesinos or the pranks with the Duke and Duchess – no definitive interpretation appears possible. Indeed, the weight of modern research shows that to seek one would be quixotic in the extreme. Yet what does emerge from a reading of these episodes and from a study of the multiple views they generate is the undeniable fact that Cervantes was a supreme master of narrative in all its forms. What is sadly lost in translation is his brilliant use of all the registers of language and style employed in his creation and treatment of character. The basin-helmet episode illustrates the point and could easily be replicated.

What is truly remarkable about the book is the influence the text has exerted on succeeding generations of writers inside and outside Spain.[19] Cervantes could not have foreseen its remarkable success – remarkable because it has been universal – but once launched he realized that a sequel was guaranteed. And yet the reasons for the novel's creation – the destruction of all poorly written novels of chivalry – are not those that explain its abiding appeal. Indeed, given the undeniable fact that nowadays few, if any, read novels of chivalry prior to their reading of *Don Quixote*, the reasons why succeeding generations have warmed to the text differ from those originally propounded by Cervantes in his relatively long and reasoned prologue to *Part One*. And because of this, as Daniel Eisenberg so lucidly argues, much of the humour of the text is lost on us, perhaps for ever.[20] Clearly the author's own views of his novel, which include the intentions that inspired him to write it, have little to do with the appreciation of today's readership. And this arises in part because Cervantes exposes the full inadequacies of the chivalresque as a genre. Given that the genre is no longer read, other reasons must explain its continuing popularity. The fact that it has become a classic is undisputed, but the reasons why have led to varying interpretations.[21]

While Cervantes turned his attention to *Part One* of his novel, there arose in Spain a new era of optimism, as the strategy of peace with its traditional enemies adopted by the Duke of Lerma in 1598–9 began to bear fruit. As well as the continuing peace with France and that with Flanders was soon to succeed, in Italy the Duke of Savoy, a traditional enemy, had become Spain's ally and, with the death of Elizabeth I in 1603, both Spain and England saw their way clear to negotiate the Treaty of London, signed in August 1604. After almost three decades of war this treaty brought a complete halt to the actions of pirates and buccaneers against Spanish ships, an end to English support of the rebels in the Low Countries, a restoration of trade with Spain and an acceptance of Spain's monopoly over the Americas. From many points of view, therefore, 1604 and 1605 may be considered golden years for the new regime.[22] Not all, of course, shared such optimism. Critics of Philip III attacked the peace accord with England and later would attack that with the Dutch Republic of 1609. They also criticized his apparent inability to resolve the Crown's financial crisis and his determination to expel the Moriscos.

On Good Friday 1605, a day considered especially auspicious by Spaniards, the child who became Philip IV was born. The consequence was a prediction of an illustrious king ushering in another Golden Age. Extraordinary festivities occurred throughout Iberia, a prelude to those planned to honour the arrival of Lord Howard of Effingham – promoted to Earl of Nottingham for his successful exploits in Cádiz in 1596 – who was coming to ratify the peace accord signed with James I of England the year before.

With Lord Howard, who spoke Spanish, came a retinue of pages, bowmen and some 350 cavalry, numbering 506 in total. It was a very ostentatious affair, and the Duke of Lerma met the English contingent, who were treated to royal fiestas, a bullfight and a play by Lope de Vega. In the parade that always preceded royal performances, the public saw the first appearance of two new characters: Don Quixote and Sancho Panza. So immediate had been the appeal of *Part One* that the knight and his squire already featured – and with Dulcinea were to become standard figures – in masquerades and public celebrations all over the country. In keeping with Cervantes' new-found popularity, it is probable that among the gifts given to Lord Howard – which included swords from Toledo, jewels and leather goods – was a copy of *Don Quixote*, now in its second edition. If not, how else can the reference to the episode with the windmills, made by George Wilkins in 1607, be explained? We know that the story of Cardenio was the source of a play – now lost – by John Fletcher and William Shakespeare which was performed at court in 1612–13.[23] Shakespeare's troupe was the one chosen to entertain the Condestable of Castile and his royal retinue of some 234 'gentlemen' who visited London between 9 to 27 August to sign the peace accord of 1604. Park Honan claims that Shakespeare's men 'were made to wait' on the party for eighteen days.[24] Was any mention made of Cervantes or *Don Quixote* during this visit? Three years later, in the festivities to mark the inauguration of the new Viceroy of Peru, the Marquis of Montesclaros, chroniclers tell us that such familiar characters as the barber, priest, Princess Micomicona were represented but so was the knight and his squire.

Cervantes, aware of such festivities at court, was busily revising a number of works that would form part of the *Exemplary Novels*. While working on these a murder took place outside the building in which he lived, an event which sucked him into its murky currents. Don Gaspar de Ezpeleta died from wounds received in a brawl on 27 June 1605. Residents in the same building as Cervantes, having found Ezpeleta dying in the street, had brought him inside to tend to his wounds while sending for the police. In their quest for clues the local mayor, who was also the magistrate, therefore questioned everyone in the building, including the Cervantes household, but he did not question Inés Hernández, with whom Ezpeleta was having an affair. Nor did he interrogate her husband, the notary Melchor Galván, who lived close by and was known to be jealous. Even though Ezpeleta's servant openly accused Melchor Galván as the assailant the magistrate focused his inquiries on those residing in the building. It was common knowledge that Ezpeleta had entered the premises on several occasions, so aspersions were cast on the character of some of the women who lived inside, in particular on the Cervantes household, which received visitors at all times of day and night. The local mayor, Villaroel, swayed by local gossip and aware of alleged scandalous relationships, imprisoned Andrea, Isabel and Constanza as well as Cervantes – Catalina escaped as she was in Esquivias at the time. The fact that that Cervantes' daughter Isabel was openly associating with Simón Méndez, a Portuguese financier, did not help matters. And doubts about her conduct seemed to be confirmed when Méndez was sent, shortly after the Ezpeleta case, to prison in Madrid for debts. What should not be forgotten is that in their actions the Cervantes women were driven by economic necessity and that more than once their liaisons – mostly unhappy ones – solved the family's money problems.[25] It seems clear that jealousy arising from adultery was the cause of the murder, and, although immorality and prostitution were common aspects of life, the authorities had no desire to publicize such matters. The outcome for Cervantes was yet another stint inside the prison in which both his father and grandfather before him had languished. No sooner had he tasted the first fruits of a long-awaited success that he ended up inside gaol. Can it be wondered why so much of his art depends on *admiratio*?

Forty-eight hours later the Cervantes household was released from prison but remained under house arrest, a situation that continued until 18 July. Despite no longer being under suspicion, Cervantes' honour had been stained. An innocent bystander, he had been ensnared in the injustices of the judicial process. The experience was to surface in a later work, for it is probably the Ezpeleta affair that animates an episode in *Persiles and Sigismunda* where Auristela and Periandro are falsely accused of a murder. The two pilgrims, while resting near a stream, suddenly see a young man stagger out of the bushes, pierced by a sword protruding through his back. He falls dead before their eyes. Periandro rushes forward and withdraws the sword, whereupon the local constabulary arrive and blame him for the murder. When all seems lost, Periandro is saved by one of those strokes of fortune that is so typical of Cervantes' writings.[26] He was a master at incorporating real-life experiences into his work, either his own or that of others, as both 'The Captive's Tale' and the fake sequel to *Don Quixote* written by Avellaneda attest.

Despite such setbacks Cervantes remained single minded, and he continued to work on his stories, including on the two most famous of all, 'The Deceitful Marriage' and 'The Colloquy of the Two Dogs'. He would have learned of yet another pirate edition of *Don Quixote* in Valencia, thus, with the two in Portugal, making a total of three to date. After the Ezpeleta affair, most of the occupants of the building moved out, thus easing Cervantes' working space. For over a year there had been talk of a return of the court to Madrid, and suddenly, in January 1606, the king and queen with the Duke of Lerma left Valladolid.

There were a number of reasons why the return to Madrid occurred. To begin with, the problems formerly experienced by the court in Madrid had reappeared in Valladolid. Despite assurances of an infrastructure adequate to a royal court, it soon became obvious that it was impossible to maintain the royal family in the decorum to which it had been accustomed. This inadequacy was the main reason why Philip III decided to return the court to Madrid in 1606.[27] None the less the routine established in Valladolid was resumed once the court returned to Madrid. Lerma bought and refurbished the Quinta del Prior, an enormous estate located in what was then a suburb of Madrid, where he again organized entertainments for the king and the royal entourage. In this way Lerma maintained his hold over the young monarch and simultaneously legitimized his own power. He also exalted his own image transforming himself, according to Feros, 'into the most powerful favourite in history'.[28]

Critics of Lerma provided other reasons for the transfer to Madrid, one of which was his need of money. Madrid offered him huge profits from renting properties, and he needed the money in order to maintain the lifestyle he had instigated for the royal household in Valladolid. Although the royal family left in January, the official move of government departments and civil servants was scheduled for after Easter. But it was obvious to those who had moved that the same problems would occur with finding accommodation as had occurred in Valladolid, and so those shrewd enough and not part of the civil service began to flee Valladolid in their droves with the king.

As a result, Madrid rapidly regained its former prestige and became the cultural city of Europe. Property developers in Valladolid were unable to sell or rent – estimates put the number of houses left empty as high as 4,000 and as high as 3,000 in Toledo – but many had made handsome fortunes. It is not known when the Cervantes womenfolk left for Madrid, but it is known that Cervantes and

Catalina went to Esquivias, where he continued work on the *Exemplary Novels* before moving to Madrid in the early autumn of 1606. One incentive for their return was the forthcoming marriage of Isabel to Don Diego Sanz, a figure shrouded in mystery. Married in December, Isabel was a mother within the year and a widow by June 1608 – what Sanz died of is not known – and had a second husband three months later. To cap it all, the father of the baby daughter, also named Isabel, was not Sanz but Juan de Urbina.

Juan de Urbina, who had a wife and children in Italy, was secretary to the House of Savoy. With an acknowledged flair for business, he had been working in Valladolid since 1602. Whereas Sanz was as unprosperous as Isabel herself, Juan de Urbina had high connections and tempted her with a taste of luxury and courtly life far above her station. Juan de Urbina's employer, the Duke of Savoy, had married Catalina, the half-sister of Philip III in 1585. Isabel then was playing for high stakes. In her desire to enjoy the good life she clearly forgot her father's bitter experiences as a court petitioner. Cervantes' disillusion with the deceit and hollowness of courtiers had solid foundation, but it meant little to a girl born out of wedlock. Profiting from his position, Juan de Urbina had acquired land and property and was very much a man about town. That Isabel should fall for such a figure is no great surprise, but how and when her affair began remains a mystery. Despite Magdalena's care and influence, Isabel cuts a rather lonely figure and would have quickly realized that she would have to fend for herself. Besides, she would have known that her cousin Constanza's illegitimacy had been accepted while hers had not. In fact, Isabel's existence had, as we have seen, been disguised and may well have been resented. And she would have wondered why.

Recent research proves that Isabel was and remains a very controversial figure.[29] There are some fifty legal documents, three dramatic works and a few short articles mainly written in the nineteenth century relating to her life. If Cervantes believed his own words, 'that daughters are the greater half of one's soul', the greater would have been the displeasure that she caused him. Isabel behaves quite other to what is typical of Cervantes' heroines who are, as Theresa Sears claims, 'normally sixteen or seventeen years old, always beautiful, always fair, and always destined for an appropriate marriage if nothing goes wrong; failing that they may head to a convent or die. This type of female occurs with such frequency that it comes to suggest a personal preference on Cervantes' own part.' On the other hand, 'sexually active, sexually *experienced* women, what we may call Lustful Ladies, who are not contained in any of the sanctioned roles – young, innocent, virgin, mother – always seem to cause a violent distaste in our author'.[30] Cervantes had a great deal to say in his writings about women and the use of free will and the choices open to them, but when it came to his daughter it was her choices and her desires that mattered, not his. He could not expect Isabel to imitate Magdalena or even Luisa, locked away in the Carmelite convent in Alcalá de Henares.

It is obvious that Isabel made his life more burdensome. She had entered a world that really did not seem to want her, and it was a feeling she would have picked up very early in her life, with an adulterous mother and cuckold father. There is no doubt that her childhood was painful, and when, at fourteen she was put to work with Magdalena, initially for a period of two years to learn sewing and be given board and lodging, she knew that she was being palmed off. In the care of Cervantes' favourite sister, however, it is reasonable to suppose that she would be protected, possibly loved. A girl of fourteen would need that, but by that age the indignation towards her father that manifested later had already taken root. In his defence her father could argue that he had to fend for five women.

Cervantes was lucky to have a sister who was free and presumably willing to undertake the responsibility of looking after Isabel. (Such willingness has prompted the far-fetched suggestion that Magdalena was in fact Isabel's real mother and Juan de Urbina the father, but nothing has come to light to support such a view.[31] Consensus has it that Cervantes was Isabel's father, a claim that both father and daughter were to make on different occasions, and that is how it remains.) The question arises, what did Isabel learn from Magdalena? To judge from the Ezpeleta murder case, not much. Neighbours reported that 'men visited her, both day and night', although she was living unmarried with Simón Méndez. Whether she had any illicit affairs with Ezpeleta is not known, although the presiding judge had her – and the rest of the household – detained but in the absence of concrete evidence released her. And yet, if we demonstrate the toler- ance that is such a hallmark of Cervantine writings, surely Isabel deserves more pity than blame. Is it really surprising that her conduct – which with regard to Juan de Urbina is a mirror image of that of Cervantes with Ana Franca, her mother – was not exemplary? Juan de Urbina was to her what Cervantes had been to Ana Franca, a fact that would have bitten deeply into her father's consciousness.

Cervantes may not have approved of Isabel's behaviour, but he could not deny that she enjoyed much more money than he ever did. We read that in December 1608 she handed over to her second hus- band Luis de Molina some 14,753 reales worth of goods which included 'six gilded portraits of saints, a ruby ring, two diamond rings, a crimson-coloured full-length satin skirt having five gold braids and all made in France, gold bracelets, a gold necklace and tapestries'. But what is odd and much more relevant to her father was 'a white satin bodice (or jerkin) made in China'. According to Krzysztof Sliwa, this may have been a gift from the Emperor 'who wanted to found a college in China in which the *Quixote* could be studied in Castilian'.[32] Was Miguel de Cervantes intended to be the first principal? Curiously enough, the second prize in the prestigious poetry competition held in Toledo in 1608 was 'a satin jerkin', which was taken by Lope de Vega who had won two first prizes. He apparently preferred the jerkin to the official first prize of six silver spoons. Called by Cervantes a 'monster of nature', a term that probably refers to the dramatist's prodigious out- put, Lope de Vega had also won first prize in a similar competition held in 1605, also in Toledo.[33] Cervantes took no part in either event although the prizes – and the recognition – were certainly worth having. He did not participate presumably because he knew that Lope de Vega had organized both events. The list of contestants in the poetry tournaments of 1605 and of 1608 is impressively long, although most names now are totally forgotten.[34] Besides, in 1605 he was more than preoccupied with the publication of *Don Quixote, Part One* and in 1608 he was preoccupied with Isabel's illicit liaison with Juan de Urbina as well as with plans of her marriage to Luis de Molina y Castilla.

What emerges from Isabel's catalogue of wealth is that she was no pauper. Her liaison with Juan de Urbina helped to keep her in comfort, an added compensation when her daughter died unexpectedly in 1610. She then became embroiled in lawsuits about money and property that dragged on for years. A document shows that not until 1622 did Juan de Urbina lose the case against her, a case involving use of the marital home. Disputes with him may have finished but not those with Luis de Molina. Her second will, drawn up on 19 September 1652, one day before she died, reveals that she, too, had joined the Tertiary Orders of the Franciscans and laid claims to the arrears owed to her 'uncle' Rodrigo which mostly remained unpaid. Also curious is the fact that when her aunt Magdalena drew up her will she made no mention whatsoever of Isabel. What had come between them? Nothing has yet come to light on the matter, but presumably the antipathy between father and bastard daughter caused Magdalena to act as she did.[35]

Accounts differ as to Isabel's looks, but her liaisons with several men point to an attraction that William Byron overlooks in his biography. It is not unreasonable to suppose that she was attractive. She obviously lacked the high-principled conduct associated with Magdalena, who had been a second mother to her, and she was also devoid of her father's robust moral fibre, but she was certainly no worse than many women of her day.[36] The fact that she kept books – she had six texts on history – indicates that she could read; this being so, she would have found in *Guzmán de Alfarache* characters infinitely worse; and she would have been aware of the scandals at court, the indiscretions of Cervantes' sisters, including Magdalena, and the plight of her own mother. Until her stay in Valladolid her father had been a distant figure, and she must have resented his wife's attitude towards her: by all accounts Doña Catalina had no time for Isabel. No doubt Catalina could argue her case, having married Cervantes unaware of his amorous past, and her hurt was probably taken out on Isabel. But Cervantes' indiscretions were hardly Isabel's fault. Initially, then, when Isabel had found a man prepared to wed her, both Cervantes and Catalina must have sighed with relief. Isabel's husband, they must have thought, could now undertake what they had found irksome to do.

Whether Sanz knew of the paternity of Isabel's child is conjecture, but it did not matter overmuch, for he did not last long. Shortly after his death the two Isabels moved into a house owned by Juan de Urbina. If the latter genuinely felt any affection for Isabel, it proved ephemeral. It is not known when Cervantes discovered Isabel's adultery, but we do know that he confronted the man and negotiated a plan of action to safeguard the future of both Isabel and her daughter. For Juan de Urbina to marry Isabel was out of the question, yet their child had to be protected, and so it was agreed that Juan de Urbina would break off his affair but leave Isabel with a comfortable dowry, some 2,000 ducats and a house to live in for life. Cervantes must have been relieved when Luis de Molina appeared. A former captive in Algiers some fifteen years after Cervantes' release, he had been nominated by a friend of Juan de Urbina. To what extent Isabel was pressurized into the marriage – would a second marriage end her illicit liaisons? – is not clear, but certainly Cervantes seemed to warm to Luis de Molina. Moreover, Cervantes was now a grandfather and over sixty, so Isabel went through with the arrangement. However, the newlyweds did not live together until March 1609, that is, some six months after the wedding. Some commentators claim that Isabel's pre-nuptial negotiations with Luis de Molina brought the Cervantes family to new depths of cynicism and depravity. To comprehend her actions, however, one must be familiar with the socio-economic reality of the day. Quite simply, women without a dowry and proof of purity of lineage were, by and large, unmarriageable. The result was that women entered into lucrative alliances that were expected to be temporary. To her credit, Isabel was very aware of the 'marriage game' and exploited its rules wherever possible. Nevertheless, in the long and rich history of Spain 1609 proves a fateful year; it was not a good year to marry.[37]

9

A FULL-TIME PROFESSIONAL WRITER
(1608–14)

Believing that his daughter's life was now in order, Cervantes could once again focus on his writing. A second part to *Don Quixote* was in the offing, and, with the reopening of literary academies in Madrid he could continue his association with contemporary writers and poets. He associated with Quevedo, Góngora, Espinel and the Argensola brothers, and a meeting with the Count of Lemos bore fruit, as he later became Cervantes' patron and staunch ally.[1] Although strongly urged by Francisco de Robles to complete the continuation of *Don Quixote* Cervantes, in a new surge of optimism, turned his attention to the theatre, where financial returns were potentially greater. He wished to complete his *Interludes* (one-act plays shown during the intervals of longer plays) and wrote possibly the finest in the genre. He would have been pleased that the claim the Treasury sent in November 1608 for the alleged deficit from his accounts from Granada in 1594 was shelved after he had proved to the officials that they were the debtors and not he. Without paying him what they owed, the matter was quietly dropped. He would also have known in that same month of Isabel's vain efforts to claim her mother's inheritance. Apparently the executor of the will opposed Isabel's claims, so she got nothing. Luckily for her, the settlement from Juan de Urbina was comprehensive; he had been generous and Isabel knew how to exploit such a rare virtue.

The stepping up of the expulsion of the Moriscos from 1609 carried the support of most Spaniards, and even Cervantes has harsh words to say about this minority group. But his feelings are mixed, for in *Don Quixote* and later in *Persiles and Sigismunda* he clearly sympathizes with their human tragedy. A massive exodus of many of the country's best

artisans, farmers, agricultural labourers and builders, it has been estimated that as many as 270,000 citizens were forced to flee the Iberian
Peninsula over the next five years. The main areas affected were
Granada, Valencia, Murcia, Andalusia and Aragón. Given thirty days,
they had to sell their homes and take their personal belongings,
although nothing in gold or silver was to leave the country. Having
invaded in 711, they had settled in Spain and, although Muslims by
religion, they considered Spain their home and Spanish their language. Naturally enough, despite their protests to the contrary and in
the face of government decrees, they adhered to their customs, rites
and traditions. In a little-known work of an Austrian traveller,
Hieronymus Münzer, who travelled around Granada in 1494–5, he
praises the skills of the Moriscos seen in their mosques, agriculture and
gardens.[2] It was precisely for such skills that the nobility of Valencia
and Aragón needed them to maintain their properties and were
consequently against the eviction.[3] Warnings of the dire economic
consequences of a wholesale expulsion came from the Valencian
nobles, but, in an act that highlights the growing conflict between the
centre and the periphery in Spain, they were ignored.[4] They were
joined in their opposition by the growing number of the enemies of the
Duke of Lerma at court, but, despite all this, the expulsion went
ahead. Decisive action against rebels and heretics was the order of
the day. Philip III would have learned from his father that no true
Christian monarch could fail to defend the Church. Besides, the
National Assembly had not forgotten Queen Isabella's dying wish in
1504 to continue the wars against the Muslims in North Africa, a wish
that, in 1575, a newly captured Cervantes would have fully endorsed.

Münzer's comments are useful in that they were written shortly
after the official expulsion of the Jews in 1492, the year that saw the fall
of Granada and nine years later the official ban on Islam. The decision
to expel the Moriscos had been taken long before 1609 by Philip II in
the wake of the uprising in the Alpujarras in 1568. This was a most cruel
conflict, in which, for readers of Cervantes, the fate of the townsfolk of

Galera is of interest in that the whole population of 2,500 was slaughtered, the town was razed and salt was poured over it.[5] When this occurred Cervantes was twenty-one, but nearly fifty years later the same image is used in *Voyage to Parnassus*, wherein Apollo pours salt over the battlefield so that from the blood of the slain – the inferior poets – offspring poetasters will not arise. This link between real and imagined events is typical of the creative work of Cervantes. The frequency of such links makes the task of biographers doubly difficult, however, because Cervantes is a master at blending both aspects. It is for this reason we have to resort to authentic historical documents whenever possible. There is simply no other way of discovering the man behind the mask.[6]

In 1501 official state policy had decreed that Muslims did not exist in Spain. The nation that was the right arm of the Pope could not allow any heretical minorities within its frontiers. In Spanish eyes therefore, all its citizens had been baptized as Catholics and were subject to the Church authorities with greater or lesser degrees of tolerance. It was this very policy that compelled Cervantes to seek speedy absolution from his two excommunications. Being banned from the sacraments was bad enough, but to be outlawed by the Church was worse.

Despite an official ban on Islam in Spain, everyone knew that in reality many Moriscos did continue to practise their faith and customs and were tolerated in so doing. Only when that tolerance collapsed, as in 1568, were there serious breaches of peace in Granada. Compared with the unsuccessful armed rebellion of Castilian cities, known as the Revolt of the Comuneros (1520–1), at the beginning of the reign of Charles V, the revolt in Granada was nothing less than a horrible civil war. Once concluded, those Moriscos who did not become slaves either fled to the Barbary States or were forcibly exiled from the kingdom of Granada and ended up in Castile. No doubt a number of the Moriscos Cervantes met in Algiers were those unfortunates who had survived the rebellion but had not escaped deportation. In September 1582, at a meeting of the Council of State in Lisbon, it was resolved to seek what some would term as the 'final solution': it was deemed right to expel all the Moriscos, whom many saw as an Ottoman Fifth Column operating in Spanish territory. In truth, the fear of the Turks hid behind this much-debated and contentious directive.

The advocates of a total expulsion, led by Archbishop Ribera of Valencia, who had the queen's support, persuaded Philip and the Duke of Lerma at the beginning of the seventeenth century of the wisdom of such a step, and so, on the day Spain signed peace with the Low Countries, Philip decreed the wholesale deportation of the Moriscos. The roads of Spain became filled with distressed people hauling valuables and whatever was portable of their worldly possessions. Unsurprisingly, the exodus gave rise to violence, robberies and murder.[7] Based on religious bigotry, the loss in economic terms of such a valuable labour force was one Spain could ill afford. The loss, equally as deep, in human terms is described touchingly in Don Quixote, Part Two, in the character of the Morisco Ricote, a neighbour of Sancho Panza. The famous squire unexpectedly meets Ricote as the latter, lamenting his fate, sets out on his road to exile, confessing that he now knows what is meant by the common saying, 'the love of one's homeland is sweet'.[8] His plight was replicated nation-wide. Commonly viewed by the Spanish at the time as a minority sub-culture, its members were rejected, like the gypsies in Castile, mainly for being different. Although comprising less than 4 per cent of the total population, the Moriscos provided some 7 per cent of the galley-slaves, their lack of religious orthodoxy providing the authorities with valid excuses to sentence them to a life on the galleys. No surprise then that groups of Moriscos resisted the expulsion order by forming themselves into bands of brigands and thus joined that ever-growing sect of delinquents associated with unpaid soldiers, indigent students, unemployed labourers and peasants driven from their lands. Seville, so it is recorded, teemed with disaffected Moriscos, vagrants, ruffians, thieves and foreigners that created a frightening sub-culture of a picaresque underworld organized into guilds and fraternities. The juxtaposition of fabulous wealth and massive poverty led to a great deal of crime, and more men from Seville served on the benches of galleys than from any other city. Galley service, despite radical changes in sea-craft and navigation, was not officially abolished in Spain until 1748.[9] The kingdom of Granada, especially after the economic devastation caused by the ruin of its silk industry in the 1560s and culminating in the rebellion in 1568, ran a close second to Seville.[10] Cervantes would have seen at first hand the lawlessness in both regions.

But 1609 was also a religious year for the Cervantes household. Andrea and Catalina both joined the Trinitarian society of which Magdalena was already a novitiate. Cervantes would have approved of this step, because after his ransom by the Trinitarians he had always felt indebted to them. Despite this, that same year he joined the Society of the Holy Sacrament, where he would rub shoulders with the greatest intellectuals of the age. Ostensibly founded in response to the acts of outrage against the Holy Eucharist by Protestants in London, which came to a head in 1607, the society was more of a club for writers, poets and artists and, significantly for a pauper like Cervantes, attracted wealthy patrons.

Greater affiliation to the Church proved opportune because a severe blow rocked the Cervantes household with the sudden and inexplicable death of Isabel Sanz in June. The fragile harmony that Cervantes had so painstakingly struck between Juan de Urbina, Isabel and Luis de Molina suddenly cracked. The two year time-span agreed by Juan de Urbina in which to pay the 2,000 ducats expired in August 1609. One direct consequence of the baby's premature death was that Juan de Urbina changed his tune. He now argued that he was legally exempt from his dowry obligation and indeed worked towards evicting Luis de Molina and allowing Isabel only to stay in what was *his* property. Isabel, desperate to hold on to the money she was owed, proved stubborn in her opposition. Having already lost her lover, she was resolved not to lose what had been at the time second best for her. She wanted everything that had been promised and, in the ensuing dispute, was to break off with her father, who found himself trapped in between the warring factions. Juan de Urbina, unwilling to pay his debt, shrewdly linked Luis de Molina to one of his business ventures; Luis de Molina, prudently or not, agreed to the proposition and became Juan de Urbina's chief steward in an iron foundry. Clearly Luis de Molina's liaison with Juan de Urbina did not please Isabel. When 28 August – the date for the 1,000 ducat balance of the funds to be remitted – had passed, Juan de Urbina must have thought that his obligation was now null and void. But, to his surprise, Luis de Molina then sued both him and Cervantes for damages, that is, for the remainder of the unpaid dowry. Cervantes, virtually penniless, had already returned to Esquivias, and so the onus fell on Juan de Urbina who paid 19,000 reales as a token gesture, but that only provoked Luis de Molina to sue him a second time. Amid the wrangling that inevitably ensued, little attention was paid to the death of Andrea in October, only four months after receiving the habit of the Tertiary Orders of St Francis. Her death was sudden, for she made no will and went to her grave the widow of the Florentine Santi Ambrosio, who had died in 1605. Cervantes took charge of her burial in the parish of San Sebastian in Madrid, paying the sum of two ducats for the privilege. Her daughter Constanza lived until 1622.[11]

Apart from the opening of new academic societies the literary event of the year 1609 was the publication of Lope de Vega's *New Art of Writing Plays*, which was to set the pattern for drama in Spain and would influence the work of the greatest of all seventeenth-century Spanish dramatists, Calderón de la Barca, born in 1600. The pervasive influence of Lope de Vega continued to rankle with Cervantes because, despite the success and growing fame of *Don Quixote*, it had done little to remove the slur that Lope de Vega had so cast on his status as a poet. In defiant mood, Cervantes soldiered on with his works for the theatre and completed eight plays and eight interludes. In the prologue to these, published in 1615, we can sense how disillusioned he felt with theatre managers who failed to approach him for work. And yet, by his own admission, Cervantes refused to pander to them, the result being that he buried his plays under lock and key. And then, deciding to complete the *Exemplary Novels*, he stayed on in the back- water of Esquivias, a decision that only served to delay the sequel to *Don Quixote*. Meanwhile, the popularity of *Part One* continued to grow, both at home and abroad.

Evidence of his much belated recognition was seen in the festivities of 1610 organized all over Spain to commemorate the beatification of St Ignatius Loyola, founder of the Jesuits.[12] In the traditional masked celebrations the figures of Don Quixote and Sancho Panza seemed to have stolen the show. It is interesting to note that both figures were seen as 'figures of fun' and little else. And as such, the two characters were to cross the Pyrenees and the Channel.[13] Although not published until 1612, the first English translation of *Don Quixote*, based on the edition produced by Roger Velpius, a bookseller in Brussels, was fin- ished 'in forty days' in 1607 by Thomas Shelton of London. In Paris in 1609 a French edition of *La Galatea* was published, as well as a trans- lation of one of the interpolated novellas, 'Misguided Curiosity', and in Milan an edition of *Don Quixote* appeared but not in translation, so well did Italians know and speak Castilian.[14] Amid the international success of *Don Quixote, Part One*, which brought fame and recognition to its author, the Count of Lemos – the 26-year-old former president of the Council Of the Indies and Lerma's nephew and favourite relative – was made Viceroy of Naples and asked Lupercio Argensola to arrange for artists, writers and intellectuals to join him in Italy. Cervantes made public his desire to be chosen, and Argensola promised him a place. Why at the age of sixty-three, when tasting the success he had yearned for and deserved, would he wish to leave his homeland to go abroad yet again? Was it to escape domestic disputes with Isabel, to revive old memories – old loves too? – or to further his writing career? This request marks one further enigma in Cervantes' biography and will remain so until research – long overdue – into his stay in Naples is undertaken. Without it, conjecture about this and about his love life while a young soldier will persist, although it is more than likely that such an intelligent and adventurous character as he had amorous liaisons when in Naples as a young soldier. After all, it was, and still is, a part and parcel of military life, especially when soldiers are abroad.

Much like his father, a great deal of what Cervantes did in life was dictated by financial need, and so for some commentators his wish to return to Naples was no more than a desire to improve his financial position. He was three years away from the publication of the *Exemplary Novels* and four years from *Don Quixote, Part Two*, and so his ambitions as a creative writer were still in full flow. None the less, his petition strongly suggests that somehow those ambitions were being frustrated. The theatres, which had reopened in 1600, had never been 'open' to him since the advent of Lope de Vega, and that hurt. It may be that in Naples he thought his works would have stood a better chance of performance. And then there were the growing pressures not only of his immediate family life but also of his extended family, with Isabel and Juan de Urbina. Such burdens must have taken their toll of his physical and psychological well-being. These may well have been compelling reasons to want a change of scene. His petition failed, but how bitter he must have felt at being snubbed by Lupercio Argensola, a lesser poet and perhaps a lesser man.

But he was long accustomed to disappointments and betrayals. He felt betrayed by Argensola. But there was more behind the rejection. The Argensola brothers were from Aragón and proud of it. Moreover they were historians and were all too aware of the long-standing enmity between the kingdoms of Aragón and Castile, despite their union by Ferdinand and Isabella. The authoritarian and dogmatic Castilianization of the Iberian Peninsula was not welcome in the other regions, strong in their allegiance to their own sense of *patria*. After all, what was Castile itself if not a composite kingdom within a monarchy that was an aggregate of monarchies? The Argensola brothers, as did Cervantes, knew about the disaffection in Aragón, Catalonia and in

Portugal in 1588, followed by the cruel suppression of riots in Saragossa in 1590–1. Lupercio Argensola was the official chronicler and reported the event. It was bad luck on Cervantes' part that, around the time of his application to join the retinue to Naples, Lupercio was busily writing the history of his own kingdom. Lupercio expressed the fear, widespread among his countrymen, of absorption by a monarchy whose view of liberty differed widely from that traditionally enjoyed by the Aragonese.[15] In rejecting Cervantes, Lupercio was possibly retaliating against the imperialist spread of Castile. The notion of retaliation warrants consideration. If political history in Spain was, and remains, contingent on the meaning of *patria*, it may well be that Cervantes' application was rejected as much on political as on personal grounds.[16] The undeniable fact that Madrid was the honey-pot in the peninsula in the seventeenth century was no reason for proud Aragonese, Catalans, Galicians or Portuguese to rejoice, all wary of Habsburg domination and absolutism. Further proof of the discontent of non-Castilians is afforded by the testimony of the Frenchman, Barthelémy Joly, who claimed that 'among themselves the Spaniards are at daggers drawn, each extolling his own province over that of his companions but should a Castilian appear among them, then see how at one they are in launching themselves upon him all together, as bulldogs upon a wolf'.[17]

Similarly disappointed was Luis de Góngora, one of the most outstanding poets of the seventeenth century. His rejection provided no solace to Cervantes, however. The exclusion of both men of genius stands as an eternal indictment on the poetical judgement and acumen of the Argensola brothers. And yet Lupercio was also an ardent opponent of the 'new comedy' and indeed abandoned the theatre after failing to halt the advance of Lope de Vega and his followers.[18] One would have thought he would have shown a fellow ally and loser in the battle of the classicists versus the moderns greater sympathy.

Nevertheless, hindsight proves to us that the exclusion of Cervantes from the entourage to Naples was a blessing. One wonders whether Cervantes was aware of the fierce political infighting that surrounded the appointment of the Count of Lemos. From the start of his reign, Lerma had demonstrated an interest in Naples, not only because of its wealth but also because of its geopolitical importance and its centrality to the conservation of the Spanish monarchy. As an ally and close family member of Lerma, Lemos, although successful in his policies, especially in terms of accruing revenue for the monarchy, could not escape the fierce recriminations and factional enmity towards Lerma that raged throughout his time in Naples and that eventually led to his resignation in 1618. Had Cervantes gone to Italy, he could not have escaped the backlash of so much backbiting and division. The fact that nothing comparable to the works of Cervantes emanated from the circle around Lemos suggests that Cervantes was more fortunate than he could have imagined. He would not have relished, for example, the ridiculous nature of some of the debates held in the *Academia de los Ociosos*, which Lemos founded in Naples: What was Achilles' name when he was disguised as a maiden? Which songs were sung by the Sirens? How many barrels of wine were drunk at Alceste's feast? The term *ocioso* means 'idle' or 'at leisure', and so the topics were possibly in keeping with the name of the academy, but to an elderly Cervantes such exercises had no place in well-run literary academies.[19]

While Cervantes was left pondering the reasons for the failure of his petition, Catalina made out her will. There is not one mention either of Isabel or of Luis de Molina. She named as her executors her brother Francisco to whom she bequeathed most of her possessions, her husband Cervantes and the local priest in Esquivias, a Dr Peña. To Cervantes she donated her deathbed, the linens and furnishings of the house and two small plots of land outside the town, the larger of which was to pass to her brother two years after Cervantes' death and the smaller immediately upon his death. The major concession to her husband was that he was to have use of the bulk of her estate during his lifetime.

To judge from her allocation of wealth and property, she clearly loved her brother far more than her husband. Despite this, the reason she gave for the items bequeathed to Cervantes – one seized upon by commentators – was 'for the great love and good companionship we both have had'. This is questionable, for we know that since her marriage she had lived more like a widow than a wife who had been greatly loved. We also know that the sentiment expressed was nothing new in such documents and is probably no more than a notarial declaration. Indeed, in the very next sentence, she uses the same expression 'for the great love' that was shown to her when a young girl by her servant, a María de Ujena, to whom she bequeaths 'all her dresses, of silk and of whatever other materials and the cloak and blouses [shirts] that she had on the day of her death'.[20] Catalina would have known of her husband's petition and would have realized that, if successful, another separation would result. Viewed at in this light her will is an act of resentment and suggests a deep breach in what up until then seems to have been a harmonious, if belated, reconciliation.

From the documentation extant there is nothing to suggest that Catalina was in any way ill or that she really believed that she might die before her husband. The consequence of this is that the few commentators who discuss the will have been hard put to explain its timing. Did the deaths of Diego Sanz in 1608 and of Andrea and of Isabel Sanz in 1609 make her reconsider her own mortality? Fears of her own fragility, if that is what inspired her will, proved groundless, for she was to live until 1625, nine years after her husband's death. Yet, given the relatively poor value of her possessions, Catalina's will is no more than a token with a built-in snub seen in her specific wish – the first real item after the notarial formalities – to be buried not with her husband but in her father's tomb in the local church in Esquivias. If we set this stipulation alongside her later claim of 'the great love and good companionship we both have had', it is plain that her love for Cervantes was not so deep but deeper than that of her own mother, who had left her estranged son-in-law nothing. As it transpired, despite the clear stipulations of her will, Catalina's desire to join her father in his tomb was not to be fulfilled.

Four months later, in October 1610, Magdalena, who was genuinely ill, drew up her will in which she made her peace with God and calmly faced death trusting in the goodness and mercy of the divine. She claimed to have no debts and, because she had no personal possessions, had no need to name heirs. Generous to the last, she bequeathed her portion of what she was due from the inheritance of her brother Rodrigo to Constanza de Figueroa, her niece. A major feature of her will is her insistence that the debt of 300 ducats owed to her by Fernando de Lodeña was still outstanding and therefore she urges her executors, one of whom was Cervantes, 'to collect the money or at least to tell him of his debt and let his conscience do the rest'. It is saddening to realize that years after her affair it still continued to rankle, proving how deeply hurt she had been.[21] The tone of Magdalena's will is quite different to that found in Catalina's. Magdalena knows that she is dying and simply asks to be buried with the minimum of ceremony and pomp. Like Catalina, however, she also excludes all mention of Isabel and Luis de Molina. Magdalena, once a mother to Cervantes' wayward daughter, had seemingly lost all contact with her former charge. She certainly would not have approved of Isabel's past liaisons with Simón Méndez in Valladolid or with Juan de Urbina in Madrid. Magdalena had also suffered at the hands of men and gradually turned her thoughts towards the next world. As a result she had sincerely tried to lead a pious life, far from the ways of *Guzmán de Alfarache* or from the numerous dubious characters found in Cervantes' short stories and works for the theatre. She died in January 1611 and was buried in the Franciscan habit, her face unveiled. The fact that her funeral was paid for by the nuns suggests that Cervantes once again found himself in financial difficulties. That this was so is corroborated twelve months later in the documented transfer of his wife's portion of the estate inherited from her mother to Francisco de Palacios, Cervantes' brother-in-law. This document, witnessed and signed by Cervantes, may be seen as a modified continuation of the will made eighteen months earlier and clearly shows the heavy debts that still burdened the family. Francisco was to be the sole beneficiary because Cervantes' mother-in-law had stipulated that her daughter could not sell what she had inherited and gave as reasons her specific desire to exclude Cervantes from profiting from any sale of such goods and property. She also stipulated that if Catalina had no children then all goods and properties should revert to Francisco and to his offspring. By 1612 it was clear to Catalina that she would remain barren, and so she transferred her portion of the inheritance to Francisco. She was right to do so for he had been dutifully paying off the family debts when and where possible.

In October 1611 Marguerite of Austria died of complications following childbirth. Seen by many as an opponent of the Duke of Lerma and of his policies she played an important role in bringing public charges against some of the duke's favourites. Mourned nationally, her funeral, with all due ceremonial, gave rise to several sermons and pamphlets that praised her qualities and virtues. As a token of respect for his wife, Philip ordered the closure of the theatres that remained in place until the summer of 1613. The queen's sudden death ushered in other changes, too. A year after her death a host of social reforms were introduced by the Duke of Lerma that aimed to curb the excesses of courtiers, excesses which the duke himself had, unwittingly or not, encouraged. Restrictions were imposed on Spaniards that governed dress, public etiquette, displays of gold and silver jewellery and wall hangings inside homes. Public carriages, drawn by four horses, were to be used by women; the only males allowed inside such vehicles were the husbands, fathers or grandfathers and small children of the female owners of the carriages. The curious reason given for this ban was that men who used them became effeminate. Needless to say, this particular measure gave rise to endless banter by its many critics, including Francisco de Quevedo. Hunting with firearms was also forbidden, especially of birds such as partridges. Finally, the Duke urged all

Spaniards to observe Spain's Code of Law, which had been established in 1567 and remained in force until its revision in 1775. Critics condemned such restrictions as window-dressing aimed to distract attention away from the consequences of the expulsion of the Moriscos, the economic crisis, the depopulation of Valladolid and Toledo and the beginning of the criminalization of the political debate.[22] The court certainly needed reform, and the measures introduced by the Duke of Lerma served that end, but they had no real application nationally. Although to the modern mind such measures may sound odd, they provide an interesting backdrop to the spate of works that Cervantes was about to produce.

Cervantes focused on his creative writing, and his output was now to be prodigious. With the theatres closed he was able to concentrate on his prose, so he returned to his revision of the *Exemplary Novels*. Despite the recent resurgence of interest in these shorter companions of *Don Quixote*, they remain unknown to many, even those supposedly educated in the humanities. This is especially true in Britain, despite the work of universities, of Spanish cultural centres and the existence of excellent translations. Without knowledge of his other works how can we begin to appreciate the man and his life?

Among cervantistas and Hispanistas the *Exemplary Novels* have aroused the most disparate interpretations. Even in his own day the antithesis implicit in the very title 'exemplary' and 'novel' would have raised many an eyebrow, mainly because the term novel, then a recent coining and clearly based on the Italian novella, had none of the respectability the term currently enjoys. Traditionally associated with salacious literature, Cervantes deliberately employs the term to surprise his readers while also showing them that the novella could become an independent vehicle for serious narrative. And it was his transformation of the traditional short narrative, which in the past formed part of a larger structure – *The Canterbury Tales* is an example in English – that led him to claim that he was 'the first to write novels in the Castilian language'.[23] He was clearly challenging the writers of other types of much longer fiction, such as novels of chivalry, the pastoral and the picaresque, which had long dominated the fiction scene in sixteenth-century Spain. The success of his stories proves that his reading public was also ready to read a new type of shorter narrative which could stand on its own and which offered them what he called harmless entertainment as well as exemplariness. And yet, despite the success, when the same type of novella was interpolated into *Don Quixote, Part One*, many readers criticized the intrusion.

According to Cervantes, the recipe for such profitable fiction lay in the subtle mixture of writing read as pleasure or as therapy, which also contained a moral message. Hence the use in the title of the notion exemplary that has provoked endless debate and reinterpretation. This is to be expected in very diverse stories that touch on identity, gender, romance, social and moral values, language and the literary game between reader and author. This list alone, bald as it is, shows not only the breadth of Cervantes' interests but also how relevant they still are to modern readers. Furthermore, close examination reveals that the novella offers us a rich synthesis of the stratagems and novelties that Cervantes employs throughout his works. An illustration of this is his claim in the prologue that the stories contain nothing harmful and could not provoke anyone into evil thoughts but that, on the contrary, the reader will find therein a 'hidden fruit'. Such a challenge engages reader participation and is a favourite Cervantine ploy. From the outset, therefore, the dual dimension of entertainment allied to a didactic message is presented seemingly unambiguously. It is common for characters to find themselves in a crisis situation brought about by human evil or adverse fate – the abduction of Leonisa by Turks in *The Liberal Lover*, the kidnapping of Isabela by Clotaldo in 'The English Spanish Girl', the violent rape of Leocadia by Rodolfo in 'The Force of Blood', Loaysa's attempts to seduce the young wife of Carrizales in 'The Jealous Old Man from Extremadura' – and very often wrongdoers go unpunished. Are we then forced to read in between the lines? Most probably, and this is because the favourite stance adopted by

Cervantes in his writings is that of being non-committal. He far prefers to leave all judgements to the discerning reader. This is clearly seen in 'The Colloquy of the Two Dogs', in which we learn that corruption indeed permeates all of society. If the two dogs are not talking, who or what is guiding the dialogue? Each of us has to make up his or her own mind.

Preciosa, the little gypsy girl in the story of that title, is clearly no gypsy; Tomás Rodaja, the protagonist in 'The Glass Graduate', is clearly not insane in his pronouncements; the heroine in 'The Illustrious Kitchen Maid', despite her occupation, turns out to be a noblewoman; 'Rinconete and Cortadillo', the two eponymous heroes, are certainly not inveterate rogues or thieves, and the two dogs, Cipión and Berganza, prove to be, as their conversation unfolds, the most 'human' of creatures in a world of violence and brutal immorality.

Speculation about the genesis of the collection have given rise to various theories, but what is known for certain is that the date of approval for publication was in July 1612.[24] Unquestionably, however, the stories were written over several years, probably from the 1590s. Although numerous events referred to in several texts point to dates from 1600 onwards, this does not necessarily mean a great deal because such events may be contemporaneous with the revisions and not with the stories as a whole. The controversy, for example, surrounding the two versions of 'The Jealous Old Man from Extremadura' typifies the difficulty of trying to be precise about the chronology of specific stories. This famous tale, together with 'Rinconete and Cortadillo', had been collected in the so-called Porras manuscript (now lost) that was compiled for the Archbishop of Seville around 1604, and both stories underwent radical revision before final publication in 1613. There are those who surmise that the two stories do not belong to Cervantes at all but are anonymous works. This is probably why Cervantes in his prologue clearly states that his twelve stories 'have not been filched; neither are they imitations'.[25] Matters of genesis apart, Cervantes, chastened by his knowledge of the several pirate editions of *Don Quixote, Part One*, ensured he obtained the licence to protect the collection; this covered the kingdom of Aragón as well as Castile, but to acquire it he had to haggle for another twelve months. That done, the censor, named Alonso Jerónimo de Salas Barbadillo, was the last hurdle, and from the lavish praise he gave to the collection he clearly became the *Exemplary Novels'* first admirer. He praises the author for his 'clear mind, unique powers of invention and abundant use of language'.[26]

Cervantes went again to Francisco de Robles to publish the book. Given that the bill of sale to him was dated September 1613, it is generally agreed that Cervantes first looked elsewhere, presumably for a better deal. Nevertheless, the 1,600 reales given to Cervantes was a pretty good sum, but consensus has it that that amount had already been swallowed up in advances paid to the struggling author. Once more Cervantes failed to profit from his genius as a writer, although he had no doubts about the value of his work. Money evaded him even at this late hour, so that necessity kept him to his pen. How he felt about this we see later in *Voyage to Parnassus*. What is of greater autobiographical interest at this time is found in the rather unflattering self-portrait offered to the reader in the witty prologue to the novels. It is the surest and best picture we have of the ageing writer.

Critics, following in the footsteps of the dramatist Tirso de Molina, a contemporary of Cervantes, label him the Spanish Boccaccio, whose *Decameron* had been published in Spain and was widely read until placed on the Index in 1559. Other Italian authors must have influenced Cervantes, too, notably Matteo Bandello, whose collection of *Tragic and Exemplary Tales* was first published in Salamanca in 1589 – the title probably suggested to Cervantes the idea of exemplariness – and Giraldi Cinzio, whose *Hecatommithi* had been published in Toledo in 1590 and which was widely read in Spain. Cervantes' study of such works and an awareness of their popularity clearly encouraged him to focus on this type of fiction, to exploit its possibilities and potential. Until Cervantes made the genre his own, his countrymen, so he tells us in his prologue, read translations, although quite often such works were adapted rather than translated.[27]

The claim that he created the short novel in Spain is now generally acknowledged, even though the themes and motives he employs are as old as literature itself. What helps to make his contribution to the genre so important, in both the evolution of prose fiction in Spain and in the creation of the short story in Spanish, was his love of experimentation and his ability to adapt and improve. His unique fusion of very different sources, styles and traditions animates these twelve stories, which became an instant success: four editions in ten months, and, by the end of the seventeenth century, twenty-three editions in total. The success did not stop there. In England and France, in particular, so popular were his short stories throughout the seventeenth century that the collection was often preferred to Don Quixote, although this changed in the eighteenth century and has never reverted. But, since that time, what has occurred is the virtual disappearance from the European mass consciousness of all knowledge of his works other than Don Quixote. For a writer so passionately concerned about literature, in particular about its uses and effects, both for good or ill, on readers, this is a sad reflection on modern taste and culture, for it would be true to say that few writers, especially in Spain, shared his deep concern about the pernicious effects bad literature has on readers, especially the young.[28] Related to this concern is his preoccupation with 'truth' in literature which results in that sense of experienced reality that his fiction conveys. And this is as true for the short stories as for Don Quixote.

The reading public thirsted for Don Quixote, Part Two, but Cervantes delayed the sequel. The success of Part One meant that he knew he could use the promise of Part Two to ensure that Francisco de Robles published his other writings. Despite the economic decline of Spain, the great fiestas associated with its phenomenal rise to supremacy in Europe continued. The celebrations to mark the beatification of St Teresa of Ávila in 1614 led to masquerades and invariably to the inclusion of the figures of Don Quixote and Sancho Panza – and now with Dulcinea as well. Fiestas in Córdoba celebrated the wedding between the knight and his fair lady – an event inconsistent with the text – and once again the point of the masquerade was fun and entertainment, an element some may think incongruous with the reason for the feast. With such popular renderings of his famous characters, Cervantes could keep his public waiting: it was clear that, in an age when advertising was unknown, *Don Quixote* would not be forgotten. And so he now focused on the completion of the *Voyage to Parnassus*, a text written in verse. When compared to *Don Quixote* and the *Exemplary Novels*, it is a work that has been neglected by critics and scholars. One solid reason for this, even though it is increasingly being considered as a major work, is its acknowledged complexity. Published in 1614, it is almost certain that work on it had begun four years earlier, at the time that Cervantes learned of the decision of the Argensola brothers not to include him in the entourage being sent to Naples. Indispensable for biographers, it is probably his most confessional work and one in which he tries to come to terms with his frustrations and constant bad luck in life. In his inclusion of what may seem to be a boring register of names, many of whom were contemporary minor poets and writers and now irrelevant to a modern readership, he shared the historian's eye for detail and accuracy, so much so that not only is this catalogue of poets, along with court officials, patrons and ecclesiastics, a faithful historical tableau of his period but it attests to the astonishing amount of reading he must have accomplished. He certainly read the major Spanish and Italian authors of his day and much more besides, as his own writings prove and as modern scholarship corroborates.[29]

When James Fitzmaurice-Kelly claimed in 1892 that as a poet Cervantes was 'Samson with his hair cut', he was continuing a vein of criticism that had begun in the poet's own lifetime, mainly the biased verdict of fellow academicians jealous of his considerable achievements. Describing himself as having 'hair as white as a swan' (*cisne en los canos*), Cervantes deftly uses the Renaissance image of the swan to point to his purity of ideal and to the fact that the swan's song improves with age. The swan, dedicated to Apollo and the Muses, represents the 'good' poet and is the insignia of those who fight alongside Apollo in the famous battle scene in Book 7 of *Voyage to Parnassus*. The swan is the major image in Luis de Carballo's influential text *Cisne de Apolo* (*Apollo's Swan*), published in 1602, and a clear precursor to Cervantes' creation. Recent studies have shown that, without a good knowledge of emblematic literature, much of the meaning of the *Voyage to Parnassus* is irremediably lost. This is because Cervantes employs, as ever, irony, wit and satire to clothe his purpose. A clear reason for writing the text is stated in the humorous prose 'Postscript'. In a scurrilous sonnet attributed to Lope de Vega the figure of Don Quixote had been attacked and not for the first time. And, although Lope de Vega later recanted in 1631, the slur remained.[30]

Bearing in mind Cervantes' socio-economic situation, age, his exclusion from the group around the Count of Lemos, his stance vis-à-vis contemporary tastes in literature and his marginalized position in the academies, the fundamental question for Cervantes was how to frame his assault on a subject he held as dear as life itself. In response to the problem, and true to his practice, he drew on a variety of sources and traditions. In the prologue to his poem he claims that Cesare Caporali's *Viaggio di Parnaso* (1582) was his literary model. It may have been, but Cervantes' intentions in writing his poem were very different to those of his model. By 1610 Cervantes had long known that Lope de Vega had been wrong in his view of *Don Quixote*. He also felt quite certain that Lope de Vega had been equally as wrong in his earlier perverse criticism about his skill as a poet.

As was his wont, Cervantes used the criticism to good effect. He made it the basis of self-questioning about his own role as a poet and the relationship of that role with regard to his peers. The answers he provides are central to his purpose in writing the text. But, to penetrate Cervantes' meaning in this poem, the reader will have to tread carefully, because the method employed by Cervantes in his reply makes it difficult to unravel. What may seem, for example, to be a litany of sweet praises for his colleagues, sprinkled with biographical facts and figures about himself, serves in fact as a smokescreen concealing the real message which only knowledge of the socio-literary practices and traditions of its times will yield. If we could employ the same presuppositions that Cervantes himself established with which to judge all his poetry, as Spadaccini and Talens recommend us to do, 'we could break a long critical tradition, initiated in Cervantes' own time, that undervalues his poetic production'.[31] This calls for a serious, objective study, unbiased by the weight of rather negative appraisals of those few critics who have bothered to read the text and publish their findings. The poem is, after all, his commendation for his longed-for return to Naples. That is why the real import of the text is concealed: he wanted to be seen making friends not enemies. To illustrate this further, when Mercury addresses Cervantes as 'O Adam of poets' or as a 'rare inventor', what exactly is Cervantes hoping to convey to his peers? We know that he was preoccupied with his public image, so can we safely discount self-adulation as an option? The subtle contradictions arising from the text as a vindication of himself as a poet worthy of Parnassus and from his frustration at being marginalized by critics such as Lope de Vega and his 'crew', as Cervantes was later to call them, adds to the complexity, so much so that it appears that the deliberate ironies, contradictions and paradoxes have been overlooked.[32]

Cervantes' attack falls squarely on the vulgar tastes of those around him who call themselves poets, in particular on Lope de Vega. Although it would be imprudent to exaggerate the rivalry between both men of genius, some of the things they have to say about each other often leave much to be desired. 'Lope', we are told, 'rained down out of a cloud / an illustrious poet whose verse or prose / is unmatched and untouched by any other.' But just prior to Lope de Vega's miraculous appearance there had been other cloudbursts that had also rained down poets who are compared to toads and frogs. Sandwiched between these poetasters and representatives of the most vulgar of poetry – a blind man, a shoemaker, a cloth cutter and a tailor – is Lope de Vega. So many 'poets' (frogs and toads?) have descended in cloudbursts and have landed on the tiny sea-vessel making its way to Parnassus that Mercury has to sift out the wheat from the chaff, otherwise all will perish. After the weeding, Lope de Vega does not reappear. The fact that he does not rise again is an attack on his nickname of 'the phoenix'. And to compound his annihilation it should be noted that the piece of stage equipment that lowered and raised actors to the stage was known as the cloud; Lope de Vega made extensive use of the cloud because, Cervantes argued, it brought in audiences: visual effects sold plays. In the poem the image of Lope de Vega descending from a cloud captures 'the entire contemporary debate concerning the theatre' in Spain.[33]

As Ellen Lokos asserts, Cervantes' criticism of Lope de Vega is aimed not at the latter's lack of talent but rather that Lope de Vega 'was a reprehensible artist because of the manner in which he chose to exert his influence'.[34] He was to blame for lowering artistic standards which in turn allowed so many inferior poets to spawn and to flourish. Whether we agree with Cervantes is not the issue. Clearly he believed Lope de Vega to be culpable, and from this censure arose the astonishing text of his major poem. What interests us now is to see how Cervantes made use of his disparaging assessment of Lope de Vega and his supporters in particular and of his fellow academicians in general. What he produced was a scathing satirical attack on the deplorable state of poetry and of poets in contemporary Spain. His assault centred on the failure of the literary academies; for far from being centres of artistic excellence they became insiders' clubs whose primary outcome – if not aim – was the profanation of poetry. In Cervantes' view the work of those most praised and rewarded was actually destroying the art and science of poetry altogether.

In his poem Cervantes plainly distances himself from the toads and frogs (the would-be poets) that slavishly follow Lope de Vega. The more striking, therefore, to discover that in his imagined journey to the sacred mountain accompanied by Apollo he can find no place there for himself. When he asks why he is left to stand when his contribution to poetry has been so great, Apollo tells him to stop complaining and to make a seat out of his cloak. It is obvious that Parnassus reflects the situation of Cervantes in Madrid, especially since beginning work on his poem. This 'moment of encounter' with Apollo occurs at the mid-point in the text and is intended to highlight Cervantes' isolation and disillusion. Even Apollo seems unable to assist. Cervantes realizes that in the society he worked in he would never ever receive his just deserts. The definition he gave of poetry in *Don Quixote, Part Two* as something made of an 'alchemy so rare that whoever knows its secrets can turn her into the purest and most precious gold' remained for him an ideal.[35] He would go on being unrewarded and unappreciated, an unwilling outsider excluded from the laurel wreath, symbol of immortality and true recognition. How different was the fate of the protagonist poet Sannio, who is crowned with the laurel, visits the Temple of Fame, is showered with riches from the underseas treasury and is finally escorted to the surface by nymphs. Composed by Juan de la Cueva in 1585, *Sannio's Journey* provided Cervantes with another literary model, but the two texts differ radically in their outcomes. When Cervantes laments in his poem that he is 'pursued by envy and ignorance and never attains the rewards he expects', he is not exaggerating and makes a similar comment in *Don Quixote, Part Two* when the chastened knight remarks to Sancho that 'when I expected palms, triumphs and crowns as the merited reward of my deeds I've found myself trampled, kicked and pounded by the hooves of vile, unclean animals', such claims could easily apply to the blows that rained upon him in some of the academies Cervantes attended.[36] Don Quixote had indeed been kicked by bulls; in the poem, however, Cervantes' attackers live in much slimier regions.

A number of literary academies had sprung up in major cities, especially in Madrid, Valencia, Saragossa, Seville and Granada.

Cervantes would frequent such academies when and wherever possible. After all, anyone who deemed himself a writer belonged to such societies. With roots in Renaissance Italy, the specific aim of literary academies – that of Marsilio Ficino in Florence, for example – was the promotion and encouragement of the arts. Even in Italy from the mid-1550s in particular, when literary academies were still flourishing, their original aims and purposes had not altered. But, to the increasing despair of Cervantes, things developed quite otherwise in Spain, where it was the custom to close sessions with the *vejamen*, the systematic mocking of all academicians. As a result, personalities clashed and bitter feuds arose. The bellicose attitude that prevailed in Spanish academies militated against the genuine desire of those few poets who sought an open forum where they could discuss poetic theory and thereby raise artistic awareness nation-wide. The literary competitions, termed 'jousts' – in context there is no more appropriate term – bear witness to the warring factions to be found inside academies. And the notion of the warrior-poet is very much evident in the *Voyage to Parnassus*. Witness the major battle between the 'good' and 'bad' poets that lies at the core of the text. To Cervantes the amazing decline in the nation's economy was no more real or more life threatening than the decline in the republic of letters. What else, indeed, did the so-called literary academies profess to be?

Designed to test the wit and skill of participants, literary jousts proved to be very popular in Golden Age Spain. The three silver spoons won by Cervantes in a poetry competition organized in Saragossa – which was also the home of a literary academy – were the prize of a literary joust.[37] Although Don Quixote informs Don Lorenzo that a first prize is all too often awarded to a favourite or a person of high social standing so that it is the second prize which carries true merit, nowhere is it said that Cervantes complained at winning.[38] At long last his poetry had won public recognition. But sadly it was to be an isolated event. By and large literary academies were no more than a poetic wilderness in which Cervantes belonged to the almost voiceless minority. The result for him was greater isolation, increasing frustration – indeed probable resentment – and disillusionment. The psychological pain suffered by Cervantes at the hands of the academicians with their antics, prejudices and mediocrity has received little attention, and yet evidence of such abounds in what was to become an enigmatic literary testament. Biographers of Cervantes have repeatedly underestimated the 'event' of the academy on his work and life. It is generally conceived that he used to spend much-deserved leisure time in the company of congenial soul-mates who were willing to listen, share and further the aims of humanistic pursuits in ideal surroundings. A careful reading of the *Voyage to Parnassus* shows that nothing could be further from the truth, for what transpired were literary wrangles, disputes, quarrels and fights.[39] The improvement in his life situation for which he yearned simply did not manifest itself. It is not surprising therefore that the poem ends on a note of sadness and dejection.

Far from being a text in the mould of Caporali's *Viaggio di Parnasso*, Cervantes' work reveals a text astonishingly frank in its declarations about himself, his society and his contemporaries. What superficially seems to be a praise of fellow-poets, including Lope de Vega, turns out to be scathing censure. The blame-through-praise technique used by satirists shows an ageing Cervantes resentful of the literary tastes of his day and of the folly of praising those whom he regards as fools. *The Praise of Folly* by Erasmus undoubtedly casts its long shadow over Cervantes' self-revelation. Much more could be said of his imagined trip to Parnassus. Long overdue are new reappraisals, for it is clear that the pen that produced such remarkable texts as the *Exemplary Novels, Don Quixote, Part Two, Persiles and Sigismunda* and the *Interludes* is the same that created the *Voyage*. It plainly deserves more respect and attention than it has hitherto been accorded. In fact it was the discrepancy between the 'magnitude of Cervantes' literary accomplishment in the poem and the scant measure of recognition it has received' that propelled Ellen Lokos to launch her pioneering study.

But 1614 was also the year that marked the death of El Greco and saw the beginning of the return of the Moriscos. They wanted, so they claimed, to retrieve the treasures they had hidden in the panic of their mass deportation in 1609. The government appointed the Count of Salazar to put a stop to the return of what the government deemed as undesirables, a task he carried out to the letter. Many of the returnees were sent to the galley-ships or simply deported a second time. Many of the women, however, in order to remain in Spain either married Christians or married Christ and became members of religious orders and communities, and because they brought much needed money promptly received the blessing of the Church authorities. Nevertheless, there are cases, and one is recorded by Cervantes in *Don Quixote, Part Two*, of Moriscos who return in disguise to Spain and retrieve their hidden wealth and leave again just as unnoticed.[40] But for Cervantes 1614 also saw the publication of a spurious sequel to *Don Quixote*, written by Avellaneda and already in the shops. It was outrageous and cruel, forcing Cervantes to face an event he could never have suspected. In his reaction we can learn a great deal about a man who all too often is hidden behind the writer's mask.

THE FINAL FLOWERING
(1614–16)

His indignation was justified, for he was by now an internationally acclaimed author. After decades on the sidelines he had finally gained the public recognition that he always felt he merited, but some upstart had suddenly emerged intent on stealing his fame and success. It was a heartless trick but one that was to backfire. Fortunately for Cervantes it was to have no impact whatsoever on his prestige abroad, as the fake text was not translated. England had been the first nation to champion his cause and, indeed, the cause of Spanish literature in general, for there were already translations of other Spanish masterpieces such as *La Celestina*, *La Cárcel de Amor* (*The Prison of Love*), *Lazarillo de Tormes*, *Guzmán de Alfarache*, the *Diana* as well as *Amadís de Gaula*. The first English edition of *Don Quixote, Part One* was translated by Thomas Shelton and was published in 1612 by William Stansby. A French edition, translated by César Oudin, appeared in 1614 and the sequel in 1618 but translated by F. de Rosset. César Oudin, a most colourful character, was the court interpreter for Spanish, Italian and German for Louis XIII and an ardent admirer of Cervantes' work. Indeed, after a journey through Spain, he had already published in France the third edition of *La Galatea*. The success of the latter with French readers persuaded Oudin to translate *Don Quixote, Part One*. [1] His translation came at a most opportune moment because it coincided with the marriage between King Louis XIII and Ana Mauricio of Spain, which took place in 1615. As one of his wedding gifts, Louis gave his Spanish bride a copy of *Don Quixote*. In 1614 a fourth edition of the *Exemplary Novels* appeared in Brussels. Such public recognition served to assuage his exasperation and to encourage him to persevere with his writing, and, in particular, the real sequel to *Don Quixote*.

It was not until he was working on Chapter 59 of his own continuation that Cervantes found out about the rival version that was illicitly published in Madrid in October 1614. We know that it was at this point because Cervantes has his knight *en route* for the jousts in Saragossa. The effect of the imitation was to make Cervantes reroute his main characters; a remarkable affair in that the publication of a work of fiction – the *Quixote* of Avellaneda – compelled the living author – Cervantes – of another work of fiction – the authentic sequel – to change tacks. In other words, Cervantes employed a real-life situation to intervene in his work of art. But that was not all. It is generally believed that Cervantes 'had written about two-thirds of the second part when the "false" sequel was published'.[2] Its presence in the shops compelled him to redouble his efforts to finish a text that demanded the calm of reflection. Add this to the agenda that Cervantes had set himself, and it is no wonder that his work was undermining his health.

Unsurprisingly, one year after the publication of the *Voyage to Parnassus* and having worked slavishly to complete *Don Quixote, Part Two*, Cervantes was described by Francisco Márquez Torres, the official appointed to authorize texts, as 'old, a soldier, a nobleman and poor'. A fuller picture of Cervantes is found in his self-portrait given in the prologue to his *Exemplary Novels* in which he claims he has 'an aquiline face, chestnut hair, a smooth unwrinkled brow, joyful eyes and a curved though well-proportioned nose'; his beard 'is silvery which not twenty years ago was golden, a large moustache but a small mouth'; he is 'of middling height . . . fresh-faced, rather fair than dark, somewhat stooping and none too light on his feet'. It is interesting to discover that Márquez Torres perceived him as a nobleman and that the soldier in him was still present, for he was to be drawn into another battle – a literary one with Avellaneda – at a time when he had far better things to do. Avellaneda's sequel had caught everybody napping, especially Cervantes. Yet other literary successes, as Canavaggio clearly shows, generated a number of imitations and spurious sequels. *La Celestina* by Fernando de Rojas had given rise to a plethora of continuations, as did the precursor of the picaresque novel *Lazarillo de Tormes*. And, as already mentioned, the success of *Guzmán de Alfarache* by Mateo Alemán led to a spurious sequel that was published while Alemán was completing his continuation.

Whatever short-term financial gains Avellaneda may have had from cashing in on Cervantes' delay in finishing the sequel, however, have become long-term losses, for his text is rarely read nowadays. Avellaneda's work is not without merit and many agree that it deserves serious study, but it is commonly dismissed as a counterfeit and has become, as a result, a much-maligned and neglected text, although that would not worry Cervantes.[3]

Alonso Fernández de Avellaneda – probably a pseudonym – was a native of Tordesillas.[4] A literary opportunist, he certainly recognized the public's growing demand for more of the knight of the sorrowful countenance accompanied by his gullible squire Sancho. Audacious, motivated by the rewards a sequel would accrue, he possibly believed that Cervantes' promise to write a second part would suffer the same fate as that promised for *La Galatea*. The temptation of quick profits proved too strong to resist, so the work was published and sold as the real article. What an extraordinary turn of events in the life of a writer struggling to make ends meet. In his response, Cervantes, as ever, resorted to humour to make his point and thus was able to turn adversity to his advantage. If the prologue to *Part One* served as an attack to destroy novels of chivalry, the prologue to *Part Two* intended the same for Avellaneda's fake. In the eyes of Cervantes, the forgery of Avellaneda was doubly offensive: first, it had been born out of envy and, second, was making untrue claims about his main characters.[5] Hence in the prologue Cervantes promises the reader that he will leave his heroic knight dead and buried thus intending to prevent further spurious sequels.

When Don Quixote, ever aware that his exploits are being

recorded, discovers Avellaneda's false biography and, worse, a false account of an equally false protagonist also called Don Quixote, he becomes larger than life and *he* decides not to go to Saragossa, where Avellaneda takes *his* hero, but to Barcelona instead! At one stroke Cervantes was able to dismiss the forgery and fuse literature and life together. What was real and what was fiction were – and still are – central issues not only in his novel but also for his society. To theologians and to humanists, in Counter-Reformation Spain in particular, the content of reading matter became an issue of intense interest and debate. Whatever the Avellaneda text said about the characters first created by Cervantes could not be true. What lies behind Cervantes' humorously spiked attack on Avellaneda was the general acceptance that literature could be morally harmful; it was for this very reason that he had made his initial onslaught against novels of chivalry. Avellaneda was an impostor, and Cervantes strove, in his completed novel, to drive home that very point. Avellaneda's name is mentioned no less than five times in *Part Two* in Chapters 59, 62, 70, 72 and 74. There was to be one major bonus arising from Avellaneda's act of plagiarism: it drove Cervantes to finish a book that was to change for ever the face of novel-writing in Europe.

While he toiled to finish his text his family circle was once again involved in litigation. Through failure to pay the marriage settlement (dowry as well as Isabel's ground rent) Luis de Molina was to sue Juan de Urbina who subsequently spent, from 12 January 1615, a total of 226 days in gaol. Fortunately for him, his contacts in officialdom ensured that he spent most of his sentence under house arrest. Despite the dishonour of incarceration, Juan de Urbina retained his post as secretary to the House of Savoy. He was treated leniently because the Duke of Savoy, Charles Emmanuel, in defiance of Spain, had captured several cities in northern Italy in 1613 and had divided the duchy into two separate parts. As a result, the Spanish authorities, faced with yet another military campaign, acted cautiously while acutely aware that their inability to end Savoy's attempts to control the north was a weapon that other European powers could use against them, a situation which riled both the Spanish monarchy and its critics from within. The Duke of Lerma's relative and ally, Juan Hurtado de Mendoza, was the governor of Milan, but he proved ineffective against Savoy's expansion. Lerma turned against Mendoza in an open attack during the meeting of the Council of State held on 28 February 1615, prior to which Mendoza's agent at court, Juan de Urbina, had been detained.[6] Mendoza signed a treaty with the Duke of Savoy in June 1615. Known as the Peace of Asti, it restored to Savoy all the territories it had lost to Spain and left the future of Mantua undecided, thus leaving an opportunity for further conflicts. The treaty also marked the beginning of the end of the rule of the Duke of Lerma. Unwittingly it seems, in their litigation against Juan de Urbina both Luis de Molina and Isabel de Cervantes Saavedra were playing with political fire and at the worst possible moment. Despite their just demands Juan de Urbina never did pay his debts in full.

With Juan de Urbina under arrest, Cervantes indirectly found himself freed from the tangle of lawsuits that were to plague Isabel, her husband and her ex-lover. After finishing *Don Quixote, Part Two* in February he then had to set about the process that both Church and state required for publication of texts. The official authorization, granted by Márquez Torres, who was in the employ of Barnardo de Sandoval y Rojas, the Archbishop of Toledo, has become famous, for it demonstrates undiluted official support for a work of fiction which, so Torres claimed, entertains and yet is morally edifying. Ever since that date, the novel has had a life of its own and it would need a separate volume to trace the numerous editions, translations, adaptations and versions with or without glossaries, illustrations or even a potted biography of the author that have appeared. When *Life* magazine listed the novel as ninety-seventh of the hundred greatest events of the millennium, its place in history had reached new heights.[7] Francisco de Robles was as pleased as Cervantes with the praise that accompanied the approval and promptly set his presses in motion.

As *Part Two* went to press, Cervantes began work on his extensive Byzantine novel *Persiles and Sigismunda*. He also decided to complete his writings for the theatre, published as *Eight Plays and Eight Interludes* in 1615. According to Cervantes, his first cycle of plays was rather well received in that they did not provoke 'uproar, shouts or the throwing of cucumbers'. Unfortunately, virtually all of his first cycle has been lost, although we do know the titles of several of them. Lost or not, it is commonly accepted that they did not excite immediate euphoria, which was a common response to the best of plays by Lope de Vega. Yet, years later, when Cervantes once again produced works for the theatre, there was no response at all from anybody: theatre managers simply ignored him. Faced with their indifference, he wisely decided to use the deserved success of *Don Quixote* as a lever to have his works printed 'so that what passes quickly on stage can be read at leisure' in order to extract the full import of the work. In other words, much of what was being written and produced by others was not, at least in his opinion, worth a second visit.

Fortunately, Cervantes' second cycle of works, which was published in 1615, are still extant, but, although they follow some of the precepts laid down by Lope de Vega in his manifesto of 1609 are rarely performed. If the accepted giants of Spanish drama – Calderón, Tirso de Molina and Lope de Vega – are not now regularly performed, the chances of seeing a play or playlet by Cervantes are indeed slim. It is true that his patriotic play *Numantia* is performed as well as a few of his playlets, but this is nothing to the extent that Shakespeare's plays are performed, season after season, at home as well as abroad. Just as the dramas of Cervantes suffered in his own day because of the phenomenal success of Lope de Vega – and because of the commercial bias of theatre managers – so today his works for the theatre suffer because of a lack of a national institution in Spain. The result is that the flowering of Spain's dramatic genius in the age of Cervantes and after is virtually unrecognized outside the circles of Hispanic studies. When in the 1980s two plays of Calderón de la Barca (1600–81) were

performed in London, 'theatre critics hailed the discovery of a remarkable new dramatist'.[8]

The mention of Shakespeare is valid, for there are those who
believe that what Ben Jonson was to Shakespeare, Cervantes was to
Lope de Vega. Jonson, like Cervantes, was strongly classical and
humanist and was undeniably eclipsed by Shakespeare. Furthermore,
and of real interest to devotees of Cervantes, is the fact that Jonson's
work had been clearly influenced by Shelton's translation of Cervantes'
masterpiece. Both Cervantes and Jonson shared a similar fate in that
they were overshadowed by contemporaries who were unquestionably
men of genius. They also shared the view that it was the popularity of
chivalric romances that impeded the development of humanist drama
based on classical principles. This was why Jonson decided to have
selected plays of his published in 1616 in the first deluxe folio edition
in the history of English literature.[9] Although never issued in a deluxe
folio edition, we now applaud Cervantes' wisdom in having his
dramatic works published in 1615. Having been under lock and key
for so long and then printed intact, it is highly probable that the
versions we have, together with their stage directions, come to us
as Cervantes intended. This is significant, for, even though stage
directions may have always existed, they were frequently omitted from
printed editions. A close study of the directions reveals his technical
knowledge of the theatre and of his desire to use space and scenery to
their best effect. They also serve to stamp the presence of a dramatist
who was neither enslaved by Lope de Vega's precepts nor was he some-
one anchored to the hackneyed notions of Spanish tragedy. His works
clearly demonstrate his love of experimentation not just in theme but
also in dress, the use of dance, song and stage machinery.[10]

Equally significant is the fact that it was the practice of both actor
and producer to amend and delete texts as they saw fit. (Shakespeare,
too, amended and altered his scripts in the light of rehearsals and performances and following discussions with actors.) In Spain, moreover,
once the text had been sold it became the possession of the new owner

– the stage manager – who might then lend or hire it out to colleagues. And, as we have seen, there was no law of copyright, a fact that gave rise to the proliferation of pirate editions. Cervantes would have known of the decree, passed in 1615, which stated that every new play had to be approved and, if necessary, expurgated and altered by a censor before being awarded a performance licence by the Council of Castile. He also would have known of the ban in 1608 of Lope de Vega's play about the conversion of St Augustine, *The Divine African*, because of its 'indecent argument'.[11] Avoiding the additional hurdle of acquiring approval for performance, Cervantes shrewdly redeemed his works from oblivion, intending thereby to attract discerning readers. To a writer who once declared that 'actors are as necessary to the republic as flowers and trees' the notion of having what he deemed good works wasting away was anathema.[12] His publisher no doubt was hoping to cash in on the name of Cervantes alone, for, as the prologue reveals, word had got around that as a poet Cervantes' work was nothing like as good as his prose. When Cervantes in the same prologue claims to Pancracio that 'plays, like songs, have their times and seasons' he could not have known that their moment would be as late as the twentieth and twenty-first centuries.

The dates given for his eight plays and interludes are between 1590 and 1615, a span of some twenty-five years. To date individual works exactly is an impossible task; the most that can be said is that, although he did not have each piece of work published as he finished it, he was indeed writing them. The explosion of creativity after 1606 did not arise out of a vacuum: he had been storing ideas and themes and had made rough drafts of texts long before final publication. We know that once he found adequate time he revised several texts – including his *Exemplary Novels* – and that adequate time was found after he retired from life as a civil servant. Unlike Shakespeare or Goethe, whose works very often directly reflect events that can be dated in their lives, the works of Cervantes in this regard are exasperatingly unchronological. We have already seen how the events recorded in the inset story 'The Captive's Tale', although historically valid, are often unchronological; he simply used anything and everything to suit the work in hand. After all, as Aristotle taught, poetical truth is of a far higher order than mere historical facts and figures. Because of the relatively long delay between his lived experience and the inclusion of it in his published works, it is extremely difficult to correlate with any worthwhile accuracy actuality and writing. The same goes for his drama. By way of contrast, however, in the playlet *The Vigilant Guardian* (often translated as *Sir Vigilant*), the depiction of Madrid as a burgeoning capitalist city filled with merchants selling their wares is what he would have experienced in early seventeenth-century Spain.[13] But Cervantes is much more interested in the problem faced in the playlet by Cristina who has to choose a husband for herself.

To his and our advantage is the fact that today drama is read a great deal and that more and better editions of his theatrical works appear almost annually. Taking a quotation from the illustrious knight Don Quixote, theatre, he asserts, is to be the 'mirror of human life, the replica of customs and the image of truth'. Such sentiments are strikingly similar to those of Hamlet who maintains that drama's purpose is 'to hold, as 'twere, the mirror up to nature; to show virtue her own feature, scorn her own image, and the very age and body of the time his form and pressure'. Cervantes follows this advice and would also have viewed the 'groundlings', as Hamlet names them, 'who, for the most part, are capable of nothing but inexplicable dumb shows and noise'. Unlike Lope de Vega and his followers, however, Cervantes would never pander to the lowest common denominator simply because they paid for their tickets. When he claims that he was the first to 'portray on stage the hidden imaginings and thoughts of the soul, by bringing allegorical figures into the theatre' he is reiterating his allegiance to his practice of combining entertainment with didacticism. Nevertheless, as numerous critical works testify, what that message may be is often difficult to ascertain.

Those who seek biographical elements in his works often turn to the writings that his captivity inspired, such as *Life in Algiers* and later 'The Captive's Tale', *The Liberal Lover*, *The Great Sultan's Wife* and *The Prisons of Algiers*. In the last-named play readers may find in the character of the sacristan the opprobrious Blanco de Paz. Portrayed as greedy, cowardly, self-centred, lax in his faith and patriotism, the sacristan flirts with Islam and even denies his Christianity. And so obnoxious is his behaviour that it occasionally provokes attacks from other captive Christians. The exasperation that Cervantes felt in his real-life association with Blanco de Paz is thus transmuted into literature. When the captive Aurelio, at the opening of *Life in Algiers* – a play from his first cycle written in the early 1580s – describes life in prison as 'a purgatory in life' and 'a hell put on earth', the reference to the work of Dante is clear, but the difference for Cervantes is that those condemned to either 'place' do so, not because of their own sinfulness or wrongdoing but by reason of a capricious coincidence in their life or from the workings of an inexplicably adverse fate. Worse for him was the fact that the wanton evil of others caused so many innocent people to suffer. And when, in the same play, he affirms that captives face this constant dilemma: 'either you lose your body or you lose your soul', he was speaking as one prepared – when in Algiers – to die for his principles. Knowing what he knew, he could not forget those he left behind, the thousands who died there forgotten by their king and country. No wonder, then, that in *Life in Algiers* Cervantes makes explicit his plea for the public to give generously for the 'redemption' of captives, and by redemption he means both physical and spiritual salvation.[14]

In his play *The Mistress*, Cervantes' rivalry with Lope de Vega fuels his attack both on the precepts for drama drawn up by his opponent and on the absurd behaviour of the character Almendárez – a parody of Lope de Vega himself? – who falls in love with Marcela Osorio at first sight. The fact that Cervantes chose the name Osorio is telling, for it was well known that Lope de Vega fell head over heels in love with Elena Osorio, the daughter of a famous contemporary actor. The parody of Lope de Vega as lover and as a dramatist of intrigue is evident throughout the play and further reveals the extent to which their feud affected Cervantes in his later work.[15] Although Lope de Vega stated that 'all errors made in love are forgivable', Cervantes disagreed, and in *The Mistress* he was to question Lope de Vega's use of the word 'love'. Much of the erratic and stupid behaviour of so-called lovers was, in the eyes of Cervantes, based on an emotional aberration far from the spiritualizing force of true love, of the sort Montemayor in his pastoral novel *Diana* describes as true and pure and which sought nothing for itself. There is no triumphant wedding to conclude *The Mistress* and yet, for Lope de Vega, as everybody knew, a happy ending was the norm.

But Cervantes attacked his own weaknesses, too. His play *The Fortunate Pimp* lends support to the view of those who claim that Cervantes suffered from an inferiority complex. Cristóbal de Lugo is the son of a tavern-keeper, and this fact tortures him because he believes that others consider such a birth and background shameful. Consequently, Lugo feels compelled to assert himself above everybody else. It is debatable whether Cervantes suffered from the same or a similar complex, but is not Lugo's background and behaviour similar to that of Isabel? In the drama Lugo repents, takes himself off to a cell and undergoes a spiritual transformation, a change that has baffled commentators and critics: in real life, as we have seen, Isabel never repented. Ever since her falling-out with her father over the Juan de Urbina affair and her second marriage to Luis de Molina she could not bring herself to forgive her father.

And to what extent may we relate his play *The Labyrinth of Love* to Cervantes' own marriage? In the play confusion arises from the lies concocted by the two protagonists, Rosamira and Dagoberto, who see their union threatened by the girl's father, the Duke of Novara, who hopes to see Manfredo as his future son-in-law. When we learn that the duke, had he known of their intention to marry, would have consented to it from the outset, it is clear that the young couple's suffering could easily have been prevented. And yet how truthful had Cervantes been in his dealings with Catalina? Equally, how truthful had her family been with him? The play concludes that the best defence against Machiavellian intrigue, deception and lies is truth, but truth allied to reason. And when the eponymous hero of *Pedro de Urdemalas* decides at long last to become an actor, we can see a possible connection with the mature Cervantes. Just as the picaresque figure of Pedro passes from master to master, further convincing him that the world is evil and that men are corrupt and that a great source of their corruption and hypocrisy is their abuse of language, Cervantes likewise has passed from master to master and after a long and weary life turned once again to the theatre. In his desire to become an actor, Pedro, as Zimic lucidly shows, sees the 'world of theatre as an alternative to the theatre of the world'.[16] And so Pedro willingly turns to the theatre where illusion and reality fuse so easily and where Cervantes can lift men's vision to a nobler concept of life. The fact that Pedro beseeches the king to regulate the theatre and ensure that not any Tom, Dick or Harry could turn actor supports the view that Cervantes was still smarting from the snub suffered at the hands of theatre managers of the day.

The publisher of his theatrical works was not Francisco de Robles but Juan de Villarroel. Astrana Marín claims that disputes over money matters led to the breach with Robles. Although never well treated by his publishers, it should not be forgotten that Cervantes was a professional writer for whom all negotiation about payment was a matter of survival; he had no prospects of a sinecure or the pension. With this in mind, he found a publisher to print his works, not one of which had ever been performed. The reasons for this are explained in the prologue that typically offers us rich autobiographical material. Indeed, it provides us also with invaluable insight into the history of the Spanish stage. That said, the publication was not a success, for there was to be no reprint of the work until 1749. With regard to his *Interludes* it was the custom to write both the main play and the interlude that was shown in the interval between the acts of the former. Interludes gave main play actors time to change costumes and scenery while the audience was entertained with what was often perceived as low comedy dealing with 'cases of honour', the staple diet of the day. Cervantes' works were to change such a perception.

In redirecting his dramatic works to a privatized reading public he was telling the world that his *Interludes* were not to be run-of-the-mill time-fillers serving only to entertain unruly spectators. His works would retain all the fun of the genre but would include food for thought. A message, so typical of his prose works, is now introduced to what had been carnivalesque slapstick comedy. With a mind impregnated with the classical precept that writing should include both a moral and be fun, he set about what was to become a radical transformation of this very popular genre, and he did so by incorporating what are clearly novelistic devices seen well, for example, in the principle of open-endedness, that is, not providing clear-cut solutions. However, his innovations went too far, so his farces gathered decades of cobwebs. Commentators rightly conclude that, with regard to his drama, he was a man condemned for being ahead of his time. Nevertheless, those who claim that his works suffer from that 'quintessential lack of a sense of what constitutes drama' and that it was this fact that 'explains why his career as a dramatist came to a premature end' need to re-examine his personal circumstances.[17]

The most recent criticism has done much to salvage the reputation of Cervantes' dramatic works, especially the *Interludes*, interpretations of which vary enormously. The bewildering range of critiques of *The Divorce Court Judge*, *The Election of the Councillors of Daganza* and *The Marvellous Puppet Show* illustrate this. Consensus now has it, however, that the comic farces are exceptional. 'I would like them to be the best in the world – or, at least, reasonably good,' wrote a tongue-in-cheek Cervantes in his prologue and no doubt would have wished them to be performed, too. Despite the fact that the priest said to the canon in *Don Quixote* that plays are 'mirrors of nonsense', it was nevertheless a genre that Cervantes, preoccupied with his public image, knew he could exploit and improve. Nonsense certainly exists in the playlets, and it is that which gives rise to entertainment, but all too often it overlies a deep human weakness that needs to be remedied before lasting happiness can be attained. When the student in *The Magic Cave of Salamanca* exclaims to the sexton that 'we're not here to commit any mortal sins' but 'to enjoy ourselves and to dine well, with God's blessing', Cervantes is echoing the wishes of his audience.[18]

The characters he portrays – judges, town councillors, soldiers, prostitutes, tricksters, pimps, gullible husbands and shrewish wives, sacristans involved in issues of marriage, divorce, deception and governance in the pursuit of individual happiness – are similar to those we find in his prose works. He ridicules superstition, jealousy and hare-brained ambition that to him were all symptoms of insatiable desire. Such passions and obsessions, the result of our fallen human nature, were ones that Cervantes knew all too well. Possibly they are ones he feared in himself and therefore lamented in others. Even his austere knight suffers from such, having to undergo tortuous punishment to exorcize himself of them as a necessary prerequisite to self-enlightenment. Compare this to the ignominious fate that befell Avellaneda's impostor-knight, who is dispatched to a mental asylum.

Marriage problems arising from the battle of the sexes tend to dominate in pieces that show a Cervantes remarkably different to the writer of pastoral romances. The pleasing harmony of idyllic nature filled with the poetical laments of lovers is far removed from the bawdiness and vulgarity of pimps and bumpkins. The variety of character is further proof of his extraordinary insight into human character in much the same way that Shakespeare created a Dogberry, a Macbeth and a Cordelia. Yet what underlies these snippets of human life is the theme of deception – appearance versus reality – and the insistence that such hoaxes are inoffensive. In fact, the theme of deception dominates half of the collection while that of choice animates the others.

In the title to the collection Cervantes designated his playlets as 'new interludes' and is probably his response to Lope de Vega's *New Art of Writing Plays*. The playlets were certainly new in that they transcended – his critics would say transgressed – conventional practice. But, being the supreme novelist he was, it was inevitable that he should bring to the stage novelistic techniques that he had so successfully incorporated into his prose. Those who argue that his playlets are 'novelized dramas' or 'novels in dialogue' certainly have a point, but more important is this: to what extent was he able to transform traditional elements – the festive, carnivalesque song-and-dance routine of stock-in-trade characters – into a literary form without shedding its intrinsic theatricality? This is not the place to trace the history of the genre or to expound on the literary merits or otherwise of each play or playlet – useful critiques on his works for the stage exist as the notes in this book reveal – suffice it to say that whatever genre he tackled he almost always transformed it for the better, and this is unquestionably so of his playlets. Rejection of them by contemporary managers forced him to reconsider their worthiness as a vehicle for the stage as well as their appropriateness as reading matter. In time he was to succeed, but neither he nor his publisher benefited from the success.

Cervantes transformed Spanish playlet-writing as much as Lope de Vega did with his manifesto for the theatre. The changes he introduced show his indebtedness to the Erasmian precept of 'curing by amusing'.[19] Compare this to Lope de Vega's confession that when he wrote plays he locked up classical precepts 'with six keys' and wrote chiefly to entertain the masses. Although in his full-length plays Cervantes did follow much of his rival's manifesto he could never forgive him for forsaking what he, Cervantes, rightly or wrongly, considered to be the true aims and art of literature; to pander to the marketplace was anathema to him and it was a principle he carried to his grave. In what is perhaps the most famous and most developed of his playlets, *The Marvellous Puppet Show*, he criticises excessive commercialization in artistic ventures. As a writer of fiction Cervantes may be called a master of ambiguity, but in drama, as in life, he was single minded vis-à-vis his dearest values.

Nevertheless, the long delay in the reprinting of his plays and playlets proves how commercially unattractive they seemed to stage managers of the day. And what was not performed was unlikely to be published. To be fair, they had solid reasons to reject Cervantes' playlets, which are, on average, three times as long as the conventional ten-minute pieces, tend to treat rather serious issues, are open-ended and in both theme and characterization would have diverted attention away from the evening's central entertainment. Cervantes had to accept the fact that Lope de Vega's works continued to monopolize the theatre and that he was to be followed by Calderón de la Barca, so it was bad luck for Cervantes that he had to compete with probably the two most colourful and creative of Spanish dramatists ever. The outstanding success of Calderón de la Barca, whose works, especially the religious *autos sacramentales*, continued to dominate theatre performances long after his death in 1681 – indeed records show that his autos were performed regularly until 1765 – largely explains the neglect and long delay in the republication of Cervantes' theatrical works.[20]

Four centuries later, however, attitudes and opinions are very different, so much so that his plays are receiving greater and fairer critical appraisal and his farces are now widely accepted as the best in Spanish. As shown by Cory A. Reed, Cervantes transformed the genre into a drama of ideas and refused to close them neatly.[21] Indeterminacy lies at the heart of these works, an aspect much appreciated by today's public but anathema to seventeenth-century theatre managers. The reader/audience is left to draw conclusions from playlets whose underlying philosophical stance is one of tolerance and compassion. The plight of those unhappily married, for example, is rectified by a return to the practice of virtue. In short, what we learn from the *Interludes* is his advocacy of humanist ideals: we are morally responsible for our actions and all progress towards self-improvement has to be encouraged. It was a theme to be reiterated in Don Quixote, Part Two.

The prologue to this, dated 1615, shows that Cervantes is seriously ill and, as ever, short of money. His financial survival was dependent on the 'favours' sent to him by the Count of Lemos – by now the son-in-law as well as nephew to the Duke of Lerma – to whom Don Quixote, Part Two was the third text dedicated by Cervantes. His other patron, likewise acknowledged, is Archbishop Sandoval y Rojas. With his tongue-in-cheek assault on Avellaneda – how can a poor imitation affect the true Don Quixote? – the ageing Cervantes reveals that he is completing Persiles and Sigismunda and has hopes of completing a sequel to La Galatea. Persiles and Sigismunda, based on an original text by Heliodorus, was not published until 1617, a year after Cervantes' death. Most probably the version of Heliodorus known to Cervantes was the translation from the French compiled by Jacques Amyot, the bishop of Auxerre. Given that the love tale, known commonly by its abridged title of the Aethiopica, proved immensely popular throughout Europe – especially in Spain where three translations were published in 1554, 1581 and 1587 – Cervantes rightly saw in it a story to exploit. As a professional writer he was always alive to the changing needs of the reading public. As a foretaste he had told us in the prologue to the Exemplary Novels that Persiles and Sigismunda was near completion and dared to compete with the work of Heliodorus; probably Cervantes believed that he would go one better than his Greek model. His deft borrowing – an offshoot of the principle of imitatio – had become a habit of mind; from a variety of sources he invented something altogether new. In short, he sustained a fictive illusion that sweeps the reader along with the pleasure of the contents.

The vast majority of the readers of Don Quixote have yet to discover Persiles and Sigismunda. A bestseller in its own day, it has been sadly ignored since then. And yet the text followed hard on the heels of Don Quixote, Part Two. Did Cervantes make drastic changes to his story-telling or was the publication of Don Quixote more than enough to satisfy the thirst of the reading public? The almost total eclipse of Cervantes' last work is a mystery to those who have made a serious study of it. It is time for critics and commentators to turn their attention away from the knight errant and the riches of the *Exemplary Novels* to focus on this encyclopaedic romance that is in many respects as sweeping and as vast in its episodic narrative as *Don Quixote*. Translations undoubtedly helped to bring *Don Quixote* to a wider European audience; the English translation especially shaped appreciation of the novel. This did not happen with *Persiles and Sigismunda*, however; the belated attempt of a translation by Louisa Stanley in 1854 was poor and now unreadable and English readers had to wait until 1989 for an intelligible translation to be made available. The differences between *Don Quixote* and *Persiles and Sigismunda* are substantial. Cervantes had destroyed the world of the chivalresque, so now he had to look elsewhere, and he chose what is commonly called the 'Byzantine novel'. And, given that he never slavishly followed any prescriptive mode of literary genre, he experimented. He exceeded the well-worn Renaissance principle of *coincidentia oppositorum* and undertook one of the most extraordinary intellectual feats ever attempted by a novelist. As Diana de Armas Wilson points out, Cervantes was 'experimenting with new structures of desire' in this astonishing *tour de force*.[22] What it has to say, *inter alia*, about cultural and gender differences is very relevant and therefore appealing to our postmodern age.

The two main characters, Persiles and Sigismunda, are royal lovers who have sinned in thought but not in deed and so, to atone, flee from their northern territories disguised as brother and sister.[23] Their goal is Rome, their journey a pilgrimage, and what befalls them on their way – shipwrecks, seductions, suicides, bewitchments, injuries, narrow escapes, betrayals and all the situations of people pushed to the brink – make up the novel's myriad contents. Sigismunda's explicit goal in heading for Rome is to learn about Christianity and, upon arrival, to convert and thereafter marry Persiles. Their plan is simple and noble, but in the attempt to make it a reality events inevitably overtake them. The geography in the novel conforms closely to the maps and knowledge of explorations at the time, and Cervantes was clearly abreast of the advances made in cartography in his own day. Not only did he know of the astounding accounts coming out of the Americas but also of journeys into the extremities of polar Europe. The exciting but exhausting expeditions led by William Barents to the Arctic Ocean, details of which were published in Amsterdam in 1598, would probably have reached his ears. And allied to such expeditions was the dependence on what may loosely be termed astrological knowledge. Indeed, astrology has been shown to be a major theme in the novel.[24]

It is clear that the storyline is based on the classical concept of *admiratio*, and it worked beyond all expectation: in its first year *Persiles and Sigismunda* went through six printings. It was more successful than *Don Quixote*, although Cervantes was not to live long enough to witness it. Within a decade it had been translated into all the major European languages, but, whereas the interest in *Don Quixote* has remained and grown, that in *Persiles and Sigismunda* declined and has almost disappeared. It is true to say that modern readers, accustomed to shorter and tighter plots, have developed different tastes and tend to ignore that which Cervantes believed to be the best of his work.

Recent translations of the novel into French and English are a useful first step in publicizing a text that touches on an astonishing range of issues: witchcraft, exorcism, abductions, mariolatry, pilgrimage, astrology, oracles, captivity and other vicissitudes suffered by the star-crossed lovers whose romance is interlaced with a dozen inset tales. Despite obvious debts to Heliodorus, Aristotle, Tasso and El Pinciano – witnessed in the core principles of surprise, variety, verisimilitude and pleasure – he brought to bear on *Persiles and Sigismunda* the full powers of his skill in story-telling. Readers who have followed *La Galatea* and the *Voyage to Parnassus* will not be surprised to find a laurel wreath crowning the head of a beautiful maiden – although the circumstances in which this occurs, her rising in the opening scene after a massacre during a banquet on board a ship now abandoned on the shore, will inevitably elicit shock and horror; or the plight of the unmarried mother, Feliciana de la Voz, as she sings her song to the Virgin Mary, a song that bears resonance with that of Calíope in *La Galatea*. All seems in keeping with the pastoral mode until we learn of her concealed pregnancy, bizarre delivery of her infant and her desperate flight into an unrefined pastoral world to take refuge in a tree. Compare this to the songs of lovesick Elicio and Erastro in *La Galatea*. If we wish to know more about the laurel-crowned maiden's tale and of Feliciana de la Voz we have to take some words of Don Quixote's to heart; 'read them and see what pleasure they bring'. What has happened and what is about to happen – everyone has a tale to tell and almost everyone likes to hear one – brings into question problems of feasibility, truth, enjoyment and didacticism.

True to their Christian principles, in *Persiles and Sigismunda* Cervantes' pious lovers undertake a pilgrimage to Rome, an act of faith, and there they marry. In their union we can see the idealism of *Don Quixote* persevering in two much younger hearts. Cervantes' readings of the Neoplatonists had served to reinforce his own deep idealistic streak, whether in poetry or in love. A life without ideals would have been no life for him. Even though his saddened knight accepted the error of his ways his creator saw that it was equally wrong to jettison his ideals. The belief that virtue – Christian virtue – triumphs, if not on earth, then surely in heaven, resonates in both texts. And we know from his various prologues written at this time that Cervantes' thoughts were heaven bound. His letter in *Persiles and Sigismunda* to his patron proves this.

But writing *Persiles and Sigismunda* had not been easy. His strength and vigour were fading, his daughter remained estranged and his money troubles continued. Despite all, his desire to complete his text was as deep as that of Persiles and Sigismunda to reach Rome and marry. The outcome of their astonishing ordeals was love and a happy marriage, an ending that differs greatly from those of his *Interludes*. For those who seek parallels between his fiction and his life there is little to suggest that the final happiness of his two lovers reflects his final years of conjugal life with Catalina. Indeed there is visibly very little that applies to his later life in these works. They are literary creations based as much on his imagination as on his experiences or on those of others. Of course we know that Cervantes had been to Rome, had experienced piracy and captivity and, if we accept his love affair in Naples, had been crossed in love. But these facts do not explain the vicissitudes of *Persiles* and *Sigismunda* or the couples in *The Divorce Court Judge* or the plight of Trampagos in *The Widowed Pimp*.

Persiles and Sigismunda has attracted a growing academic and literary interest of late. This is a good sign, because there may arise new perspectives and insights of use to the modern reader. The fact that virtue can and often does ultimately triumph is a lesson modern readers need to consider. Whatever we care to make of *Persiles and Sigismunda*, what should not be overlooked is that not only did he consider it to be his finest work but he sensed it would be his final gift to his readers. Indeed, when working on the text and suffering from failing health, he was advised to visit Esquivias to take the pure airs of the countryside but within a week had repaired to Madrid, allegedly 'more dead than alive'. He was given the last rites on 18 April and on the 19th wrote what has now become his famous letter to the Count of Lemos. It was filled with an awareness of last things and when paraphrased begins, 'With one foot already in the grave'. Surprisingly, on that same day he also wrote the prologue to *Persiles*. Both the letter and the prologue can be considered his last message to the world. Curiously enough, one aspect of that message, the desire to 'tell the truth' in literature, found its way into the now famous work of the seventeenth-century chronicler Tamayo de Vargas, who claimed that it was his job 'to tell the truth' as well as offer moral instruction and advice. For him, the writing of history was a humanistic discipline. Indeed the writing of history in Habsburg Spain – the work of royal chroniclers – and its relationship and impact on secular writers of fiction is an unexplored field. And yet at the heart of both is the alleged claim to uphold the truth.[25] But royal chroniclers were court officials first and historians second; Pedro de Navarra was well aware of the delicate balancing act royal chroniclers had to perform in their desire to tell the truth and yet present the monarch in the best possible light. Likewise, the problem was known to the novelist Cervantes, who had to persuade us that what he wrote was true, although we all know it is fiction and thus, by definition, not fact.[26]

But what does this book tell us of Cervantes' experiences in his final years? We know that the Spain he knew was drowning in pessimism. Criticism of the Duke of Lerma was mounting and worsened when his own son, the Duke of Uceda, turned against him and joined forces with Luis de Aliaga, Philip III's confessor and former Inquisitor-General. In 1615, after two years of fighting, Philip III's government came away with a loss of political reputation that announced to other European powers that Spain's control in Italy – if not elsewhere – was weakening.[27] More alarming for the court favourite was the fact that the king, incensed at the loss of Savoy and the Peace of Asti, began to free himself from Lerma's spell. The same year that saw the publication of *Don Quixote, Part Two,* was also the year of irreconcilable divisions in Philip's court, witnessed especially in the publication of Fray Juan de Santa María's *República y Policía Christiana,* described as 'the finest and most influential attempt by Lerma's opponents to challenge the political discourse he had promoted'.[28] Not even the double weddings of Louis XIII and Anne of Austria, Philip's daughter, and of Prince Philip and Isabelle of Bourbon could conceal the breaches. Seemingly immune to such events, Cervantes raced against time to finish his text. This he achieved but was to die before the eventual ousting of the Duke of Lerma by his son the Duke of Uceda, who, in 1618, followed his now demoralized father's footsteps and became the king's new favourite.

It is commonly accepted that Cervantes died on 22 April 1616. Extant medical records support the view that he died from an advanced state of diabetes, an untreatable disease at that time. Perhaps the true cause of his passing was too much living. Appropriately enough, in that same month and year Shakespeare was to die in England. To the pious-minded, heaven received at one stroke two illustrious souls. We know that around Cervantes' deathbed he had several well-wishers and visitors – the one notable exception being his daughter Isabel. To the literary-minded, a comparison can be made with the deathbed scene of his famous knight, surrounded by Sancho, the priest, the barber, the scribe and other locals. The ending of the novel is truly moving. Having at long last gained his sanity, Don Quixote acknowledges the error of his ways and thus closes his eyes on a world that, for him, has lost all its flavour. Compare this to the final days of Charles V, perhaps the last warrior-king who spent 'night and day in adjusting and setting his countless clocks, and did little else'.[29] Cervantes, always sane, retained to the last that serene outlook on a world that had treated him harshly. He was worthy of more than it had given him, but what he failed to have in life – fame, prestige and true public appreciation – he has gained posthumously, and increasingly so.

If Cervantes was able to write letters to his patron, he would also have had the energy to write his final will, but there is no trace of one in any of the records. A few years before his death he had joined the tertiary orders of the Franciscans – the same as Catherine of Aragón who, so it is reported, wore the habit of the order under her robes of state – and by all accounts carried out the duties and responsibilities of a lay-brother assiduously. The appeal of the order with its emphasis on simplicity and poverty struck a deep chord within him; in the light of his life experiences it is not difficult to see why. There is no account of his funeral, but it is likely that he would have been carried in his coarse brown habit with his face uncovered to the sky on the shoulders of other friars to his tomb.[30] No stone or cross was set to mark the grave. By way of contrast, when Lope de Vega died in 1635 he was afforded a princely burial; three bishops officiated and the solemnities lasted three days. From being the talk of the town with the publication of

Don Quixote, Part One his passing did not provoke national interest, a court obituary or a day of remembrance. Within a few decades he had become a forgotten figure.

Catalina stayed on in the family home in Madrid, although documentation about her after the posthumous publication of *Persiles and Sigismunda* in 1617 disappears until the years 1625–6. This is not surprising, because with the passing of her husband the interest – never deep or constant – of officialdom also died, and what remained concerned the progress of his works. Although literate, a rare attribute among females in her day, she was of no interest to the court, the literary academies or to the Church, and so she returned to her former obscurity. Not being a part of the literary world known to her husband, she was unaware of the final irony associated with the publication of the text. Thanks to Francisco de Ávila – he who had written the playlet about Don Quixote's invincible exploits – she obtained the licence and copyright to publish *Persiles and Sigismunda*. She had no knowledge of Ávila's association with either Lope de Vega or with Barrionuevo. It was Ávila who made sure that *Persiles and Sigismunda* and *Part Eight* of Lope de Vega's plays were on sale at the same time. Although Lope de Vega had recanted, Cervantes was never to know of either his recantation or that he shared equal space with him on the shelves of bookshops in 1617. Happily for Doña Catalina she received all the royalties from the several editions of *Persiles and Sigismunda* and was therefore able to keep house in Madrid.

She was alive to witness the death in 1621 of Philip III, a passing that gave rise to enormous political upheaval on the Iberian Peninsula. Philip IV ascended the throne at the worst possible moment in the nation's affairs. Bureaucracy was excessive, production at home decreased alarmingly, trade was hampered by piratical attacks – especially from Holland and England – taxes were crippling and there were the wars abroad. The fall of the Duke of Lerma three years earlier had proved disastrous, as the Duke of Uceda was an even greater liability than his father. More saddening for Cervantes would have been the dismissal of the Count of Lemos from the court after he had returned from Naples to Madrid in 1617–18. Disillusioned, the Count took himself and his wife to their stately home in remotest Galicia where he died in seclusion in 1622. Catalina died in 1626, and her death passed unnoticed, her remains joining those of her husband's in the Church of the Holy Trinity. It is worth recording that when the church was being rebuilt in 1694 that amid all the pious sermons and thanksgiving for the new building not one mention was made of Cervantes. Eighty years after his passing and he was already forgotten. Of course we know that there was no direct descendant of Cervantes, but he did have relatives. What has become of the descendants of María de Cervantes, the daughter of Juan de Cervantes? She had an illegitimate child, Martina, by Martín de Mendoza. And what became of Constanza de Ovando, another bastard daughter, whose mother was Andrea de Cervantes? History is unkind to the offspring of illicit liaisons, but without adequate research we shall never discover the fate of the descendants of the Cervantes family. The fact that Cervantes' remains and those of his patient wife remained in an unnamed tomb is a sad indictment of what his contemporaries in Spain thought of him. The writer who had made his countrymen smile and laugh with his creation of *Don Quixote* and his squire could raise no response with his passing

Isabel, with her money, could easily have paid for a headstone that would have marked where her father was buried and could have also paid to have the tomb removed in 1639 when the nuns changed residence. But her contrary attitude towards her father remained to the end. Well-to-do, she lived off the income gained from renting her properties, and, when she died aged about sixty-eight – the same age as her father – in 1652, she passed even more quickly into obscurity. Anonymity surrounds Cervantes' last resting-place, a poor reward for an extraordinary Spaniard who, had he been born English, would have been honoured as a poet with pride of place in Westminster.

Modern interest remains robustly tied to the creative works

Cervantes laboured to complete amid harrowing economic and often trying personal circumstances. The world was never his oyster, but that did not turn him into a Blanco de Paz or an Avellaneda; adversity and pain brought due reward of love and compassion towards his fellow man. How many of those who claim that he produced priceless pearls are aware of the muddy waters he had to inhabit so as to be able to produce these? The tide of time that ebbs and flows through nations reached its peak when he was at his. Spain was a major player in an era when Europe was creating the modern world. That world, although long removed from knights-errant and courtly love, owes much more than it has acknowledged to date to one of Spain's noblest sons.

NOTES

1 HUMBLE ORIGINS: THE MAKINGS OF A HERO (1547–69)

1. Luis Astrana Marín, *Vida Ejemplar y Heroica de Miguel de Cervantes Saavedra*, Vol. 1, Madrid: Reus, 1948–58, Ch. 4. For more on the life, times and achievements of Juan de Mena see María Rosa Lida de Malkiel, *Juan de Mena: Poeta del Prerrenacimiento*, Mexico City: El Colegio de México, 1984.

2. Krzysztof Sliwa, 'Falsificaciones de Documentos Cervantinos', *Actas del Primer Convivio Internacional de Locos Amenos*, Salamanca: Ediciones Universidad de Salamanca y Universitat de Illes Balears, 1999, pp. 493–503.

3. Krzysztof Sliwa and Daniel Eisenberg, 'El licenciado Juan de Cervantes, abuelo de Miguel de Cervantes Saavedra', in *Anales Cervantinos* (Centro de Estusios Cervantinos), 1997, Vol. 17, pp. 106–14.

4. Krzysztof Sliwa, *Efemérides del Licenciado Juan de Cervantes: Documentos y Datos para una Biografía del Abuelo Paterno del Autor del Quijote*, Kassel: Reichenberger, 2001, p. 19.

5. Ibid., pp. 26–39.

6. Sliwa and Eisenberg, 'El licenciado Juan de Cervantes', p. 108.

7. Sliwa, *Efemérides del Licenciado Juan de Cervantes*, p. 161.

8. Cristóbal Zaragoza, *Cervantes: Vida y Semblanza*, Madrid: Mondadori, 1991, pp. 39–42.

9. Krzysztof Sliwa, *Documentos Cervantinos*, New York: Peter Lang, 2000, p. 53.

10. R.L. Kagan, *Spanish Cities of the Golden Age*, Berkeley, California: University of California Press, 1989, pp. 74, 237.

11. See the drawings of Alcalá de Henares by Anton van den Wyngaerde in Kagan, *Spanish Cities*, p. 234, and in the plate section of this book.

12. Sliwa, *Efemérides del Licenciado*, p. 35.

13. For differing views of this episode see the relevant chapters in William Byron, *Cervantes: A Biography*, New York: Doubleday, 1978; Melveena McKendrick, *Cervantes*, Cambridge: Cambridge University Press, 1980; and Zaragoza, *Cervantes*.

14. Such physical impediments are left undiscussed by other biographers.

15. Jean Canavaggio, *Cervantes* (revised edn), Madrid: Espasa-Calpe, 1997, p. 30.

16. Sliwa, *Efemérides del Licenciado*, p. 23.

17. Francisco Rodríguez-Marín, *Estudios Cervantinos*, Madrid: Atlas, 1947, p. 332. See also the work of Luis de Ávila Lobera, whose *Libro de las Cuatro Enfermedades Cortesanas*, published in 1544, was the obvious choice for Miguel's father to study.

18. Canavaggio, *Cervantes*, p. 38.

19. I.A.A. Thompson, *War and Society in Habsburg Spain*, Essay XV, Aldershot, Hampshire: Ashgate Publishing, 1992, p. 59.

20. Francisco Rodríguez-Marín, *Nuevos Documentos Cervantinos*, Madrid: Real Academia Española, 1914, p. 99.

21. Sliwa, *Documentos Cervantinos*, p. 71.

22. Vassberg, *The Village and the Outside World*, Cambridge: Cambridge University Press, 1996, pp. 82–3.

23. Ibid., p. 65.

24. Anastasio Rojo Vega, *Enfermos y Sanadores en la Castilla del Siglo XVI*, Valladolid: Universidad de Valladolid, 1993, p. 28.

25. Sliwa, *Documentos Cervantinos*, p. 47.

26. Krzysztof Sliwa, *Documentos de Miguel de Cervantes Saavedra*, Pamplona: Universidad de Navarra, 1999, p. 18.

27. See Astrana Marín, *Vida Ejemplar y Heroica*; Byron, *Cervantes*; Canavaggio, *Cervantes*; and Zaragoza, *Cervantes*.

28. John Lynch, *Spain 1516–1598: From Nation State to World Empire*, Oxford: Oxford University Press, 1991, pp. 26–38.

29. Krzysztof Sliwa, 'La Dualidad de Leonor de Cortinas, Madre de Miguel de Cervantes Saavedra, Genio de la Literatura Española', in *Actas del XIII Congreso Internacional de Hispanistas*, Madrid: Universidad Autónoma de Madrid, 1999, pp. 1–12.

30. Henry Kamen, *Philip II of Spain*, New Haven and London: Yale University Press, 1997, p. 34.

31. Sliwa, *Documentos de Miguel de Cervantes Saavedra*, p. 37.

32. Francisco Rodríguez-Marín, 'Cervantes Estudió en Sevilla', in *Estudios Cervantinos*, Madrid: Atlas, 1947, p. 55.

33. Canavaggio, *Cervantes*, pp. 36–7.

34. Melveena McKendrick, *Theatre in Spain: 1490–1700*, Cambridge: Cambridge University Press, 1989, p. 52.

35. Canavaggio, *Cervantes*, p. 50.

36. Ibid., p. 52.

37. See *St Teresa of Ávila: The Complete Works of St Teresa of Jesus*, New York: Sheed and Ward, 1946, for an absorbing insight into such austerities.

38. Kagan, *Spanish Cities*, p. 110.

39. For more on the achievements of the Catholic Monarchs see Zaragoza, *Cervantes*, and Kamen, *Spain 1469–1714: A Society in Conflict*, London: Longman, 1991.

40. Kagan, *Spanish Cities*, p. 110.

41. Vassberg, *The Village and the Outside World*, p. 32.

42. Juan López de Hoyos compiled the collection which contained Cervantes' first four poems in the *Historia y Relación Verdadera de la Enfermedad, Felicissimo Tránsito y Sumptuosas Exequias Funerables de la Serenissima Reyna de Espana Doña Isabel de Valoys, Nuestra Señora en Madrid*, Madrid: Pierres Cosin, 1569.

43. Astrana Marín, *Vida Ejemplar y Heroica*, Vol. 2, p. 182.

2 EXILE AND THE FORTUNES OF WAR (1569–75)

1. Krzysztof Sliwa, *Documentos de Miguel de Cervantes Saavedra*, pp. 38–9.

2. Kamen, *Philip II*, p. 131.

3. Astrana Marín, *Vida Ejemplar y Heroica*, Vol. 2, Ch. 19.

4. Zaragoza, *Cervantes*, pp. 87–8.

5. The classic account on this aspect is Albert A. Sicroff, *Les Controverses des Statuts de 'Pureté de Sang' en Espagne du XVᵉ au XVIIᵉ Siècle*, Paris: Didier, 1960.

6. Ellen Lokos, 'The Politics of Identity and the Enigma of Cervantine Genealogy', in Anne J. Cruz and Carroll B. Johnson (eds), *Cervantes and His Postmodern Constituencies*, New York and London: Garland Publishing, 1999, p. 119.

7. Thompson, *War and Society in Habsburg Spain*, Essay XV, pp. 53–78.

8. Martín de Riquer, *Cervantes, Passamonte y Avellaneda*, Barcelona: Sirmio, 1988, p. 21.

9. Information abounds on this topic. See Emilio Sola and José F. de la Peña, *Cervantes y la Berbería*, Madrid and Mexico City: Fondo de Cultura Económica, 1996, pp. 170–3.

10. Byron, *Cervantes*, p. 72.

11. Canavaggio, *Cervantes*, pp. 72–3. See also the portrait of Don John by Titian in the plate section of this book.

12. This curious fact, not picked up by biographers, clearly requires further research.

13. Thompson, *War and Society in Habsburg Spain*, Essay XIV, pp. 379–83.

14. *The Captive's Tale*, Donald McCrory (tr. and ed.), Warminster, Wiltshire: Aris and Phillips, 1994, p. 16.

15. John F. Guilmartin, *Gunpowder and Galleys: Changing Technology and Mediterranean Warfare at Sea in the Sixteenth Century*, Cambridge: Cambridge University Press, 1974, pp. 236–8.

16. Kamen, *Philip II*, p. 11.

17. Thompson, *War and Society in Habsburg Spain*, Essay III, pp. 274–5.

18. Sliwa, *Documentos Cervantinos*, p. 1.

19. Guilmartin, *Gunpowder and Galleys*, p. 152.

20. Geoffrey Parker, *The Army of Flanders and the Spanish Road*, Cambridge: Cambridge University Press, 1972, p. 47.

21. Guilmartin, *Gunpowder and Galleys*, pp. 147, 153, 160, 168, 298.

22. Luis de Góngora, *Los Romances de Góngora*, sonnet no.11, Antonio Carreño (ed.), Madrid: Cátedra, 1985, p. 123.

23. See Guilmartin, *Gunpowder and Galleys*, pp. 221–52, and Thompson, *War and Society in Habsburg Spain*, Essay I, pp. 13–21.

24. Guilmartin, *Gunpowder and Galleys*, pp. 86–8.

25. Interesting accounts of this episode can be found in Byron, *Cervantes*, and Richard Predmore, *Cervantes*, New York: Dodd, Mead, 1973.

26. Geoffrey Parker, *The Grand Strategy of Philip II*, New Haven and London: Yale University Press, 1998, pp. 100–1.

27. Sliwa, *Documentos de Miguel de Cervantes Saavedra*, pp. 42–3.

28. Thompson, *War and Society in Habsburg Spain*, Essay XIV, p. 381.

29. Guilmartin, *Gunpowder and Galleys*, p. 235.

30. J.B. Wolf provides these figures and much else in his authoritative text on

life in Barbary: *The Barbary Coast*, New York: W.W. Norton, 1979.

31. Most biographers appear to accept Cervantes' fondness for card-playing and dice, and they were the favourite pastimes of the age. Tudor England also indulged in similar pursuits: see Peter Ackroyd, *The Life of Thomas More*, London: Chatto and Windus, 1998, p. 210.

32. Sliwa, *Documentos Cervantinos*, p. 95.

33. Canavaggio, *Cervantes,* 1997, p. 91.

34. Juan Batista de Avalle-Arce, 'La Captura de Cervantes', in *Boletín Real de la Academia Española*, 1968, No. 48, 237–80.

35. Guilmartin, *Gunpowder and Galleys*, pp. 245–51.

36. Sliwa, *Documentos de Miguel de Cervantes Saavedra*, pp. 46–7.

37. Alexander Solzhenitsyn, *The Gulag Archipelago*, London: Collins, 1973.

38. Heretics were also regularly burned in England during this period.

39. For more on this see Sola and de la Peña, *Cervantes y la Berbería*, and Wolf, *The Barbary Coast*.

40. Byron, *Cervantes*, pp. 185–90.

41. For more on this see Pierre Dan, *Histoire de Barbarie et ses Corsairs*, Paris, 1637; Predmore, *Cervantes*; and Ahmed Abi-Ayad, 'Argel: Una Etapa Decisiva en la Obra y Pensamiento de Cervantes', in *Actas del II Congreso Internacional de la Asociación de Cervantistas*, Naples: Istituto Universitario Orientale, 1995, pp. 133–42.

42. Astrana Marín, *Vida Ejemplar y Heroica*, Vol. 2, Ch. 2.

43. Sola and de la Peña, *Cervantes y la Berbería*, pp. 13–50.

44. For more see F.D. Haedo, *Topographia e Historia General de Argel*, Madrid: Sociedad de Bibliófilos Españoles, 1927–9.

45. Wolf, *The Barbary Coast*, pp. 53–67, and Canavaggio, *Cervantes*, pp. 101–8.

46. A number of maps of the Algiers known to Cervantes still survive. See the map in the plate section of this book.

47. See Wolf, *The Barbary Coast*.

48. For more details refer to relevant chapters in Sola and de la Peña, *Cervantes y la Berbería*, and Byron, *Cervantes*.

49. A document called *Información II* (a sort of affidavit), consisting of twenty-five separate questions about Cervantes' conduct in Algiers, was drawn up by him and signed by twelve bona fide witnesses. The text in full has been published by P. Torres Lanzas, *Información de Miguel de Cervantes de lo que Ha Servido a S.M.*, Madrid: Colección Cervantina, 1981. *Información I*

refers to the 'purity of blood' document sent to Cardinal Acquaviva in Rome, 1569. See Sliwa, *Documentos de Miguel de Cervantes Saavedra*, pp. 40–2.

3 CAPTIVITY IN ALGIERS (1575–80)

1. There is a great deal more fascinating material to be found in Sola and de la Peña, *Cervantes y la Berbería*, pp. 156–86.

2. A striking modern parallel is found in the New Age teachings of Maitreya. See Benjamin Creme, *The Teachings of Maitreya*, Vol. 3, London: Share International Foundation, 1997.

3. The role of providence, in the general sense of divine will, is commonplace in Cervantine writings.

4. See Brian Keenan, *An Evil Cradling*, London: Hutchinson, 1992, p. 32.

5. Byron, *Cervantes*, p. 159.

6. Ibid., p. 200.

7. Widowhood was common in Habsburg Spain. See Linda Martz, *Poverty and Welfare in Habsburg Spain*, Cambridge: Cambridge University Press, 1983, pp. 104–5.

8. Luis Astrana Marín's description of Cervantes' life as 'heroic and exemplary' has validity.

9. De Sosa claims that Cervantes wrote several poems in Algiers. As nothing is said about *La Galatea* or works for the theatre, who knows whether or not he was working on such projects.

10. Canavaggio, *Cervantes*, p. 113.

11. Astrana Marín, *Vida Heroica y Ejemplar*, Vol. 2, p. 59.

12. Sola and de la Peña, *Cervantes y la Berbería*, pp. 134–5.

13. Accounts of the second escape attempt differ widely.

14. Sliwa, *Documentos de Miguel de Cervantes Saavedra*, pp. 49–55.

15. Sliwa, *Documentos Cervantinos*, p. 102.

16. To compare ransoms see *The Captive's Tale*, McCrory (tr. and ed.), p. 20.

17. Sola and de la Peña, *Cervantes y la Berbería*, pp. 156–86.

18. What part did the Cervantine theme of providence play in the failure to escape a third time?

19. There is much more on this crucial issue in John Edwards, *Christian Córdoba: The City and Its Region in the Late Middle Ages*, Cambridge: Cambridge University Press, 1982, pp. 183–7.

20. For more on this remarkable figure see Sola and de la Peña, *Cervantes y la Berbería*, pp. 83–5, 99–105, 160–5, 169–74.

21. Some commentators have speculated that Miguel may have been homosexual. For consideration of this in recent works see Fernando Arrabal, *Un Esclavo Llamado Cervantes*, Madrid: Espasa-Calpe, 1996, pp. 15, 199; Rosa Rossi, *Sulle Tracce di Cervantes: Profilo Inedito dell'Autore del Chisciotte*, Rome: Editori Riuniti, 1997, pp. 18–19; and Stephen Marlowe, *The Death and Life of Miguel de Cervantes: A Novel*, New York: Arcade Publishing, 1996, pp. 185, 345.

22. Sola and de la Peña, *Cervantes y la Berbería*, pp. 132–3.

23. *The Captive's Tale*, McCrory (tr. and ed.), p. 81.

24. Magdalena's will, dated 11 October 1610, shows that Fernando de Lodeña still owed her 300 ducats. See Sliwa, *Documentos de Miguel de Cervantes Saavedra*, pp. 345–6.

25. For more on the Cervantes women see Lokos, 'The Politics of Identity and the Enigma of Cervantine Genealogy', in *Cervantes and His Postmodern Constituencies*, pp. 121–6.

26. Could not Cervantes' nail-biting eleventh-hour ransom be another illustration of providence at work?

27. For a detailed account of the ransom negotiations see Byron, *Cervantes*, pp. 244–7.

28. *Información II.*

29. For more see Sola and de la Peña, *Cervantes y la Berbería*, pp. 187–217.

30. Sliwa, *Documentos de Miguel de Cervantes Saavedra*, p. 108.

31. Sliwa, *Documentos Cervantinos*, p. 112.

32. Sola and de la Peña, *Cervantes y la Berbería*, p. 166.

4 THE CAPTIVE'S RETURN (1580–6)

1. Lynch, *Spain 1516–1598*, pp. 429–39.

2. Canavaggio, *Cervantes*, p. 122.

3. For more on the enmity between France and Spain see Sola and de la Peña, *Cervantes y la Berbería*, pp. 83–106.

4. Ibid., pp. 83–5, 99–105, 160–5, for more on this colourful character.

5. Kamen, *Philip II*, p. 214.

6. The undying love expressed by characters in several of the *Exemplary Novels* contrasts sharply with the real-life experiences of Cervantes' sisters.

7. G.L. Stagg, 'La Galatea, Cervantes', in *Cervantes: Bulletin of the Cervantes Society of America*, October 1994, Vol. 14, No. 2, pp. 9–26.

8. An argument in favour of *La Galatea* as poetry is Seiji Honda, 'Sobre La Galatea como Égloga', in *Actas del II Congreso Internacional de la Asociación de Cervantistas*, pp. 197–212.

9. Stanislav Zimic, *El Teatro de Cervantes*, Madrid: Castalia, 1992, p. 12.

10. James McConica, *Erasmus*, Oxford: Oxford University Press, 1991, pp. 2–3.

11. María C. Columbi, *Los Refranes en el Quijote*, Potomac, Maryland: Scripta Humanistica, 1989.

12. *Don Quixote*, Anthony Close (tr.), Cambridge: Cambridge University Press, 1990, pp. 48–51.

13. Although new material is continually coming to light there is a vast amount still untouched in Spanish archives.

14. M.J. Rodríguez-Salgado, 'The Court of Philip II of Spain', in R.G. Asch and A.M. Birke (eds), *Princes, Patronage, and the Nobility: The Court at the Beginning of the Modern Age, c. 1450–1650*, Oxford: Oxford University Press, 1991, pp. 205–44.

15. Antonio Feros, *Kingship and Favoritism in the Spain of Philip III, 1598–1621*, Cambridge: Cambridge University Press, 2000, p. 36.

16. Ibid., p. 42.

17. Rodríguez-Salgado, 'The Court of Philip II of Spain', in *Princes, Patronage, and the Nobility*, p. 228.

18. Sliwa, *Documentos de Miguel de Cervantes Saavedra*, pp. 124–5.

19. A much quoted edition is that translated and edited by Juan Bautista de Avalle-Arce, Madrid: Espasa-Calpe, 1987.

20. Francisco Márquez Villanueva, 'Sobre el Contexto Religioso de *La Galatea*', in *Actas del II Congreso Internacional de la Asociación de Cervantistas*, p. 186.

21. Ibid., p. 187.

22. Ibid., p. 188.

23. *La Galatea*, Avalle-Arce (tr.), p. 409.

24. Anthony Close, 'Cervantes: Pensamiento, Personalidad, Cultura', in *Don Quijote de la Mancha*, Francisco Rico (ed.), Barcelona: Instituto Cervantes, 1988, pp. lxxiv–v.

25. For an authoritative account of this crucial topic see Thompson, *War and Society in Habsburg Spain*, pp. 244–67.

26. Vassberg, *The Village and the Outside World*, and Martz, *Poverty and Welfare*

in Habsburg Spain, provide vivid portrayals of village life in Castile.

27. Dominic Finello, *Cervantes: Essays on Social and Literary Polemics*, London: Tamesis, 1998, p. 10.

28. Canavaggio, *Cervantes*, p. 161.

29. Paul Lewis-Smith, 'Cervantes' Numancia as Tragedy and as Tragicomedy', in *Bulletin of Hispanic Studies* (University of Liverpool), 1987, Vol. 64, pp. 15–26. Also Jean Canavaggio, *Cervantès Dramaturge: Un Théâtre à Naître*, Paris: Presses Universitaires de France, 1977.

30. Carmen Peraita, 'Idea de la Historia y Providencialismo en Cervantes: Las Profecías Numantinas', in *Actas del II Congreso Internacional de la Asociación de Cervantistas*, p. 143.

31. Sliwa, *Documentos de Miguel de Cervantes Saavedra*, p. 125.

32. The general consensus is that Ana Franca's husband was rather dull. This seems to be conjecture, however, and is probably based on his acceptance of his wife's child as his.

33. Vassberg, *The Village and the Outside World*, p. 132.

34. Ibid., p. 136.

35. For those who enjoy reading imaginative literature the pastoral genre offers ample scope.

36. *La Galatea*, Avalle-Arce (tr.), p. 276.

37. The Spanish reads: 'Quien va lejos a casar / Va engañando o va a engañar.'

38. Ortiz Domínguez, *The Golden Age of Spain*, James Casey (tr.), London: Weidenfeld and Nicolson, 1971.

39. David Vassberg, *Land and Society in Golden Age Castile*, Cambridge: Cambridge University Press, 1984, pp. 138–43.

40. Vassberg, *Land and Society*, pp. 158–64.

41. For the dowry (dated 9 August 1568) see Sliwa, *Documentos de Miguel de Cervantes Saavedra*, p. 138.

42. T.L. Darby, 'Cervantes in England', in *Bulletin of Hispanic Studies* (University of Liverpool), 1997, Vol. 74, pp. 425–41.

33. It is true that little or nothing was published for twenty years. But must we therefore assume that nothing was written during that time?

44. Sliwa, *Documentos de Miguel de Cervantes Saavedra*, pp. 143–4.

45. Canavaggio, *Cervantes*, p. 182.

46. William Shakespeare, *The Complete Works*, Peter Alexander (ed.), London: Collins, 1979, p. 275.

47. Park Honan, *Shakespeare: A Life*, Oxford: Oxford University Press, 1998, pp. 9–92.

48. Jacinto Hermúa, in *Cervantes: Administrador Militar*, Madrid, 1879, p. 18, talks of Cervantes' 'negra necesidad'.

49. The Armada, piracy in the Caribbean, unrest in the Low Countries and unpopularity in Portugal among other things.

5 PRECARIOUS YEARS IN ANDALUSIA (1586–90)

1. Vassberg, *Land and Society in Golden Age Spain* and *The Village and the Outside World*. See also Thompson, *War and Society in Habsburg Spain*, and Martz, *Poverty and Welfare in Habsburg Spain*.

2. This is a statement seized upon by commentators but all too often misinterpreted.

3. For more read Vassberg, *The Village and the Outside World*, pp. 24–47, and Thompson, *War and Society in Habsburg Spain*, Essay III, pp. 265–70.

4. Guilmartin, *Gunpowder and Galleys*, p. 270.

5. Thompson, *War and Society in Habsburg Spain*, Essay IX, p. 81.

6. For an informed introduction to a wide and complex issue see Martz, *Poverty and Welfare in Habsburg Spain*, and, in particular, Vassberg, *Land and Society in Golden Age Spain* and *The Village and the Outside World*. See also Lynch, *Spain 1516–1598*.

7. For more see Canavaggio, *Cervantes*, pp. 197–203, and Zaragoza, *Cervantes*, pp. 228–30.

8. For more on this crucial aspect of Cervantine writing, refer to the work of E.C. Riley, *Cervantes' Theory of the Novel*, Oxford: Oxford University Press, 1962, and to B.W. Ife, *Reading and Fiction in Golden Age Spain*, Cambridge: Cambridge University Press, 1985.

9. Such questions animate this work and are best answered by social historians.

10. Hermúa, in *Cervantes, Administrador Militar*, p. 29, claims that he did have them.

11. Even with our patchy knowledge of the nature of his tasks as purveyor and tax collector, it seems remarkable that more errors were not made.

12. Guilmartin, *Gunpowder and Galleys*, pp. 253–73.

13. Thompson, *War and Society in Habsburg Spain*, Essay IX, pp. 71–2.

14. A. Domínguez Ortiz, 'La España del Quijote', *Don Quijote de la Mancha*,

Francisco Rico (ed.), Barcelona: Instituto Cervantes, 1998, p. xcvii.

15. *The Captive's Tale*, McCrory (tr. and ed.), pp. 16–18, 48–9.

16. Geoffrey Parker, 'David or Goliath: Philip II and His World in the 1580s', R.L. Kagan and G. Parker (eds), *Spain, Europe and the Atlantic Worlds*, Cambridge: Cambridge University Press, 1995, p. 256.

17. Thompson, *War and Society in Habsburg Spain*, Essay IX, pp. 88–90.

18. Ibid., Essay II, p. 18.

19. Despite his zeal Cervantes most certainly would have preferred to write for a living.

20. *Don Quijote, Part 2*, Burton Raffel (tr.), New York and London: W.W. Norton, 1999, pp. 406–12.

21. For more on this see Astrana Marín, *Vida Heroica y Ejemplar*, and Byron, *Cervantes*.

22. Vassberg, *The Village and the Outside World*, pp. 117–19.

23. Zimic, *El Teatro de Cervantes*, pp. 325–36, and Cory A. Reed, *The Novelist as Playwright*, New York: Peter Lang, 1993, pp. 101–13.

24. Vassberg, *The Village and the Outside World*, pp. 133–4. For those who read Spanish the autobiographical account covering the period 1597–1630, entitled *Vida del Capitán Alonso de Contreras*, Manuel Criado del Val (ed.), Barcelona: Fontamara, 1982, Ch. 10, is interesting.

25. Barthelémy Joly, in *Viajes de Extranjeros por España y Portugal*, Vol. 2, J. García Mercadal (tr. and ed.), Madrid: Aguilar, 1952.

26. 'The Illustrious Kitchen-Maid', 'Rinconete and Cortadillo' and 'The Little Gypsy Girl' provide examples. For the English translations of all the novels see *The Exemplary Novels*, 4 vols, B.W. Ife (ed.), Warminster, Wiltshire: Aris and Philips, 1992.

27. Sliwa, *Documentos Cervantinos*, p. 136.

28. Ibid., p. 203.

29. See McKendrick, *Theatre in Spain*; D.R. Larson, *The Honour Plays of Lope de Vega*, Cambridge, Massachusetts: Harvard University Press, 1977; and J.E. Varey, *Cosmovisión y Escenografía: El Teatro Español en el Siglo de Oro*, Madrid: Castalia, 1988.

30. Thompson, *War and Society in Habsburg Spain*, Essay II, p. 18.

31. For more on the possible motives of Philip II see the relevant chapters in Lynch, *Spain 1516–1598*, and Kamen, *Philip II*.

32. Thompson, *War and Society in Habsburg Spain*, Essay V, p. 201.

33. Mary Tudor had been the second wife of Philip II.

34. Rodríguez-Salgado, 'The Court of Philip II of Spain', in R.G. Asch and A.M. Birke (eds), *Princes, Patronage, and the Nobility*, p. 205.

35. Ibid., p. 205.

36. Thompson, *War and Society in Habsburg Spain*, Essay V, pp. 197–216.

37. Kamen, *Philip II*, p. 166.

38. Thompson, *Crown and Cortes*, Aldershot, Hampshire: Ashgate Publishing, 1982, pp. 69–98.

39. For more on this serious social problem see Martz, *Poverty and Welfare in Habsburg Spain*, pp. 119–58.

40. Astrana Marín, *Vida Ejemplar y Heroica*, Vol. 4, p. 202.

41. Bobadilla's letter, quoted by Thompson in *War and Society in Habsburg Spain*, Essay VIII, p. 17.

42. Ibid., Essay V, p. 202.

43. William Giles, *The Story of Weather*, London: HMSO, 1990, pp. 102–7.

44. Honan, *Shakespeare*, p. 125.

45. Thompson, *War and Society in Habsburg Spain*, Essay V, pp. 210–12.

46. *Cervantes Saavedra, Poesías Completas*, Vol. II, Vincente Gaos (ed.), Madrid: Castalia, 1981, pp. 325–6, 337–46. Also Geoffrey Parker, *The Grand Strategy of Philip II*, New Haven and London: Yale University Press, 1998, p. 205.

47. Geoffrey Parker, 'David or Goliath: Philip II and His World in the 1580s', in Kagan and Parker (eds), *Spain, Europe and the Atlantic Worlds*, p. 261.

48. Astrana Marín, *Vida Ejemplar y Heroica*, Vol. 4, pp. 455–6.

6 THE VEXATIOUS LIFE OF A GOVERNMENT TAX INSPECTOR (1590–8)

1. For more about J. de Quadros and similar characters read Felipe Fernández-Armesto, *Philip II's Empire: A Decade at the Edge* (Annual Lecture, 1998), London: Hakluyt Society, 1999, pp. 3–16.

2. Thompson, *War and Society in Habsburg Spain*, Essay XIV, p. 387.

3. The governorship of Sancho has obvious links with the various notions of ideal societies that flourished in the Renaissance; St Thomas More's *Utopia* illustrates this. Another influence on Cervantes may have been Juan de Castillo y Aguayo's text *The Perfect Governor*, published in Salamanca in 1586.

4. For more on this read Anthony Pagden, *Lords of All the World*, New Haven and London: Yale University Press, 1995, p. 2.

5. Thompson, *Crown and Cortes*, p. 227.

6. Ibid., p. 2.

7. Martz, *Poverty and Welfare in Habsburg Spain*, p. 33.

8. Ibid., pp. 104–5. Studies of poverty, welfare and crime in Castile show why emigration was popular.

9. Anthony Pagden, 'Empire and Its Discontents', in Kagan and Parker (eds), *Spain, Europe and the Atlantic Worlds*, p. 318.

10. Martz, *Poverty and Welfare in Habsburg Spain*, p. 153.

11. For more on this fascinating character read, J.S. Cummins, *Las Casas Goes East*, London: Hakluyt Society, 1985, pp. 14–17.

12. *Don Quixote*, J.M. Cohen (tr.), Harmondsworth: Penguin, 1982, p. 171.

13. A system of meritocracy would have suited Cervantes.

14. Pagden, *Lords of All the World*, p. 68.

15. The execution of colleagues shows how dangerous a tightrope Cervantes walked.

16. Canavaggio, *Cervantes*, p. 204.

17. *Don Quijote, Part 2*, Raffel (tr.), pp. 406–12.

18. Krzysztof Sliwa, 'Un Documento Inédito Sobre el Cautiverio de Miguel de Cervantes', in *Anales Cervantinos* (Centro de Estudios Cervantinos), 1998, Vol. 34, pp. 343–7.

19. Canavaggio, *Cervantes*, pp. 214–15.

20. Feros, *Kingship and Favoritism in the Spain of Philip III*, pp. 152–6.

21. See Joly, *Viajes de Extranjeros por España y Portugal*, Vol. 2, García Mercadal (tr. and ed.); and Marcellin de Fourneaux, *La Vida Cotidiana en la España del Siglo de Oro*, Barcelona: Argos Vergara, 1983.

22. I.A.A. Thompson and B. Yun Casalilla, *The Castilian Crisis of the Seventeenth Century*, Cambridge: Cambridge University Press, 1994, p. 204.

23. Ibid., p. 171.

24. See 'The Colloquy of the Two Dogs' in *The Exemplary Novels*, Vol. 4, Ife (ed.).

25. For an interesting parallel and comparison see Leeds Barroll, *Politics, Plague and Shakespeare's Theater*, Ithaca, NY: Cornell University Press, 1991, Ch. 3.

26. Thompson and Casalilla, *The Castilian Crisis*, p. 35.

27. Mateo Alemán, *Guzmán de Alfarache*, Book 2, Benito Brancaforte (ed.), Madrid: Akal, 1996, p. 169.

28. Sliwa, *Documentos Cervantinos*, p. 187.

29. The year 1571 was therefore momentous but not only on account of Lepanto.

30. Banditry was a serious social phenomenon in sixteenth-century Spain. See J.A. Amelang, 'The Mental World of Jeroni Pujades', in Kagan and Parker (eds), *Spain, Europe and the Atlantic Worlds*, p. 213.

31. Krzysztof Sliwa, *Documentos de Miguel de Cervantes Saavedra*, pp. 298–9.

32. See 'The Illustrious Kitchen-Maid' in *The Exemplary Novels*, Vol. 3, Ife (ed.), p. 87.

33. Byron, *Cervantes*, p. 386.

34. Thompson, *Crown and Cortes*, p. 96.

35. Cervantes' achievements – not merely literary – deserve much more recognition. Even in terms of literature, it is unjust that the novel *Don Quixote* alone carries the burden of representing his greatness.

36. It is generally acknowledged by scholars of Cervantes that his favourite sister was Magdalena.

7 THE IMPULSE TO WRITE (1598–1604)

1. For more on this see the relevant chapters in Kamen, *Philip II*, and Parker, *The Grand Strategy of Philip II*.

2. Critics of and commentators on Cervantes' play *Numantia* offer interesting perspectives on this issue. See Peraita, 'Idea de la Historia y Providencialismo en Cervantes', in *Actas del II Congreso Internacional de la Asociación de Cervantistas*, pp. 149–52.

3. E.C. Graf, 'Humanism on Philip II's Tomb', in *Cervantes: Bulletin of the Cervantes Society of America*, 1999, Vol. 19, No. 1, p. 67.

4. Fernández-Armesto, *Philip II's Empire: A Decade at the Edge*, p. 16.

5. Zaragoza, *Cervantes*, p. 256.

6. For more see the articles by R.L. Kagan and G. Parker in Kagan and Parker (eds), *Spain, Europe and the Atlantic Worlds*.

7. Feros, *Kingship and Favoritism in the Spain of Philip III*, p. 48.

8. Ibid., p. 2. See also Antonio Feros, 'Twin Souls: Monarchs and Favourites in Early Seventeenth-Century Spain', in Kagan and Parker (eds), *Spain, Europe and the Atlantic Worlds*, pp. 8, 14, and John Elliott, *The World of the Favourite*, New Haven and London: Yale University Press, 1999.

9. Our interpretations of portraits owe much to the important early work of

Thomas Hyll, A Brief and Most Pleasant Epitome of the Whole Art of Phisiognomie, London, 1556.

10. The theme of kingly conduct is discussed in Antonio Feros, 'Vicedioses, Pero Humanos: El Drama del Rey', in Cuadernos de Historia Moderna (Editorial Complutense, Madrid), 1993, No. 14, pp. 103–31.

11. Shakespeare, The Complete Works, Alexander (ed.), p. 499.

12. Kagan, Spanish Cities of the Golden Age, p. 14.

13. Vassberg, The Village and the Outside World, p. 37.

14. See the maps of Spain and Andalusia in the plate section of this book.

15. R.A. Stradling, The Armada of Flanders: Spanish Maritime Policy and European War, 1568–1668, Cambridge: Cambridge University Press, 1998, p. 12.

16. Thompson, War and Society in Habsburg Spain, pp. 265, 274.

17. Such dread of soldiers is well attested. For more on the contemporary view of soldiers and billeting see the various works of Vassberg and Thompson; also S.J. Watts, A Social History of Western Europe, 1450–1720: Tensions and Solidarities Among Rural People, London: Hutchinson, 1984.

18. For an adaptation see Adrian Mitchell, The Mayor of Zalamea, Edinburgh: Salamander Press, 1981. A useful critical edition in Spanish is that of José María Díez Borque, Madrid: Castalia, 1976.

19. Vassberg, The Village and the Outside World, pp. 111–12, and Parker, The Grand Strategy of Philip II, p. 10.

20. Fernández-Armesto, Philip II's Empire: A Decade at the Edge, p. 16, and J.H. Elliott, Spain and Its World, 1500–1700, New Haven and London: Yale University Press, 1989, pp. 215, 246–8.

21. Ife, Reading and Fiction in Golden Age Spain, pp. 117–43.

22. The bilingual edition of The Exemplary Novels, Ife (ed.), goes some way towards redressing this imbalance.

23. Sliwa, Documentos Cervantinos, pp. 198–205.

24. Kamen, Philip II, p. 180.

25. The Ezpeleta affair remains an enigma. Its occurrence, however, shows how often in Miguel's life events overtook him.

26. Martz, Poverty and Welfare in Habsburg Spain, p. 103.

27. H.J. de Blij and P.O. Muller, Geography: Realms, Regions and Concepts (8th edn), New York: Wiley, 1998, pp. 245–7.

28. Sliwa, *Documentos Cervantinos*, p. 203.

29. Canavaggio, *Cervantes*, p. 257.

30. Daniel Eisenberg, *A Study of Don Quixote*, Newark, Delaware: Juan de la
    Cuesta, 1987 – now in a revised version in Spanish: *La Interpretación
    Cervantina del 'Quijote'*, Isabel Verdaguer (tr.), Madrid: Compañía Literaria,
    1995 – and G. Brown and G. Yule, *Analysis of Discourse*, Cambridge:
    Cambridge University Press, 1983.

8 DON QUIXOTE, THE KNIGHT ERRANT OF LA MANCHA (1604–8)

1. Francisco Rico, 'Historia del texto', in *Don Quijote de la Mancha*, Rico
   (ed.), p. cxcix.

2. Ife, *Reading and Fiction in Golden Age Spain*, p. 17.

3. Eisenberg, *A Study of Don Quixote*, p. 32.

4. Kenji Inamoto, 'Sobre un Tomo del Homenaje "Satírico" a Cervantes', in
   Actas del II Congreso de la Asociación de Cervantistas, p. 75.

5. Interest in the novel *Don Quixote* seems to be endless. The bibliographical
   annual on Cervantes, *El Anuario Bibliográfico Cervantino*, published since
   1996 by Eduardo Urbina of Texas A and M University, College Station,
   Texas, shows how wide that interest is.

6. Ife, *Reading and Fiction in Golden Age Spain*, pp. 25–6.

7. 'The Little Gypsy Girl', in *The Exemplary Novels*, Vol. 1, Ife (ed.), p. 45.

8. Peter Ackroyd, *The Life of Thomas More*, pp. 231–46.

9. These are much-quoted lines from *El Viage del Parnaso*, E.L. Rivers (ed.),
   Madrid: Espasa-Calpe, 1991, p. 151.

10. For more on a much-neglected topic read P.A. Neville-Sington and
    Anthony Payne, *Richard Hakluyt and His Books*, London: Hakluyt Society,
    1997, p. 13.

11. Ibid., p. 13.

12. Dominic Finello, *Cervantes: Essays on Social and Literary Polemics*, London:
    Tamesis, 1998.

13. Other Spanish picaresque novels demonstrate the difference, too. See
    Ch. 8, note 6 above and 'The Deceitful Marriage' and 'The Colloquy of
    the Two Dogs' in *The Exemplary Novels*, Ife (ed.).

14. James McConica, *Erasmus*, p. 49.

15. Eisenberg, *A Study of Don Quixote*, p. 41.

16. For more on this see Anthony Pagden, 'Heeding Heraclides: Empire and Its Discontents', in Kagan and Parker (eds), *Spain, Europe and the Atlantic Worlds*, p. 321. See also Richard Tuck, *Philosophy and Government 1572–1651*, Cambridge: Cambridge University Press, 1993, p. 66.

17. T.S. Eliot, *The Use of Criticism*, London: Faber and Faber, 1964, p. 151.

18. For more on these central issues read Ann Moss, *Printed Common-place Books and the Structuring of Renaissance Thought*, Oxford: Oxford University Press, 1996.

19. See the Close translation of *Don Quixote* and Eisenberg, *A Study of Don Quixote*, pp. 205–23.

20. Eisenberg, ibid., p. 106.

21. The Close translation of *Don Quixote* and Eisenberg, *A Study of Don Quixote*, illustrate the point here. See also Riley, *Cervantes' Theory of the Novel*, and P.E. Russell, *Cervantes*, Oxford: Oxford University Press, 1985.

22. Feros, *Kingship and Favoritism in the Spain of Philip III*, pp. 163–4.

23. Honan, *Shakespeare*, pp. 375–6.

24. Ibid., p. 312.

25. Lokos, 'The Politics of Identity', in *Cervantes and His Postmodern Constituencies*, p. 122.

26. *Persiles y Sigismunda*, Book 3, Juan Bautista de Avalle-Arce (ed.), Madrid: Castalia, 1969, pp. 300–1.

27. Feros, *Kingship and Favoritism*, p. 88.

28. Ibid., p. 91.

29. Krzysztof Sliwa, 'Hija y Nieta de Miguel de Cervantes Saavedra, Isabel de Cervantes y Saavedra e Isabel Sanz', in *Actas del VIII Coloquio Internacional de la Asociación de Cervantistas*, El Toboso: Ediciones Dulcinea del Toboso, 1998, pp. 267–74.

30. T.A. Sears, 'Sacrificial Lambs and Domestic Goddesses, or, Did Cervantes Write Chick Lit?', in *Cervantes: Bulletin of the Cervantes Society of America*, 2000, Vol. 20, No. 1, p. 54.

31. Canavaggio, *Cervantes*, pp. 165, 297.

32. Sliwa, 'Hija y Nieta', pp. 267–73.

33. Joaquín de Entrambasaguas, *Lope de Vega en las Justas Poéticas Toledanas de 1605 y 1608*, Madrid: Gráficas Uguina, 1969, p. 124.

34. Ibid., pp. 150–2.

35. Sliwa, 'Hija y Nieta', pp. 267–73.

36. Lokos, 'The Politics of Identity', in *Cervantes and His Postmodern Constituencies*, p. 123.

37. Although 1609 saw the signing of the Twelve Year Truce with the Low Countries it also marked the vigorous expulsion of the Moriscos, with a loss over five years of nearly 300,000 people.

9 A FULL-TIME PROFESSIONAL WRITER (1608–14)

1. Dominic Finello and J. Robbins (eds), *The Challenges of Uncertainty*, London: Duckworth, 1998, pp. 30–1.

2. Colin Smith, *Christians and Moors in Spain: Vol. 2, 1195–1614*, Warminster: Aris and Phillips, 1989, p. 153.

3. James Casey, 'Patriotism in Early Valencia', in Kagan and Parker (eds), *Spain, Europe and the Atlantic Worlds*, pp. 188–210.

4. Ibid., p. 205.

5. Kamen, *Philip of Spain*, pp. 130–1.

6. *The Captive's Tale*, McCrory (tr. and ed.), pp. 127–57.

7. Thompson, *War and Society in Habsburg Spain*, Essay XI, pp. 244–67.

8. *Don Quijote, Part 2*, Raffel (tr.), p. 647.

9. Thompson, *War and Society in Habsburg Spain*, Essay XI, p. 247.

10. Ibid., pp. 247–9.

11. Sliwa, *Documentos Cervantinos*, p. 212.

12. For more see Antonio de Nicolas, *Ignatius: A Hermeneutic of St Ignatius de Loyola*, Albany, NY: State University of New York Press, 1986.

13. For examples read the several articles in *Actas del II Congreso de la Asociación de Cervantes*, pp. 727–929.

14. Canavaggio, *Cervantes*, p. 309.

15. Xavier Gil, 'Aragonese Constitutionalism and Habsburg Rule: The Varying Meanings of Liberty', in Kagan and Parker (eds), *Spain, Europe and the Atlantic Worlds*, p. 168.

16. I.A.A. Thompson, 'Castile, Spain and the Monarchy: The Political Community from Patria to Patria Nacional', in Kagan and Parker (eds), *Spain, Europe and the Atlantic Worlds*, p. 125.

17. Joly, *Viajes de Extranjeros por España y Portugal*, Vol. 2, García Mercadal (tr. and ed.), p. 125.

18. McKendrick, *Theatre in Spain*, p. 202.

19. Teresa Cirillo, 'Nápoles en el *Viaje del Parnaso* Cervantino y en Dos

Parnasos Partenopeos', in *Actas del II Congreso de la Asociación de Cervantes*, p. 71.

20. Sliwa, *Documentos de Miguel de Cervantes Saavedra*, pp. 342–5.

21. Ibid., pp. 345–7.

22. Casey, 'Patriotism in Early Valencia', in Kagan and Parker (eds), *Spain, Europe and the Atlantic Worlds*, p. 205.

23. *The Exemplary Novels*, Vol. I, Ife (ed.), p. vii.

24. Sliwa, *Documentos de Miguel de Cervantes Saavedra*, p. 354.

25. Canavaggio, *Cervantes*, p. 321.

26. Ibid., p. 318.

27. Ibid., p. 322.

28. Eisenberg, *A Study of Don Quixote*, p. 40.

29. Close, 'Cervantes: Pensamiento, Personalidad, Cultura', in *Don Quijote*, Rico (ed.), pp. lxxi–ii.

30. N. Marín López (ed.), *Las Cartas de Lope de Vega*, Madrid: Clásicos Castilla, 1985, pp. 68, 110.

31. Nicolás Spadaccini and Jenaro Talens, *Cervantes and the Self-Made World*, Minneapolis: University of Minnesota Press, 1993, p. 4.

32. Ellen Lokos, *The Solitary Journey: Cervantes' Voyage to Parnassus*, New York: Peter Lang, 1991, pp. 100–2.

33. Ibid., pp. 151–2.

34. Ibid., p. 92.

35. *Don Quijote, Part 2*, Raffel (tr.), p. 440.

36. *Don Quijote, Part 2*, Raffel (tr.), p. 670.

37. De Entrambasaguas, *Lope de Vega*, pp. 18–22, 114–26.

38. *Don Quijote, Part 2*, Raffel (tr.), p. 451.

39. Lokos, *The Solitary Journey*, p. 102.

40. *Don Quijote, Part 2*, Raffel (tr.), p. 647.

10 THE FINAL FLOWERING (1614–16)

1. Canavaggio, *Cervantes*, pp. 309, 314.

2. E.H. Friedman, 'Insincere Flattery: Imitation and the Growth of the Novel', in *Cervantes: Bulletin of the Cervantes Society of America*, 2000, Vol. 20, No. 1, p. 109.

3. T.A. Sears, in the *Newsletter of the Cervantes Society of America*, January 2001, p. 2.

4. Tordesillas is famous, not because of Avellaneda but on account of the treaty signed there in 1494 by which Portugal and Spain agreed to the division, set by the Pope, of their colonies in South America.

5. For more see Martín de Riquer, *Cervantes, Passamonte y Avellaneda*, Barcelona: Sirmio, 1988.

6. Feros, *Kingship and Favoritism in the Spain of Philip III*, p. 233.

7. E.S. Knotek, 'Don Quijote and the Modern Undergraduate Student', review article in *Cervantes: Bulletin of the Cervantes Society of America*, 2000, Vol. 20, No. 1, p. 180.

8. McKendrick, *Theatre in Spain*, pp. 262–5.

9. For more see Yumiko Yamada, *Ben Jonson and Cervantes: Tilting Against Chivalric Romances*, Tokyo: Maruzen, 2000.

10. Aurelio González, 'Las Acotaciones: Elementos de la Construcción Teatral en las Comedias Cervantinas', *Actas del II Congreso de la Asociación de Cervantes*, pp. 155–67.

11. McKendrick, *Theatre in Spain*, p. 185.

12. *The Exemplary Novels*, Vol. 2, Ife (ed.), pp. 2–5.

13. *Eight Interludes*, D.L. Smith (tr.), London: Everyman, 1996, pp. 55–72.

14. Enrique Fernández, 'Los Tratos de Argel: Obra Testimonial, Denuncia Política y Literature Terapéutica', in *Cervantes: Bulletin of the Cervantes Society of America*, 2000, Vol. 20, No. 1, pp. 14–15.

15. Zimic, *El Teatro de Cervantes*, pp. 221–62.

16. Ibid., p. 285.

17. McKendrick, *Theatre in Spain*, p. 64.

18. *Eight Interludes*, Smith (tr.), p. 123.

19. McConica, *Erasmus*, p. 89.

20. McKendrick, *Theatre in Spain*, p. 259.

21. Reed, *The Novelist as Playwright*, p. 122.

22. *Persiles and Sigismunda*, Diana de Armas Wilson (tr.), Princeton: Princeton University Press, 1991, p. xix.

23. A useful introduction to the text is provided by Maurice Molho in his translation into French, *Les Travaux de Persille et Sigismonde*, Paris: José Corti, 1994.

24. Maurice Molho, 'Filosofía Natural o Filosofía Racional: Sobre el Concepto de Astrología en Los Trabajos de Persiles y Sigismunda', *Actas del II Congreso de la Asociación de Cervantes*, pp. 673–9.

25. R.L. Kagan, 'Clio and the Crown: Writing History in Habsburg Spain', in Kagan and Parker (eds), *Spain, Europe and the Atlantic Worlds*, p. 76.
26. Ibid., pp. 76–99.
27. Feros, *Kingship and Favoritism in the Spain of Philip III*, pp. 233–5.
28. Ibid., p. 236.
29. Kamen, *Philip of Spain*, p. 54.
30. Ackroyd, *The Life of Thomas More*, p. 195.

A BRIEF CHRONOLOGY OF THE LIFE OF MIGUEL DE CERVANTES

1547 Miguel de Cervantes Saavedra born in Alcalá de Henares on ?29 September to Rodrigo de Cervantes and Leonor de Cortinas

1551 The Cervantes family leaves for Valladolid, then capital of Spain

1553 The Cervantes family moves to Córdoba

1556 Death of Juan de Cervantes (grandfather); the abdication of Charles V and the coronation of Philip II

1557 Death of Leonor Fernández de Torreblanca (paternal grandmother)

1561 Madrid is made the capital of Spain

1564 The Cervantes family moves to Seville; William Shakespeare born

1565 His sister Luisa enters the Carmelite convent in Alcalá de Henares

1566 The Cervantes family moves to Madrid

1567 First poems published

1569 Flees Madrid following a duel with Antonio de Sigura

1570 Arrives in Italy and joins the household of the prelate Giulio Acquaviva in Rome

1571 Joins the army in Naples with his brother Rodrigo and is wounded at the Battle of Lepanto

1572 In Sicily, Corfu and Modón

1574 In Sardinia(?), Sicily and Naples

1575 Cervantes and Rodrigo captured by pirates and taken to Algiers

1576 First escape attempt

1577 Ransom of Rodrigo and Cervantes' second escape attempt; Hasan Pasha appointed Bey (governor) of Algiers

1578 Third escape attempt; death of Don John of Austria

1579 Fourth escape attempt; opening of the first theatres in Madrid

1580 Cervantes ransomed; lands in Valencia and returns to Madrid, then leaves for Portugal where Philip II has established his court

1581 First mission for the Crown sends him back to North Africa; becomes court petitioner in Lisbon

1584 Affair with Ana Franca de Rojas, resulting in the birth of of a daughter, Isabel de Cervantes Saavedra; marries Catalina de Salazar in Esquivias

1585 Publication of *La Galatea*; death of his father

1587–94 Works as a civil servant in Andalusia

    1588 The Armada sets out; death of Catalina de Palacios (mother-in-law)

    1590 Seeks a post in the New World but is turned down; 'The Captive's Tale' probably written

    1592 Imprisoned in Castro del Río

    1593 Death of his mother

    1594 Works as a tax collector in Granada

    1595 Wins a national poetry tournament in Saragossa

    1597 In prison in Seville

    1598 Death of Ana Franca de Rojas; death of Philip II; coronation of Philip III and the beginning of the rule of the Duke of Lerma; theatres closed in Spain

    1600 Death of his brother; theatres reopened

    1601 Moves once again to Valladolid, following the court

    1602 Problems with the Treasury; begins writing *Don Quixote*

    1604 Feud with Lope de Vega becomes public

    1605 Publication of *Don Quixote, Part One*

    1606 Moves back to Madrid, following the court; his daughter marries Diego Sanz

    1607 Birth of Isabel Sanz (granddaughter)

    1608 Death of Diego Sanz; his daughter marries Luis de Molina

    1609 The Cervantes household joins religious societies; deaths of his sister Andrea and his granddaughter

    1610 Count of Lemos appointed Viceroy of Naples; Cervantes' application to go to Naples is rejected

    1611 Death of his sister Magdalena; growing success throughout Europe of *Don Quixote, Part One*; death of Marguerite of Austria (Philip III's wife) leads to the temporary closure of theatres

    1613 *Exemplary Novels* published; Cervantes joins the tertiary orders of St Francis

    1614 *Voyage to Parnassus* published; Avellaneda's fake sequel to *Don Quixote* published; Cervantes' own sequel, *Don Quixote, Part Two*, published

    1615 *Eight Plays and Eight Interludes* published

    1616 Makes a final dedication to his patron the Count of Lemos in *Persiles and Sigismunda*; Cervantes dies on 22 April

    1617 Posthumous publication of *Persiles and Sigismunda*

APPENDIX 2
THE CERVANTES FAMILY TREE

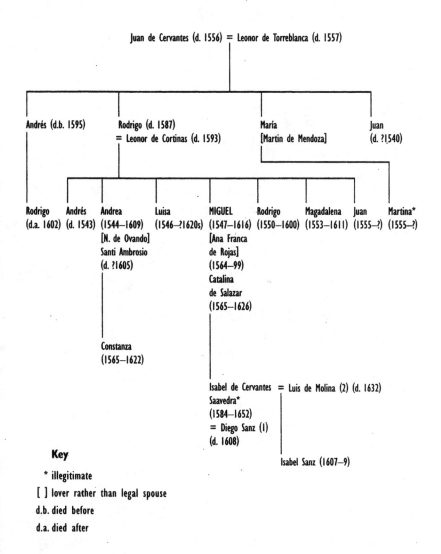

Juan de Cervantes (d. 1556) = Leonor de Torreblanca (d. 1557)

Andrés (d.b. 1595)   Rodrigo (d. 1587)   María   Juan
= Leonor de Cortinas (d. 1593)   [Martin de Mendoza]   (d. ?1540)

Rodrigo   Andrés   Andrea   Luisa   MIGUEL   Rodrigo   Magadalena   Juan   Martina*
(d.a. 1602)   (d. 1543)   (1544–1609)   (1546–?1620s)   (1547–1616)   (1550–1600)   (1553–1611)   (1555–?)   (1555–?)
[N. de Ovando]   [Ana Franca
Santi Ambrosio   de Rojas]
(d. ?1605)   (1564–99)
Catalina
de Salazar
(1565–1626)

Constanza
(1565–1622)

Isabel de Cervantes   = Luis de Molina (2) (d. 1632)
Saavedra*
(1584–1652)
= Diego Sanz (1)
(d. 1608)

Isabel Sanz (1607–9)

Key

* illegitimate
[ ] lover rather than legal spouse
d.b. died before
d.a. died after

APPENDIX 3
A NOTE ON CURRENCY

In 1497 Ferdinand and Isabella, the Catholic Monarchs, passed a decree, 'La Ordenanza de Medina del Campo', in an attempt to put the rather chaotic Castilian monetary system into some semblance of order. However, it remained somewhat complicated and unstable in terms of both real values and the relationships between different units of coinage. An important factor in this was the inflow of gold and silver from the Americas, particularly the flood of silver from Potosí towards the end of the sixteenth century. Another was the heavy expenditures by Charles V and Philip II on their diplomatic and military adventures abroad. The result of these and other developments was a disastrous inflation that raised price levels fourfold during the century, leading to a progressive debasement of currency and a sharp rise in the cost of living. This was accompanied by increasingly harsh taxation and strenuous efforts to extract the last maravedí from the unfortunate taxpayer.

The ordinance defined coins of gold, silver and of an alloy of silver and copper called vellón (billon). These were measured in a unit of currency called a maravedí. This coin is often mentioned by Cervantes in his writings, although it is conspicuous by its absence in 'The Captive's Tale'. In the reign of Philip II the standard coins were the gold escudo and the silver real. Nevertheless older coins, notably the ducado (gold ducat) and the dobla (double-ducat or doubloon), still circulated. Although it would be impossible to give simple and accurate equivalents of these coins for the period, the values in the following list appear to be those most widely accepted by critics and commentators.

Ardite A small copper coin withdrawn in the early sixteenth century.
Dobla Better known as the doblón, this gold coin minted by the Crown was in common usage in the sixteenth century. The Spanish doubloons of the seventeenth century were gold coins representing various multiples of the escudo, the most famous being the doblones a ocho, the 'pieces of eight' of pirate lore.

Ducado Although in origin Italian – the ducato being a gold coin imprinted with the portrait of the Doge of Venice – it was used in Spain throughout the sixteenth century. The ducado served for a time as the basis of the currency system, but after 1534 it became a money of account, valued at 375 maravedís.

Escudo The name comes from the Spanish word for shield, and it was also known as the corona (crown). This common coin was introduced into Spain by Charles V in 1537, and it was minted from gold of 22 carats fine. It was originally valued at 350 maravedís but raised to 400 in 1566 and to 440 in 1609. In Castilian accounts, the escudo usually referred to was the escudo de diez reales, worth 340 maravedís.

Maravedí This started out as a small copper coin but later became the smallest unit of account.

Real The name comes from the word *rey*, meaning king. It was a widely circulated small silver coin, roughly akin to the English sixpence of the same period, and was worth 34 maravedís. It was eventually debased to copper. The so-called reales de vellón contained a tiny fraction of silver.

Vellón In addition to the above there was a heavy billon coinage of progressively debased copper-silver alloy in varying proportions circulating in various units of value. It was calculated as equivalent to 4 maravedís.

Readers will observe that the currency of the maravedí is mentioned throughout this text. The following items taken from Francisco Rico's definitive edition of *Don Quixote, Book One*, p. 3, gives prices for the year 1605 as follows:

12 eggs = 63 maravedís
12 oranges = 54 maravedís
1 chicken = 55 maravedís
1 hen = 127 maravedís
1 ream of paper = 28 maravedís

SELECT BIBLIOGRAPHY

So much has been written about the works of Cervantes that it would take more than a lifetime to keep up with it all. Fortunately Professor Eduardo Urbina's mammoth undertaking – *Cervantes Proyecto 2001* – has as its main aim the compilation of an up-to-date and fully comprehensive bibliography. This has been aided by the publication of his *Anuario Bibliográfico Cervantino* which was started in 1996. For the general reader, however, select bibliographies are more useful. In this text I have attempted to slant the references towards the biography of Cervantes as well as towards the needs of the non-Spanish reader. For this reason I have also exempted references relating to the extensive materials to be found on the economic, political, military and religious aspects of sixteenth-century Spain. The texts mentioned in the notes commonly carry extensive bibliographies on such matters.

Without doubt the best work currently on Cervantes and his writings is published in the *Anales Cervantinos* and in *Cervantes: The Bulletin of the Cervantes Society of America*. Both journals deal specifically with all things Cervantine. For the serious student and specialist there is the Association of Cervantistas that promotes all aspects of his life and work. It is true to say that the creative works of Cervantes have spawned a major industry; the findings of original research into archives – an area still much neglected – of conferences and learned societies are published regularly.

BIOGRAPHIES OF CERVANTES
The nine major biographies studied by Dr Krzysztof Sliwa (see the introduction to this book) are given in chronological order so that readers can trace the development of interest in the life of Cervantes.

Mayáns y Siscar, Gregorio, *Vida de Miguel de Cervantes Saavedra*, Madrid: Briga Real, 1737

De los Ríos, Vicente, *Vida de Miguel de Cervantes Saavedra*, Madrid: Real Academia Española, 1773

Pellicer y Pillares, J.A., *Vida de Miguel de Cervantes Saavedra*, Madrid: G. de Sancha, 1798–1800

Fernández de Navarrete, M., *Vida de Miguel de Cervantes Saavedra*, Madrid: Imprenta Real, 1819

Morán, Jerónimo, *Vida de Cervantes*, Madrid: Imprenta Nacional, 1862–3

Máinez, León Ramón, *Vida de Miguel de Cervantes Saavedra*, Cádiz: Tipografía la Mercantil, 1876

Fitzmaurice-Kelly, J., *Miguel de Cervantes Saavedra: A Memoir*, Oxford: Clarendon Press, 1913

Astrana Marín, Luis, *Vida Ejemplar y Heroica de Miguel de Cervantes Saavedra*, Madrid: Reus, 1948–58

Canavaggio, Jean, *Cervantes*, Madrid: Espasa-Calpe, 1986 (revised 1997)

These biographies are useful stepping-stones towards that synthesis which we seek. There were and are other biographies, but those studied by Dr Sliwa were deemed to have made the most significant contribution to the life of Cervantes. Each text offers very different interpretations. Those of William Byron and of Cristóbal Zaragoza, cited below, carry extensive bibliographies.

It should be mentioned that the modern trend is for biographers and researchers to study original documents wherever possible. Renewed interest in the historical document is most welcome, seen especially well in a number of recent articles that examine, for example, Cervantes' family, both immediate and extended.

Arrabal, Fernando, *Un Esclavo Llamado Cervantes*, Madrid: Espasa-Calpe, 1996

Byron, William, *Cervantes: A Biography*, New York: Doubleday, 1978

Durán, M., *Cervantes*, Boston, Massachusetts: Twayne World Author Series, 1974

Marlowe, Stephen, *The Death and Life of Miguel de Cervantes: A Novel*, New York: Arcade Publishing, 1996

McKendrick, Melveena, *Cervantes*, Boston, Massachusetts: Little, Brown and Company, 1980

Predmore, Richard, *Cervantes*, New York: Dodd, Mead, 1973

Rey Hazas, A., and F. Sevilla, *Vida de Cervantes*, Madrid: Alianza, 1995

Rossi, Rosa, *Sulle Tracce di Cervantes*, Rome: Editori Riuniti, 1997

Trapiello, A., *Las Vidas de Cervantes*, Barcelona: Planeta, 1993

Zaragoza, Cristóbal, *Cervantes: Vida y Semblanza*, Madrid: Mondadori, 1991

LITERARY CRITICISM

A widely consulted edition of the complete works of Cervantes is *Las Obras Completas de Miguel de Cervantes Saavedra*, published by Aguilar of Madrid in 1986, edited by Valbuena Prat. As such it is the recommended edition for all of Cervantes' works. Nevertheless, other editions of individual texts are also recommended.

LA GALATEA

Despite the unpopularity of the pastoral novel, *La Galatea* continues to attract ever increasing attention. In the findings of the International Congress of Cervantistas held in Naples in 1994 (*Actas del II Congreso Internacional de la Asociación de Cervantes*, Naples: Istituto Orientale Universitario, 1995) there were as many articles – seven – devoted to *La Galatea* as to the highly popular *Exemplary Novels*. It is articles, however, rather than full-scale studies that contribute the most to the theme of the bucolic in Spain. A much quoted Spanish edition of *La Galatea* is that of Juan Bautista de Avalle-Arce, Madrid: Espasa-Calpe, 1987, which should be complemented with his *La Galatea de Cervantes Cuatrocientos Años Después*, Newark, Delaware: Juan de la Cuesta, 1985.

Honda, Seiji, 'Sobre *La Galatea* como Égloga', *Actas del II Congreso Internacional de la Asociación de Cervantistas*, Naples: Istituto Universitario Orientale, 1995, pp. 197–212

Poggioli, R., *The Oaten Flute: Essays on Pastoral Poetry and the Pastoral Ideal*, Cambridge, Massachusetts: Harvard University Press, 1975

Rhodes, E., 'Sixteenth Century Pastoral Books: Narrative Structure and *La Galatea* of Cervantes', *Bulletin of Hispanic Studies* (University of Liverpool), 1989, Vol. 66, pp. 351–60

EXEMPLARY NOVELS

The twelve novellas that make up the collection are:

'The Little Gypsy Girl', 'The Liberal Lover', 'The English-Spanish Girl', 'The Glass Graduate', 'The Force of Blood', 'The Jealous Old Man from Extremadura', 'The Illustrious Kitchen-Maid', 'The Two Damsels', 'Lady Cornelia', 'The Deceitful Marriage', 'Rinconete and Cortadillo' and 'The Colloquy of the Two Dogs'.

An enormous amount of research has been poured into the *Exemplary Novels*, with the result that the modern reader has a variety of excellent individual studies on offer. For a useful compendium of the major interpretations of the novels refer to D.B. Drake, *Cervantes' Novelas Ejemplares: A Selective, Annotated Bibliography*, New York: Garland, 1981. A standard Spanish edition is the three-volume edition edited by Juan Bautista de Avalle-Arce, Madrid: Castalia, 1985.

A useful bilingual edition is the four-volume one edited by B.W. Ife, Warminster, Wiltshire: Aris and Philips, 1992. Although not part of the collection, my own edition of *The Captive's Tale* (1994), also published by Aris and Philips and now distributed through donald_mccrory@yahoo.co.uk, provides a useful addition to the series edited by Professor Ife. In analysing the differences between the fictional and factual, I show to what extent autobiographical elements animate the tale. The edition also discusses the background, sources, themes, characters, narrative techniques and problems of literary appreciation in a text that has been much neglected.

Amezúa y Mayo, A.G. de, *Cervantes, Creador de la Novela Corta Española*, 2 vols, Madrid: Instituto Miguel de Cervantes, 1982

Clamurro, W., *Beneath the Fiction: The Contrary Worlds of Cervantes' Novelas Ejemplares*, New York: Peter Lang, 1997

Gilman, S., *The Novel According to Cervantes*, Berkeley, California: University of California Press, 1989

Osterc, L., *La Verdad Sobre las Novelas Ejemplares*, Mexico City: Gernika, 1985

Ricapito, J., *Cervantes' Novelas Ejemplares: Between History and Creativity*, West Lafayette, Indiana: Purdue University Press, 1996

Rodrigo-Luis, J., *Novedad y Ejemplo de las Novelas de Cervantes*, 2 vols, Madrid: Porrua Turanzas, 1980–4

Sánchez, F.J., *Lectura y Representación: Análisis Culturales de las Novelas Ejemplares de Cervantes*, New York: Peter Lang, 1993

Zimic, Stanislav, *Las Novelas Ejemplares de Cervantes*, Madrid: Siglo Veintiuno, 1996

DON QUIXOTE

Cervantes' major text has created a seemingly inexhaustible treasure house of critical commentaries and interpretations, so much so that to keep abreast of the literature is almost a full-time occupation in itself. The major translations into English continue to be those of J. Ormsby, New York: W.W. Norton, 1981, and Burton Raffel, New York: W.W. Norton, 1999. Of the various editions in Spanish few can match that of the two-volume text from the Instituto Cervantes edited by Francisco Rico, *Don Quijote de la Mancha*, Barcelona: Crítica Biblioteca Clásica, 1998, with accompanying CD-ROM. This edition is exhaustively comprehensive, the fruit of the labour of over fifty cervantistas and clearly the text for the new millennium. I have chosen to list those critical works which I believe offer new and or interesting perspectives. Much of the modern criticism depends largely on the works of Bakhtin, Calvino, Deleuze and Derrida.

Close, Anthony, *Don Quixote*, Cambridge: Cambridge University Press, 1990

Cruz, Anne J. and Carroll B. Johnson (eds), *Cervantes and His Postmodern Constituencies*, New York and London: Garland, 1999

Eisenberg, Daniel, *A Study of Don Quixote*, Newark, Delaware: Juan de la Cuesta, 1987. A revised version is available in Spanish: *La Interpretación Cervantina del Quijote*, Isabel Verdaguer (tr.), Madrid: Compañía Literaria, 1995

Haley, G. (ed.), *El Quijote de Cervantes*, Madrid: Taurus, 1984

Márquez Villanueva, Francisco, *Personajes y Temas del Quijote*, Madrid: Taurus, 1975

Riley, E.C., *Don Quixote*, London: Allen and Unwin, 1986

Salazar Rincón, J., *El Mundo Social del Quijote*, Madrid: Gredos, 1986

Urbina, Eduardo, *El Sin par Sancho Panza: Parodia y Creación*, Barcelona: Anthropos, 1991

Welsh, A., *Reflections on the Hero as Quixote*, Princeton, New Jersey: Princeton University Press, 1981

THE THEATRE

A useful edition of Cervantes' dramas is that of F. Sevilla Arroyo and A. Rey Hazas, *Teatro Completo*, Barcelona: Planeta, 1987. Of the twenty or thirty plays Cervantes claims to have written in his first cycle of theatrical works only two remain: *Numantia* and *Life in Algiers*. The titles of the eight plays and eight playlets published in 1615 are as follows:

Plays

The Fortunate Pimp, The House of Jealousy, The Labyrinth of Love, The Gallant

Spaniard, The Dungeons of Algiers, Pedro de Urdemalas, The Sultan's Wife and *The Mistress.*

Playlets

The Vigilant Guardian, The Divorce Court Judge, The Marvellous Puppet Show, The Election of the Councillors of Daganza, The Widowed Pimp, The Man Who Pretended to Be from Biscay, The Magic Cave of Salamanca and *The Jealous Old Man.*

For more general studies see:

Allen, J.J., *The Reconstruction of a Spanish Golden Age Playhouse: El Corral del Príncipe 1583–1749*, New York: New York University Press, 1988

Canavaggio, Jean, *Cervantes Dramaturge: Un Théatre à Naître*, Paris: Presses Universitaires de France, 1977

Friedman, E.H., *The Unifying Concept: Approaches to the Structure of Cervantes' Comedias*, York, South Carolina: Spanish Literature Publications Co., 1981

García Martín, M., *Cervantes y la Comedia Española en el Siglo XVII*, Salamanca: Universidad de Salamanca, 1980

McKendrick, Melveena, *Theatre in Spain, 1490–1700*, Cambridge: Cambridge University Press, 1989

Zimic, Stanislav, *El Teatro de Cervantes*, Madrid: Castalia, 1992

INTERLUDES/PLAYLETS

Smith, D.L., *Eight Interludes*, London: Everyman, 1996 (a useful translation with an introduction)

Reed, C.A., *The Novelist as Playwright: Cervantes and the Entremés Nuevo*, New York: Peter Lang, 1993

VOYAGE TO PARNASSUS

This is probably the most neglected of all of Cervantes' works, and very few studies have been dedicated to this, his longest poem. Those who refer to it generally do so to censure it or to compare it unfavourably with the 'Postscript' ('Adjunta') written in prose. Some ignore it altogether: in the revised edition of the Canavaggio biography of Cervantes there is no mention of it whatsoever in the bibliography.

The negative appraisal of Cervantes' poetry arose mainly out of the jealousy of his fellow-poets at the success of *Don Quixote*. A total re-evaluation of the *Voyage to Parnassus* is found in the study by Ellen Lokos, whose work is the best to date and one that should initiate further scholarly studies. The disparaging remarks made by those few critics who have bothered to study the text echo the very negative comments Cervantes was made to suffer during his own lifetime. A useful edition is that of E.L. Rivers, *Viage del Parnaso: Poesías Varias*, Madrid: Espasa-Calpe, 1991.

Canavaggio, Jean, 'La Dimensión Autobiográfica del Viaje del Parnaso', *Cervantes: Bulletin of the Cervantes Society of America*, 1981, Vol. 1, No. 1, pp. 29–41

Lokos, Ellen D., *The Solitary Journey*, London: Peter Lang, 1991

Márquez Villanueva, Francisco, 'El Retorno del Parnaso', *Nueva Revista de Filología Hispánica*, Vol. 38, Mexico City: El Colegio de México, 1990, pp. 693–732

Sansone, G. E., '*El Viaje del Parnaso*: Testimonio de una Discontinuidad', *Actas del II Congreso Internacional de la Asociación de Cervantes*, Naples: Istituto Orientale Universitario, 1995, pp. 57–64

Stagg, G., 'Propaganda and Poetics on Parnassus: Cervantes' *Viaje del Parnaso*', *Cervantes: Bulletin of the Cervantes Society of America*, 1988, Vol. 8, No. 8, pp. 23–38

Talens, Jenaro, 'Poetry as Autobiography: Theory and Poetic Practice in Cervantes', *Autobiography in Early Modern Spain*, Minneapolis, Minnesota: Prisma Institute, 1988, pp. 215–46

PERSILES AND SIGISMUNDA

The edition edited by Carlos Romero Muñoz – Madrid: Cátedra, 1997 – is probably the best to date and is the text to have for anyone seriously interested in what is Cervantes' second most important work. Another edition is that of Maurice Molho, whose translation of the novel into French – *Les Travaux de Persille et Sigismonde*, Paris: José Corti, 1994 – includes a useful preface. Also recommended is the new translation into English, the first since 1854, by Celia E. Weller and Clark A. Colahan, *The Trials of Persiles and Sigismunda*, Berkeley, California: University of California Press, 1989.

de Armas Wilson, Diana, *Allegories of Love: Cervantes' 'Persiles and Sigismunda'*, Princeton, New Jersey: Princeton University Press, 1991

El Saffar, Ruth, *Beyond Fiction*, Berkeley, California: University of California

Press, 1984, pp. 127–69

Forcione, A.K., *Cervantes' Christian Romance: A Study of Persiles y Sigismunda*, Princeton, New Jersey: Princeton University Press, 1972

CERVANTES' POETRY

The poetry of Cervantes is the most neglected aspect of his work, and yet he wrote verse throughout his life. His inclination towards poetry was expressed in *La Galatea* and was reiterated in the *Voyage to Parnsassus*.

There is an edition of his poetry edited by Vincente Gaos, *Cervantes Saavedra, Poesías Completas*, Madrid: Castalia, 1981. A useful supplement to this is the work of E.L. Rivers (ed.), *Viage del Parnaso y Poesías Varias*, Madrid: Espasa-Calpe, 1991. Two recent articles which provide an exhaustive bibliography for all aspects of Cervantes' poetry – themes, use of language, influences, sources and so on – are to be found in the *Actas del II Congreso Internacional de la Asociación de Cervantes*, Naples: Istituto Universitario Orientale, 1995: A. Bernat Vistarini, 'Algunos Motivos Emblemáticos en la Poesía de Cervantes', pp. 83–95, and M. García-Page, 'El Cultismo Sintáctico en Cervantes', pp. 97–122. Other useful texts are:

Gaos, Vincente, *Cervantes: Novelista, Dramaturgo, Poeta*, Barcelona: Planeta, 1979

Martin, A.L., *Cervantes and the Burlesque Sonnet*, Berkeley, California: University of California Press, 1991

Ynduráin, F., 'La Poesía de Cervantes: Aproximaciones', *Edad de Oro*, No. 4, Madrid: Universidad Autónoma de Madrid, 1985, pp. 211–35

INDEX

A CATALOG OF SELECTED
DOVER BOOKS
IN ALL FIELDS OF INTEREST

A CATALOG OF SELECTED DOVER
BOOKS IN ALL FIELDS OF INTEREST

CONCERNING THE SPIRITUAL IN ART, Wassily Kandinsky. Pioneering work by father of abstract art. Thoughts on color theory, nature of art. Analysis of earlier masters. 12 illustrations. 80pp. of text. 5⅜ x 8½.   0-486-23411-8

CELTIC ART: The Methods of Construction, George Bain. Simple geometric techniques for making Celtic interlacements, spirals, Kells-type initials, animals, humans, etc. Over 500 illustrations. 160pp. 9 x 12. (Available in U.S. only.)   0-486-22923-8

AN ATLAS OF ANATOMY FOR ARTISTS, Fritz Schider. Most thorough reference work on art anatomy in the world. Hundreds of illustrations, including selections from works by Vesalius, Leonardo, Goya, Ingres, Michelangelo, others. 593 illustrations. 192pp. 7⅛ x 10¼.   0-486-20241-0

CELTIC HAND STROKE-BY-STROKE (Irish Half-Uncial from "The Book of Kells"): An Arthur Baker Calligraphy Manual, Arthur Baker. Complete guide to creating each letter of the alphabet in distinctive Celtic manner. Covers hand position, strokes, pens, inks, paper, more. Illustrated. 48pp. 8¼ x 11.   0-486-24336-2

EASY ORIGAMI, John Montroll. Charming collection of 32 projects (hat, cup, pelican, piano, swan, many more) specially designed for the novice origami hobbyist. Clearly illustrated easy-to-follow instructions insure that even beginning papercrafters will achieve successful results. 48pp. 8¼ x 11.   0-486-27298-2

BLOOMINGDALE'S ILLUSTRATED 1886 CATALOG: Fashions, Dry Goods and Housewares, Bloomingdale Brothers. Famed merchants' extremely rare catalog depicting about 1,700 products: clothing, housewares, firearms, dry goods, jewelry, more. Invaluable for dating, identifying vintage items. Also, copyright-free graphics for artists, designers. Co-published with Henry Ford Museum & Greenfield Village. 160pp. 8¼ x 11.   0-486-25780-0

THE ART OF WORLDLY WISDOM, Baltasar Gracian. "Think with the few and speak with the many," "Friends are a second existence," and "Be able to forget" are among this 1637 volume's 300 pithy maxims. A perfect source of mental and spiritual refreshment, it can be opened at random and appreciated either in brief or at length. 128pp. 5⅜ x 8½.   0-486-44034-6

JOHNSON'S DICTIONARY: A Modern Selection, Samuel Johnson (E. L. McAdam and George Milne, eds.). This modern version reduces the original 1755 edition's 2,300 pages of definitions and literary examples to a more manageable length, retaining the verbal pleasure and historical curiosity of the original. 480pp. 5³⁄₁₆ x 8¼.   0-486-44089-3

ADVENTURES OF HUCKLEBERRY FINN, Mark Twain, Illustrated by E. W. Kemble. A work of eternal richness and complexity, a source of ongoing critical debate, and a literary landmark, Twain's 1885 masterpiece about a barefoot boy's journey of self-discovery has enthralled readers around the world. This handsome clothbound reproduction of the first edition features all 174 of the original black-and-white illustrations. 368pp. 5⅜ x 8½.   0-486-44322-1

STICKLEY CRAFTSMAN FURNITURE CATALOGS, Gustav Stickley and L. & J. G. Stickley. Beautiful, functional furniture in two authentic catalogs from 1910. 594 illustrations, including 277 photos, show settles, rockers, armchairs, reclining chairs, bookcases, desks, tables. 183pp. 6½ x 9¼. 0-486-23838-5

AMERICAN LOCOMOTIVES IN HISTORIC PHOTOGRAPHS: 1858 to 1949, Ron Ziel (ed.). A rare collection of 126 meticulously detailed official photographs, called "builder portraits," of American locomotives that majestically chronicle the rise of steam locomotive power in America. Introduction. Detailed captions. xi+ 129pp. 9 x 12. 0-486-27393-8

AMERICA'S LIGHTHOUSES: An Illustrated History, Francis Ross Holland, Jr. Delightfully written, profusely illustrated fact-filled survey of over 200 American lighthouses since 1716. History, anecdotes, technological advances, more. 240pp. 8 x 10¾. 0-486-25576-X

TOWARDS A NEW ARCHITECTURE, Le Corbusier. Pioneering manifesto by founder of "International School." Technical and aesthetic theories, views of industry, economics, relation of form to function, "mass-production split" and much more. Profusely illustrated. 320pp. 6⅛ x 9¼. (Available in U.S. only.) 0-486-25023-7

HOW THE OTHER HALF LIVES, Jacob Riis. Famous journalistic record, exposing poverty and degradation of New York slums around 1900, by major social reformer. 100 striking and influential photographs. 233pp. 10 x 7⅞. 0-486-22012-5

FRUIT KEY AND TWIG KEY TO TREES AND SHRUBS, William M. Harlow. One of the handiest and most widely used identification aids. Fruit key covers 120 deciduous and evergreen species; twig key 160 deciduous species. Easily used. Over 300 photographs. 126pp. 5⅜ x 8½. 0-486-20511-8

COMMON BIRD SONGS, Dr. Donald J. Borror. Songs of 60 most common U.S. birds: robins, sparrows, cardinals, bluejays, finches, more–arranged in order of increasing complexity. Up to 9 variations of songs of each species.
Cassette and manual 0-486-99911-4

ORCHIDS AS HOUSE PLANTS, Rebecca Tyson Northen. Grow cattleyas and many other kinds of orchids–in a window, in a case, or under artificial light. 63 illustrations. 148pp. 5⅜ x 8½. 0-486-23261-1

MONSTER MAZES, Dave Phillips. Masterful mazes at four levels of difficulty. Avoid deadly perils and evil creatures to find magical treasures. Solutions for all 32 exciting illustrated puzzles. 48pp. 8¼ x 11. 0-486-26005-4

MOZART'S DON GIOVANNI (DOVER OPERA LIBRETTO SERIES), Wolfgang Amadeus Mozart. Introduced and translated by Ellen H. Bleiler. Standard Italian libretto, with complete English translation. Convenient and thoroughly portable–an ideal companion for reading along with a recording or the performance itself. Introduction. List of characters. Plot summary. 121pp. 5¼ x 8½. 0-486-24944-1

FRANK LLOYD WRIGHT'S DANA HOUSE, Donald Hoffmann. Pictorial essay of residential masterpiece with over 160 interior and exterior photos, plans, elevations, sketches and studies. 128pp. 9¼ x 10¾. 0-486-29120-0

THE CLARINET AND CLARINET PLAYING, David Pino. Lively, comprehensive work features suggestions about technique, musicianship, and musical interpretation, as well as guidelines for teaching, making your own reeds, and preparing for public performance. Includes an intriguing look at clarinet history. "A godsend," *The Clarinet,* Journal of the International Clarinet Society. Appendixes. 7 illus. 320pp. 5⅜ x 8½. 0-486-40270-3

HOLLYWOOD GLAMOR PORTRAITS, John Kobal (ed.). 145 photos from 1926-49. Harlow, Gable, Bogart, Bacall; 94 stars in all. Full background on photographers, technical aspects. 160pp. 8⅜ x 11¼. 0-486-23352-9

THE RAVEN AND OTHER FAVORITE POEMS, Edgar Allan Poe. Over 40 of the author's most memorable poems: "The Bells," "Ulalume," "Israfel," "To Helen," "The Conqueror Worm," "Eldorado," "Annabel Lee," many more. Alphabetic lists of titles and first lines. 64pp. 5 3/16 x 8¼. 0-486-26685-0

PERSONAL MEMOIRS OF U. S. GRANT, Ulysses Simpson Grant. Intelligent, deeply moving firsthand account of Civil War campaigns, considered by many the finest military memoirs ever written. Includes letters, historic photographs, maps and more. 528pp. 6⅛ x 9¼. 0-486-28587-1

ANCIENT EGYPTIAN MATERIALS AND INDUSTRIES, A. Lucas and J. Harris. Fascinating, comprehensive, thoroughly documented text describes this ancient civilization's vast resources and the processes that incorporated them in daily life, including the use of animal products, building materials, cosmetics, perfumes and incense, fibers, glazed ware, glass and its manufacture, materials used in the mummification process, and much more. 544pp. 6⅛ x 9¼. (Available in U.S. only.) 0-486-40446-3

RUSSIAN STORIES/RUSSKIE RASSKAZY: A Dual-Language Book, edited by Gleb Struve. Twelve tales by such masters as Chekhov, Tolstoy, Dostoevsky, Pushkin, others. Excellent word-for-word English translations on facing pages, plus teaching and study aids, Russian/English vocabulary, biographical/critical introductions, more. 416pp. 5⅜ x 8½. 0-486-26244-8

PHILADELPHIA THEN AND NOW: 60 Sites Photographed in the Past and Present, Kenneth Finkel and Susan Oyama. Rare photographs of City Hall, Logan Square, Independence Hall, Betsy Ross House, other landmarks juxtaposed with contemporary views. Captures changing face of historic city. Introduction. Captions. 128pp. 8¼ x 11. 0-486-25790-8

NORTH AMERICAN INDIAN LIFE: Customs and Traditions of 23 Tribes, Elsie Clews Parsons (ed.). 27 fictionalized essays by noted anthropologists examine religion, customs, government, additional facets of life among the Winnebago, Crow, Zuni, Eskimo, other tribes. 480pp. 6⅛ x 9¼. 0-486-27377-6

TECHNICAL MANUAL AND DICTIONARY OF CLASSICAL BALLET, Gail Grant. Defines, explains, comments on steps, movements, poses and concepts. 15-page pictorial section. Basic book for student, viewer. 127pp. 5⅜ x 8½. 0-486-21843-0

THE MALE AND FEMALE FIGURE IN MOTION: 60 Classic Photographic Sequences, Eadweard Muybridge. 60 true-action photographs of men and women walking, running, climbing, bending, turning, etc., reproduced from rare 19th-century masterpiece. vi + 121pp. 9 x 12. 0-486-24745-7

ANIMALS: 1,419 Copyright-Free Illustrations of Mammals, Birds, Fish, Insects, etc., Jim Harter (ed.). Clear wood engravings present, in extremely lifelike poses, over 1,000 species of animals. One of the most extensive pictorial sourcebooks of its kind. Captions. Index. 284pp. 9 x 12. 0-486-23766-4

1001 QUESTIONS ANSWERED ABOUT THE SEASHORE, N. J. Berrill and Jacquelyn Berrill. Queries answered about dolphins, sea snails, sponges, starfish, fishes, shore birds, many others. Covers appearance, breeding, growth, feeding, much more. 305pp. 5¼ x 8¼. 0-486-23366-9

ATTRACTING BIRDS TO YOUR YARD, William J. Weber. Easy-to-follow guide offers advice on how to attract the greatest diversity of birds: birdhouses, feeders, water and waterers, much more. 96pp. 5³⁄₁₆ x 8¼. 0-486-28927-3

MEDICINAL AND OTHER USES OF NORTH AMERICAN PLANTS: A Historical Survey with Special Reference to the Eastern Indian Tribes, Charlotte Erichsen-Brown. Chronological historical citations document 500 years of usage of plants, trees, shrubs native to eastern Canada, northeastern U.S. Also complete identifying information. 343 illustrations. 544pp. 6½ x 9¼. 0-486-25951-X

STORYBOOK MAZES, Dave Phillips. 23 stories and mazes on two-page spreads: Wizard of Oz, Treasure Island, Robin Hood, etc. Solutions. 64pp. 8¼ x 11.
0-486-23628-5

AMERICAN NEGRO SONGS: 230 Folk Songs and Spirituals, Religious and Secular, John W. Work. This authoritative study traces the African influences of songs sung and played by black Americans at work, in church, and as entertainment. The author discusses the lyric significance of such songs as "Swing Low, Sweet Chariot," "John Henry," and others and offers the words and music for 230 songs. Bibliography. Index of Song Titles. 272pp. 6½ x 9¼. 0-486-40271-1

MOVIE-STAR PORTRAITS OF THE FORTIES, John Kobal (ed.). 163 glamor, studio photos of 106 stars of the 1940s: Rita Hayworth, Ava Gardner, Marlon Brando, Clark Gable, many more. 176pp. 8⅜ x 11¼. 0-486-23546-7

YEKL and THE IMPORTED BRIDEGROOM AND OTHER STORIES OF YIDDISH NEW YORK, Abraham Cahan. Film Hester Street based on *Yekl* (1896). Novel, other stories among first about Jewish immigrants on N.Y.'s East Side. 240pp. 5⅜ x 8½. 0-486-22427-9

SELECTED POEMS, Walt Whitman. Generous sampling from *Leaves of Grass*. Twenty-four poems include "I Hear America Singing," "Song of the Open Road," "I Sing the Body Electric," "When Lilacs Last in the Dooryard Bloom'd," "O Captain! My Captain!"–all reprinted from an authoritative edition. Lists of titles and first lines. 128pp. 5³⁄₁₆ x 8¼. 0-486-26878-0

SONGS OF EXPERIENCE: Facsimile Reproduction with 26 Plates in Full Color, William Blake. 26 full-color plates from a rare 1826 edition. Includes "The Tyger," "London," "Holy Thursday," and other poems. Printed text of poems. 48pp. 5¼ x 7.
0-486-24636-1

THE BEST TALES OF HOFFMANN, E. T. A. Hoffmann. 10 of Hoffmann's most important stories: "Nutcracker and the King of Mice," "The Golden Flowerpot," etc. 458pp. 5⅜ x 8½. 0-486-21793-0

THE BOOK OF TEA, Kakuzo Okakura. Minor classic of the Orient: entertaining, charming explanation, interpretation of traditional Japanese culture in terms of tea ceremony. 94pp. 5⅜ x 8½. 0-486-20070-1

FRENCH STORIES/CONTES FRANÇAIS: A Dual-Language Book, Wallace Fowlie. Ten stories by French masters, Voltaire to Camus: "Micromegas" by Voltaire; "The Atheist's Mass" by Balzac; "Minuet" by de Maupassant; "The Guest" by Camus, six more. Excellent English translations on facing pages. Also French-English vocabulary list, exercises, more. 352pp. 5⅜ x 8½. 0-486-26443-2

CHICAGO AT THE TURN OF THE CENTURY IN PHOTOGRAPHS: 122 Historic Views from the Collections of the Chicago Historical Society, Larry A. Viskochil. Rare large-format prints offer detailed views of City Hall, State Street, the Loop, Hull House, Union Station, many other landmarks, circa 1904-1913. Introduction. Captions. Maps. 144pp. 9⅜ x 12¼. 0-486-24656-6

OLD BROOKLYN IN EARLY PHOTOGRAPHS, 1865-1929, William Lee Younger. Luna Park, Gravesend race track, construction of Grand Army Plaza, moving of Hotel Brighton, etc. 157 previously unpublished photographs. 165pp. 8⅞ x 11¾. 0-486-23587-4

THE MYTHS OF THE NORTH AMERICAN INDIANS, Lewis Spence. Rich anthology of the myths and legends of the Algonquins, Iroquois, Pawnees and Sioux, prefaced by an extensive historical and ethnological commentary. 36 illustrations. 480pp. 5⅜ x 8½. 0-486-25967-6

AN ENCYCLOPEDIA OF BATTLES: Accounts of Over 1,560 Battles from 1479 B.C. to the Present, David Eggenberger. Essential details of every major battle in recorded history from the first battle of Megiddo in 1479 B.C. to Grenada in 1984. List of Battle Maps. New Appendix covering the years 1967-1984. Index. 99 illustrations. 544pp. 6½ x 9¼. 0-486-24913-1

SAILING ALONE AROUND THE WORLD, Captain Joshua Slocum. First man to sail around the world, alone, in small boat. One of great feats of seamanship told in delightful manner. 67 illustrations. 294pp. 5⅜ x 8½. 0-486-20326-3

ANARCHISM AND OTHER ESSAYS, Emma Goldman. Powerful, penetrating, prophetic essays on direct action, role of minorities, prison reform, puritan hypocrisy, violence, etc. 271pp. 5⅜ x 8½. 0-486-22484-8

MYTHS OF THE HINDUS AND BUDDHISTS, Ananda K. Coomaraswamy and Sister Nivedita. Great stories of the epics; deeds of Krishna, Shiva, taken from puranas, Vedas, folk tales; etc. 32 illustrations. 400pp. 5⅜ x 8½. 0-486-21759-0

MY BONDAGE AND MY FREEDOM, Frederick Douglass. Born a slave, Douglass became outspoken force in antislavery movement. The best of Douglass' autobiographies. Graphic description of slave life. 464pp. 5⅜ x 8½. 0-486-22457-0

FOLLOWING THE EQUATOR: A Journey Around the World, Mark Twain. Fascinating humorous account of 1897 voyage to Hawaii, Australia, India, New Zealand, etc. Ironic, bemused reports on peoples, customs, climate, flora and fauna, politics, much more. 197 illustrations. 720pp. 5⅜ x 8½. 0-486-26113-1

THE PEOPLE CALLED SHAKERS, Edward D. Andrews. Definitive study of Shakers: origins, beliefs, practices, dances, social organization, furniture and crafts, etc. 33 illustrations. 351pp. 5⅜ x 8½. 0-486-21081-2

THE MYTHS OF GREECE AND ROME, H. A. Guerber. A classic of mythology, generously illustrated, long prized for its simple, graphic, accurate retelling of the principal myths of Greece and Rome, and for its commentary on their origins and significance. With 64 illustrations by Michelangelo, Raphael, Titian, Rubens, Canova, Bernini and others. 480pp. 5⅜ x 8½. 0-486-27584-1

PSYCHOLOGY OF MUSIC, Carl E. Seashore. Classic work discusses music as a medium from psychological viewpoint. Clear treatment of physical acoustics, auditory apparatus, sound perception, development of musical skills, nature of musical feeling, host of other topics. 88 figures. 408pp. 5⅜ x 8½.   0-486-21851-1

LIFE IN ANCIENT EGYPT, Adolf Erman. Fullest, most thorough, detailed older account with much not in more recent books, domestic life, religion, magic, medicine, commerce, much more. Many illustrations reproduce tomb paintings, carvings, hieroglyphs, etc. 597pp. 5⅜ x 8½.   0-486-22632-8

SUNDIALS, Their Theory and Construction, Albert Waugh. Far and away the best, most thorough coverage of ideas, mathematics concerned, types, construction, adjusting anywhere. Simple, nontechnical treatment allows even children to build several of these dials. Over 100 illustrations. 230pp. 5⅜ x 8½.   0-486-22947-5

THEORETICAL HYDRODYNAMICS, L. M. Milne-Thomson. Classic exposition of the mathematical theory of fluid motion, applicable to both hydrodynamics and aerodynamics. Over 600 exercises. 768pp. 6⅛ x 9¼.   0-486-68970-0

OLD-TIME VIGNETTES IN FULL COLOR, Carol Belanger Grafton (ed.). Over 390 charming, often sentimental illustrations, selected from archives of Victorian graphics–pretty women posing, children playing, food, flowers, kittens and puppies, smiling cherubs, birds and butterflies, much more. All copyright-free. 48pp. 9¼ x 12¼.
0-486-27269-9

PERSPECTIVE FOR ARTISTS, Rex Vicat Cole. Depth, perspective of sky and sea, shadows, much more, not usually covered. 391 diagrams, 81 reproductions of drawings and paintings. 279pp. 5⅜ x 8½.   0-486-22487-2

DRAWING THE LIVING FIGURE, Joseph Sheppard. Innovative approach to artistic anatomy focuses on specifics of surface anatomy, rather than muscles and bones. Over 170 drawings of live models in front, back and side views, and in widely varying poses. Accompanying diagrams. 177 illustrations. Introduction. Index. 144pp. 8⅜ x11¼.   0-486-26723-7

GOTHIC AND OLD ENGLISH ALPHABETS: 100 Complete Fonts, Dan X. Solo. Add power, elegance to posters, signs, other graphics with 100 stunning copyright-free alphabets: Blackstone, Dolbey, Germania, 97 more–including many lower-case, numerals, punctuation marks. 104pp. 8⅛ x 11.   0-486-24695-7

THE BOOK OF WOOD CARVING, Charles Marshall Sayers. Finest book for beginners discusses fundamentals and offers 34 designs. "Absolutely first rate . . . well thought out and well executed."–E. J. Tangerman. 118pp. 7¾ x 10⅝.   0-486-23654-4

ILLUSTRATED CATALOG OF CIVIL WAR MILITARY GOODS: Union Army Weapons, Insignia, Uniform Accessories, and Other Equipment, Schuyler, Hartley, and Graham. Rare, profusely illustrated 1846 catalog includes Union Army uniform and dress regulations, arms and ammunition, coats, insignia, flags, swords, rifles, etc. 226 illustrations. 160pp. 9 x 12.   0-486-24939-5

WOMEN'S FASHIONS OF THE EARLY 1900s: An Unabridged Republication of "New York Fashions, 1909," National Cloak & Suit Co. Rare catalog of mail-order fashions documents women's and children's clothing styles shortly after the turn of the century. Captions offer full descriptions, prices. Invaluable resource for fashion, costume historians. Approximately 725 illustrations. 128pp. 8⅜ x 11¼.
0-486-27276-1

HOW TO DO BEADWORK, Mary White. Fundamental book on craft from simple projects to five-bead chains and woven works. 106 illustrations. 142pp. 5⅜ x 8.
0-486-20697-1

THE 1912 AND 1915 GUSTAV STICKLEY FURNITURE CATALOGS, Gustav Stickley. With over 200 detailed illustrations and descriptions, these two catalogs are essential reading and reference materials and identification guides for Stickley furniture. Captions cite materials, dimensions and prices. 112pp. 6½ x 9¼. 0-486-26676-1

EARLY AMERICAN LOCOMOTIVES, John H. White, Jr. Finest locomotive engravings from early 19th century: historical (1804–74), main-line (after 1870), special, foreign, etc. 147 plates. 142pp. 11⅜ x 8¼. 0-486-22772-3

LITTLE BOOK OF EARLY AMERICAN CRAFTS AND TRADES, Peter Stockham (ed.). 1807 children's book explains crafts and trades: baker, hatter, cooper, potter, and many others. 23 copperplate illustrations. 140pp. 4⁵/₈ x 6.
0-486-23336-7

VICTORIAN FASHIONS AND COSTUMES FROM HARPER'S BAZAR, 1867–1898, Stella Blum (ed.). Day costumes, evening wear, sports clothes, shoes, hats, other accessories in over 1,000 detailed engravings. 320pp. 9⅜ x 12¼.
0-486-22990-4

THE LONG ISLAND RAIL ROAD IN EARLY PHOTOGRAPHS, Ron Ziel. Over 220 rare photos, informative text document origin (1844) and development of rail service on Long Island. Vintage views of early trains, locomotives, stations, passengers, crews, much more. Captions. 8⅞ x 11¾. 0-486-26301-0

VOYAGE OF THE LIBERDADE, Joshua Slocum. Great 19th-century mariner's thrilling, first-hand account of the wreck of his ship off South America, the 35-foot boat he built from the wreckage, and its remarkable voyage home. 128pp. 5⅜ x 8½.
0-486-40022-0

TEN BOOKS ON ARCHITECTURE, Vitruvius. The most important book ever written on architecture. Early Roman aesthetics, technology, classical orders, site selection, all other aspects. Morgan translation. 331pp. 5⅜ x 8½. 0-486-20645-9

THE HUMAN FIGURE IN MOTION, Eadweard Muybridge. More than 4,500 stopped-action photos, in action series, showing undraped men, women, children jumping, lying down, throwing, sitting, wrestling, carrying, etc. 390pp. 7⅞ x 10⅝.
0-486-20204-6 Clothbd.

TREES OF THE EASTERN AND CENTRAL UNITED STATES AND CANADA, William M. Harlow. Best one-volume guide to 140 trees. Full descriptions, woodlore, range, etc. Over 600 illustrations. Handy size. 288pp. 4½ x 6⅜. 0-486-20395-6

GROWING AND USING HERBS AND SPICES, Milo Miloradovich. Versatile handbook provides all the information needed for cultivation and use of all the herbs and spices available in North America. 4 illustrations. Index. Glossary. 236pp. 5⅜ x 8½.
0-486-25058-X

BIG BOOK OF MAZES AND LABYRINTHS, Walter Shepherd. 50 mazes and labyrinths in all–classical, solid, ripple, and more–in one great volume. Perfect inexpensive puzzler for clever youngsters. Full solutions. 112pp. 8⅛ x 11. 0-486-22951-3

PIANO TUNING, J. Cree Fischer. Clearest, best book for beginner, amateur. Simple repairs, raising dropped notes, tuning by easy method of flattened fifths. No previous skills needed. 4 illustrations. 201pp. 5⅜ x 8½. 0-486-23267-0

HINTS TO SINGERS, Lillian Nordica. Selecting the right teacher, developing confidence, overcoming stage fright, and many other important skills receive thoughtful discussion in this indispensible guide, written by a world-famous diva of four decades' experience. 96pp. 5⅜ x 8½. 0-486-40094-8

THE COMPLETE NONSENSE OF EDWARD LEAR, Edward Lear. All nonsense limericks, zany alphabets, Owl and Pussycat, songs, nonsense botany, etc., illustrated by Lear. Total of 320pp. 5⅜ x 8½. (Available in U.S. only.) 0-486-20167-8

VICTORIAN PARLOUR POETRY: An Annotated Anthology, Michael R. Turner. 117 gems by Longfellow, Tennyson, Browning, many lesser-known poets. "The Village Blacksmith," "Curfew Must Not Ring Tonight," "Only a Baby Small," dozens more, often difficult to find elsewhere. Index of poets, titles, first lines. xxiii + 325pp. 5⅝ x 8¼. 0-486-27044-0

DUBLINERS, James Joyce. Fifteen stories offer vivid, tightly focused observations of the lives of Dublin's poorer classes. At least one, "The Dead," is considered a masterpiece. Reprinted complete and unabridged from standard edition. 160pp. 5 3/16 x 8¼. 0-486-26870-5

GREAT WEIRD TALES: 14 Stories by Lovecraft, Blackwood, Machen and Others, S. T. Joshi (ed.). 14 spellbinding tales, including "The Sin Eater," by Fiona McLeod, "The Eye Above the Mantel," by Frank Belknap Long, as well as renowned works by R. H. Barlow, Lord Dunsany, Arthur Machen, W. C. Morrow and eight other masters of the genre. 256pp. 5⅜ x 8½. (Available in U.S. only.) 0-486-40436-6

THE BOOK OF THE SACRED MAGIC OF ABRAMELIN THE MAGE, translated by S. MacGregor Mathers. Medieval manuscript of ceremonial magic. Basic document in Aleister Crowley, Golden Dawn groups. 268pp. 5⅜ x 8½. 0-486-23211-5

THE BATTLES THAT CHANGED HISTORY, Fletcher Pratt. Eminent historian profiles 16 crucial conflicts, ancient to modern, that changed the course of civilization. 352pp. 5⅜ x 8½. 0-486-41129-X

NEW RUSSIAN-ENGLISH AND ENGLISH-RUSSIAN DICTIONARY, M. A. O'Brien. This is a remarkably handy Russian dictionary, containing a surprising amount of information, including over 70,000 entries. 366pp. 4½ x 6⅛. 0-486-20208-9

NEW YORK IN THE FORTIES, Andreas Feininger. 162 brilliant photographs by the well-known photographer, formerly with *Life* magazine. Commuters, shoppers, Times Square at night, much else from city at its peak. Captions by John von Hartz. 181pp. 9¼ x 10¾. 0-486-23585-8

INDIAN SIGN LANGUAGE, William Tomkins. Over 525 signs developed by Sioux and other tribes. Written instructions and diagrams. Also 290 pictographs. 111pp. 6⅛ x 9¼. 0-486-22029-X

ANATOMY: A Complete Guide for Artists, Joseph Sheppard. A master of figure drawing shows artists how to render human anatomy convincingly. Over 460 illustrations. 224pp. 8⅜ x 11¼. 0-486-27279-6

MEDIEVAL CALLIGRAPHY: Its History and Technique, Marc Drogin. Spirited history, comprehensive instruction manual covers 13 styles (ca. 4th century through 15th). Excellent photographs; directions for duplicating medieval techniques with modern tools. 224pp. 8⅜ x 11¼. 0-486-26142-5

DRIED FLOWERS: How to Prepare Them, Sarah Whitlock and Martha Rankin. Complete instructions on how to use silica gel, meal and borax, perlite aggregate, sand and borax, glycerine and water to create attractive permanent flower arrangements. 12 illustrations. 32pp. 5⅜ x 8½. 0-486-21802-3

EASY-TO-MAKE BIRD FEEDERS FOR WOODWORKERS, Scott D. Campbell. Detailed, simple-to-use guide for designing, constructing, caring for and using feeders. Text, illustrations for 12 classic and contemporary designs. 96pp. 5⅜ x 8½.
0-486-25847-5

THE COMPLETE BOOK OF BIRDHOUSE CONSTRUCTION FOR WOOD-WORKERS, Scott D. Campbell. Detailed instructions, illustrations, tables. Also data on bird habitat and instinct patterns. Bibliography. 3 tables. 63 illustrations in 15 figures. 48pp. 5¼ x 8½. 0-486-24407-5

SCOTTISH WONDER TALES FROM MYTH AND LEGEND, Donald A. Mackenzie. 16 lively tales tell of giants rumbling down mountainsides, of a magic wand that turns stone pillars into warriors, of gods and goddesses, evil hags, powerful forces and more. 240pp. 5⅜ x 8½. 0-486-29677-6

THE HISTORY OF UNDERCLOTHES, C. Willett Cunnington and Phyllis Cunnington. Fascinating, well-documented survey covering six centuries of English undergarments, enhanced with over 100 illustrations: 12th-century laced-up bodice, footed long drawers (1795), 19th-century bustles, 19th-century corsets for men, Victorian "bust improvers," much more. 272pp. 5⅜ x 8¼. 0-486-27124-2

ARTS AND CRAFTS FURNITURE: The Complete Brooks Catalog of 1912, Brooks Manufacturing Co. Photos and detailed descriptions of more than 150 now very collectible furniture designs from the Arts and Crafts movement depict davenports, settees, buffets, desks, tables, chairs, bedsteads, dressers and more, all built of solid, quarter-sawed oak. Invaluable for students and enthusiasts of antiques, Americana and the decorative arts. 80pp. 6½ x 9¼. 0-486-27471-3

WILBUR AND ORVILLE: A Biography of the Wright Brothers, Fred Howard. Definitive, crisply written study tells the full story of the brothers' lives and work. A vividly written biography, unparalleled in scope and color, that also captures the spirit of an extraordinary era. 560pp. 6⅛ x 9¼. 0-486-40297-5

THE ARTS OF THE SAILOR: Knotting, Splicing and Ropework, Hervey Garrett Smith. Indispensable shipboard reference covers tools, basic knots and useful hitches; handsewing and canvas work, more. Over 100 illustrations. Delightful reading for sea lovers. 256pp. 5⅜ x 8½. 0-486-26440-8

FRANK LLOYD WRIGHT'S FALLINGWATER: The House and Its History, Second, Revised Edition, Donald Hoffmann. A total revision—both in text and illustrations—of the standard document on Fallingwater, the boldest, most personal architectural statement of Wright's mature years, updated with valuable new material from the recently opened Frank Lloyd Wright Archives. "Fascinating"–The New York Times. 116 illustrations. 128pp. 9¼ x 10¾. 0-486-27430-6

PHOTOGRAPHIC SKETCHBOOK OF THE CIVIL WAR, Alexander Gardner. 100 photos taken on field during the Civil War. Famous shots of Manassas Harper's Ferry, Lincoln, Richmond, slave pens, etc. 244pp. 10⅝ x 8¼. 0-486-22731-6

FIVE ACRES AND INDEPENDENCE, Maurice G. Kains. Great back-to-the-land classic explains basics of self-sufficient farming. The one book to get. 95 illustrations. 397pp. 5⅜ x 8½. 0-486-20974-1

A MODERN HERBAL, Margaret Grieve. Much the fullest, most exact, most useful compilation of herbal material. Gigantic alphabetical encyclopedia, from aconite to zedoary, gives botanical information, medical properties, folklore, economic uses, much else. Indispensable to serious reader. 161 illustrations. 888pp. 6½ x 9¼. 2-vol. set. (Available in U.S. only.)   Vol. I: 0-486-22798-7   Vol. II: 0-486-22799-5

HIDDEN TREASURE MAZE BOOK, Dave Phillips. Solve 34 challenging mazes accompanied by heroic tales of adventure. Evil dragons, people-eating plants, blood-thirsty giants, many more dangerous adversaries lurk at every twist and turn. 34 mazes, stories, solutions. 48pp. 8¼ x 11.   0-486-24566-7

LETTERS OF W. A. MOZART, Wolfgang A. Mozart. Remarkable letters show bawdy wit, humor, imagination, musical insights, contemporary musical world; includes some letters from Leopold Mozart. 276pp. 5⅜ x 8½.   0-486-22859-2

BASIC PRINCIPLES OF CLASSICAL BALLET, Agrippina Vaganova. Great Russian theoretician, teacher explains methods for teaching classical ballet. 118 illus-trations. 175pp. 5⅜ x 8½.   0-486-22036-2

THE JUMPING FROG, Mark Twain. Revenge edition. The original story of The Celebrated Jumping Frog of Calaveras County, a hapless French translation, and Twain's hilarious "retranslation" from the French. 12 illustrations. 66pp. 5⅜ x 8½.
0-486-22686-7

BEST REMEMBERED POEMS, Martin Gardner (ed.). The 126 poems in this superb collection of 19th- and 20th-century British and American verse range from Shelley's "To a Skylark" to the impassioned "Renascence" of Edna St. Vincent Millay and to Edward Lear's whimsical "The Owl and the Pussycat." 224pp. 5⅜ x 8½.
0-486-27165-X

COMPLETE SONNETS, William Shakespeare. Over 150 exquisite poems deal with love, friendship, the tyranny of time, beauty's evanescence, death and other themes in language of remarkable power, precision and beauty. Glossary of archaic terms. 80pp. 5³⁄₁₆ x 8¼.   0-486-26686-9

HISTORIC HOMES OF THE AMERICAN PRESIDENTS, Second, Revised Edition, Irvin Haas. A traveler's guide to American Presidential homes, most open to the public, depicting and describing homes occupied by every American President from George Washington to George Bush. With visiting hours, admission charges, travel routes. 175 photographs. Index. 160pp. 8¼ x 11.   0-486-26751-2

THE WIT AND HUMOR OF OSCAR WILDE, Alvin Redman (ed.). More than 1,000 ripostes, paradoxes, wisecracks: Work is the curse of the drinking classes; I can resist everything except temptation; etc. 258pp. 5⅜ x 8½.   0-486-20602-5

SHAKESPEARE LEXICON AND QUOTATION DICTIONARY, Alexander Schmidt. Full definitions, locations, shades of meaning in every word in plays and poems. More than 50,000 exact quotations. 1,485pp. 6½ x 9¼. 2-vol. set.
Vol. 1: 0-486-22726-X   Vol. 2: 0-486-22727-8

SELECTED POEMS, Emily Dickinson. Over 100 best-known, best-loved poems by one of America's foremost poets, reprinted from authoritative early editions. No comparable edition at this price. Index of first lines. 64pp. 5³⁄₁₆ x 8¼. 0-486-26466-1

THE INSIDIOUS DR. FU-MANCHU, Sax Rohmer. The first of the popular mys-tery series introduces a pair of English detectives to their archnemesis, the diabolical Dr. Fu-Manchu. Flavorful atmosphere, fast-paced action, and colorful characters enliven this classic of the genre. 208pp. 5³⁄₁₆ x 8¼.   0-486-29898-1

THE MALLEUS MALEFICARUM OF KRAMER AND SPRENGER, translated by Montague Summers. Full text of most important witchhunter's "bible," used by both Catholics and Protestants. 278pp. 6⅝ x 10.   0-486-22802-9

SPANISH STORIES/CUENTOS ESPAÑOLES: A Dual-Language Book, Angel Flores (ed.). Unique format offers 13 great stories in Spanish by Cervantes, Borges, others. Faithful English translations on facing pages. 352pp. 5⅜ x 8½.

0-486-25399-6

GARDEN CITY, LONG ISLAND, IN EARLY PHOTOGRAPHS, 1869–1919, Mildred H. Smith. Handsome treasury of 118 vintage pictures, accompanied by carefully researched captions, document the Garden City Hotel fire (1899), the Vanderbilt Cup Race (1908), the first airmail flight departing from the Nassau Boulevard Aerodrome (1911), and much more. 96pp. 8⅞ x 11¾.   0-486-40669-5

OLD QUEENS, N.Y., IN EARLY PHOTOGRAPHS, Vincent F. Seyfried and William Asadorian. Over 160 rare photographs of Maspeth, Jamaica, Jackson Heights, and other areas. Vintage views of DeWitt Clinton mansion, 1939 World's Fair and more. Captions. 192pp. 8⅞ x 11.   0-486-26358-4

CAPTURED BY THE INDIANS: 15 Firsthand Accounts, 1750-1870, Frederick Drimmer. Astounding true historical accounts of grisly torture, bloody conflicts, relentless pursuits, miraculous escapes and more, by people who lived to tell the tale. 384pp. 5⅜ x 8½.   0-486-24901-8

THE WORLD'S GREAT SPEECHES (Fourth Enlarged Edition), Lewis Copeland, Lawrence W. Lamm, and Stephen J. McKenna. Nearly 300 speeches provide public speakers with a wealth of updated quotes and inspiration—from Pericles' funeral oration and William Jennings Bryan's "Cross of Gold Speech" to Malcolm X's powerful words on the Black Revolution and Earl of Spenser's tribute to his sister, Diana, Princess of Wales. 944pp. 5⅜ x 8⅜.   0-486-40903-1

THE BOOK OF THE SWORD, Sir Richard F. Burton. Great Victorian scholar/adventurer's eloquent, erudite history of the "queen of weapons"—from prehistory to early Roman Empire. Evolution and development of early swords, variations (sabre, broadsword, cutlass, scimitar, etc.), much more. 336pp. 6⅛ x 9¼.

0-486-25434-8

AUTOBIOGRAPHY: The Story of My Experiments with Truth, Mohandas K. Gandhi. Boyhood, legal studies, purification, the growth of the Satyagraha (nonviolent protest) movement. Critical, inspiring work of the man responsible for the freedom of India. 480pp. 5⅜ x 8½. (Available in U.S. only.)   0-486-24593-4

CELTIC MYTHS AND LEGENDS, T. W. Rolleston. Masterful retelling of Irish and Welsh stories and tales. Cuchulain, King Arthur, Deirdre, the Grail, many more. First paperback edition. 58 full-page illustrations. 512pp. 5⅜ x 8½.   0-486-26507-2

THE PRINCIPLES OF PSYCHOLOGY, William James. Famous long course complete, unabridged. Stream of thought, time perception, memory, experimental methods; great work decades ahead of its time. 94 figures. 1,391pp. 5⅜ x 8½. 2-vol. set.
Vol. I: 0-486-20381-6   Vol. II: 0-486-20382-4

THE WORLD AS WILL AND REPRESENTATION, Arthur Schopenhauer. Definitive English translation of Schopenhauer's life work, correcting more than 1,000 errors, omissions in earlier translations. Translated by E. F. J. Payne. Total of 1,269pp. 5⅜ x 8½. 2-vol. set.   Vol. 1: 0-486-21761-2   Vol. 2: 0-486-21762-0

MAGIC AND MYSTERY IN TIBET, Madame Alexandra David-Neel. Experiences among lamas, magicians, sages, sorcerers, Bonpa wizards. A true psychic discovery. 32 illustrations. 321pp. 5⅜ x 8½. (Available in U.S. only.) 0-486-22682-4

THE EGYPTIAN BOOK OF THE DEAD, E. A. Wallis Budge. Complete reproduction of Ani's papyrus, finest ever found. Full hieroglyphic text, interlinear transliteration, word-for-word translation, smooth translation. 533pp. 6½ x 9¼. 0-486-21866-X

HISTORIC COSTUME IN PICTURES, Braun & Schneider. Over 1,450 costumed figures in clearly detailed engravings–from dawn of civilization to end of 19th century. Captions. Many folk costumes. 256pp. 8⅜ x 11¾. 0-486-23150-X

MATHEMATICS FOR THE NONMATHEMATICIAN, Morris Kline. Detailed, college-level treatment of mathematics in cultural and historical context, with numerous exercises. Recommended Reading Lists. Tables. Numerous figures. 641pp. 5⅜ x 8½. 0-486-24823-2

PROBABILISTIC METHODS IN THE THEORY OF STRUCTURES, Isaac Elishakoff. Well-written introduction covers the elements of the theory of probability from two or more random variables, the reliability of such multivariable structures, the theory of random function, Monte Carlo methods of treating problems incapable of exact solution, and more. Examples. 502pp. 5⅜ x 8½. 0-486-40691-1

THE RIME OF THE ANCIENT MARINER, Gustave Doré, S. T. Coleridge. Doré's finest work; 34 plates capture moods, subtleties of poem. Flawless full-size reproductions printed on facing pages with authoritative text of poem. "Beautiful. Simply beautiful."–*Publisher's Weekly*. 77pp. 9¼ x 12. 0-486-22305-1

SCULPTURE: Principles and Practice, Louis Slobodkin. Step-by-step approach to clay, plaster, metals, stone; classical and modern. 253 drawings, photos. 255pp. 8⅛ x 11. 0-486-22960-2

THE INFLUENCE OF SEA POWER UPON HISTORY, 1660–1783, A. T. Mahan. Influential classic of naval history and tactics still used as text in war colleges. First paperback edition. 4 maps. 24 battle plans. 640pp. 5⅜ x 8½. 0-486-25509-3

THE STORY OF THE TITANIC AS TOLD BY ITS SURVIVORS, Jack Winocour (ed.). What it was really like. Panic, despair, shocking inefficiency, and a little heroism. More thrilling than any fictional account. 26 illustrations. 320pp. 5⅜ x 8½. 0-486-20610-6

ONE TWO THREE . . . INFINITY: Facts and Speculations of Science, George Gamow. Great physicist's fascinating, readable overview of contemporary science: number theory, relativity, fourth dimension, entropy, genes, atomic structure, much more. 128 illustrations. Index. 352pp. 5⅜ x 8½. 0-486-25664-2

DALÍ ON MODERN ART: The Cuckolds of Antiquated Modern Art, Salvador Dalí. Influential painter skewers modern art and its practitioners. Outrageous evaluations of Picasso, Cézanne, Turner, more. 15 renderings of paintings discussed. 44 calligraphic decorations by Dalí. 96pp. 5⅜ x 8½. (Available in U.S. only.) 0-486-29220-7

ANTIQUE PLAYING CARDS: A Pictorial History, Henry René D'Allemagne. Over 900 elaborate, decorative images from rare playing cards (14th–20th centuries): Bacchus, death, dancing dogs, hunting scenes, royal coats of arms, players cheating, much more. 96pp. 9¼ x 12¼. 0-486-29265-7

MAKING FURNITURE MASTERPIECES: 30 Projects with Measured Drawings, Franklin H. Gottshall. Step-by-step instructions, illustrations for constructing handsome, useful pieces, among them a Sheraton desk, Chippendale chair, Spanish desk, Queen Anne table and a William and Mary dressing mirror. 224pp. 8⅛ x 11¼. 0-486-29338-6

NORTH AMERICAN INDIAN DESIGNS FOR ARTISTS AND CRAFTSPEOPLE, Eva Wilson. Over 360 authentic copyright-free designs adapted from Navajo blankets, Hopi pottery, Sioux buffalo hides, more. Geometrics, symbolic figures, plant and animal motifs, etc. 128pp. 8⅜ x 11. (Not for sale in the United Kingdom.) 0-486-25341-4

THE FOSSIL BOOK: A Record of Prehistoric Life, Patricia V. Rich et al. Profusely illustrated definitive guide covers everything from single-celled organisms and dinosaurs to birds and mammals and the interplay between climate and man. Over 1,500 illustrations. 760pp. 7½ x 10⅛. 0-486-29371-8

VICTORIAN ARCHITECTURAL DETAILS: Designs for Over 700 Stairs, Mantels, Doors, Windows, Cornices, Porches, and Other Decorative Elements, A. J. Bicknell & Company. Everything from dormer windows and piazzas to balconies and gable ornaments. Also includes elevations and floor plans for handsome, private residences and commercial structures. 80pp. 9⅜ x 12¼. 0-486-44015-X

WESTERN ISLAMIC ARCHITECTURE: A Concise Introduction, John D. Hoag. Profusely illustrated critical appraisal compares and contrasts Islamic mosques and palaces–from Spain and Egypt to other areas in the Middle East. 139 illustrations. 128pp. 6 x 9. 0-486-43760-4

CHINESE ARCHITECTURE: A Pictorial History, Liang Ssu-ch'eng. More than 240 rare photographs and drawings depict temples, pagodas, tombs, bridges, and imperial palaces comprising much of China's architectural heritage. 152 halftones, 94 diagrams. 232pp. 10¾ x 9⅞. 0-486-43999-2

THE RENAISSANCE: Studies in Art and Poetry, Walter Pater. One of the most talked-about books of the 19th century, *The Renaissance* combines scholarship and philosophy in an innovative work of cultural criticism that examines the achievements of Botticelli, Leonardo, Michelangelo, and other artists. "The holy writ of beauty."–Oscar Wilde. 160pp. 5⅜ x 8½. 0-486-44025-7

A TREATISE ON PAINTING, Leonardo da Vinci. The great Renaissance artist's practical advice on drawing and painting techniques covers anatomy, perspective, composition, light and shadow, and color. A classic of art instruction, it features 48 drawings by Nicholas Poussin and Leon Battista Alberti. 192pp. 5⅜ x 8½. 0-486-44155-5

THE MIND OF LEONARDO DA VINCI, Edward McCurdy. More than just a biography, this classic study by a distinguished historian draws upon Leonardo's extensive writings to offer numerous demonstrations of the Renaissance master's achievements, not only in sculpture and painting, but also in music, engineering, and even experimental aviation. 384pp. 5⅜ x 8½. 0-486-44142-3

WASHINGTON IRVING'S RIP VAN WINKLE, Illustrated by Arthur Rackham. Lovely prints that established artist as a leading illustrator of the time and forever etched into the popular imagination a classic of Catskill lore. 51 full-color plates. 80pp. 8⅜ x 11. 0-486-44242-X

HENSCHE ON PAINTING, John W. Robichaux. Basic painting philosophy and methodology of a great teacher, as expounded in his famous classes and workshops on Cape Cod. 7 illustrations in color on covers. 80pp. 5⅜ x 8½. 0-486-43728-0

LIGHT AND SHADE: A Classic Approach to Three-Dimensional Drawing, Mrs. Mary P. Merrifield. Handy reference clearly demonstrates principles of light and shade by revealing effects of common daylight, sunshine, and candle or artificial light on geometrical solids. 13 plates. 64pp. 5⅜ x 8½. 0-486-44143-1

ASTROLOGY AND ASTRONOMY: A Pictorial Archive of Signs and Symbols, Ernst and Johanna Lehner. Treasure trove of stories, lore, and myth, accompanied by more than 300 rare illustrations of planets, the Milky Way, signs of the zodiac, comets, meteors, and other astronomical phenomena. 192pp. 8⅜ x 11. 0-486-43981-X

JEWELRY MAKING: Techniques for Metal, Tim McCreight. Easy-to-follow instructions and carefully executed illustrations describe tools and techniques, use of gems and enamels, wire inlay, casting, and other topics. 72 line illustrations and diagrams. 176pp. 8¼ x 10⅞. 0-486-44043-5

MAKING BIRDHOUSES: Easy and Advanced Projects, Gladstone Califf. Easy-to-follow instructions include diagrams for everything from a one-room house for bluebirds to a forty-two-room structure for purple martins. 56 plates; 4 figures. 80pp. 8¾ x 6⅜. 0-486-44183-0

LITTLE BOOK OF LOG CABINS: How to Build and Furnish Them, William S. Wicks. Handy how-to manual, with instructions and illustrations for building cabins in the Adirondack style, fireplaces, stairways, furniture, beamed ceilings, and more. 102 line drawings. 96pp. 8¾ x 6⅜ 0-486-44259-4

THE SEASONS OF AMERICA PAST, Eric Sloane. From "sugaring time" and strawberry picking to Indian summer and fall harvest, a whole year's activities described in charming prose and enhanced with 79 of the author's own illustrations. 160pp. 8¼ x 11. 0-486-44220-9

THE METROPOLIS OF TOMORROW, Hugh Ferriss. Generous, prophetic vision of the metropolis of the future, as perceived in 1929. Powerful illustrations of towering structures, wide avenues, and rooftop parks–all features in many of today's modern cities. 59 illustrations. 144pp. 8¼ x 11. 0-486-43727-2

THE PATH TO ROME, Hilaire Belloc. This 1902 memoir abounds in lively vignettes from a vanished time, recounting a pilgrimage on foot across the Alps and Apennines in order to "see all Europe which the Christian Faith has saved." 77 of the author's original line drawings complement his sparkling prose. 272pp. 5⅜ x 8½. 0-486-44001-X

THE HISTORY OF RASSELAS: Prince of Abissinia, Samuel Johnson. Distinguished English writer attacks eighteenth-century optimism and man's unrealistic estimates of what life has to offer. 112pp. 5⅜ x 8½. 0-486-44094-X

A VOYAGE TO ARCTURUS, David Lindsay. A brilliant flight of pure fancy, where wild creatures crowd the fantastic landscape and demented torturers dominate victims with their bizarre mental powers. 272pp. 5⅜ x 8½. 0-486-44198-9

Paperbound unless otherwise indicated. Available at your book dealer, online at **www.doverpublications.com**, or by writing to Dept. GI, Dover Publications, Inc., 31 East 2nd Street, Mineola, NY 11501. For current price information or for free catalogs (please indicate field of interest), write to Dover Publications or log on to **www.doverpublications.com** and see every Dover book in print. Dover publishes more than 500 books each year on science, elementary and advanced mathematics, biology, music, art, literary history, social sciences, and other areas.